STRUGGLING WITH GOD IN THE DISTANT I*S*L*A*N*D*S

GREG BRUCKERT

RIVERSTONE GROUP PUBLISHING

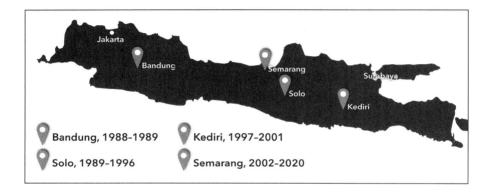

"I will set a sign among them, and I will send some of those who survive to the nations—to Tarshish, to the Libyans and Lydians (famous as archers), to Tubal and Greece, and to the distant islands that have not heard of my fame or seen my glory. They will proclaim my glory among the nations."

— Isaiah 66:19

DEDICATION

*Dedicated to my three children,
whom all three went through a time
of "struggling" (bergumul) with the Lord
about coming to and serving in
Indonesia as Missionaries.
We praise the Lord
that all three of them, Jennifer,
Jonathan and Jamie Marie love the Lord
with all of their hearts
and likewise love Indonesians.*

ACKNOWLEDGEMENTS

To **Rev Rimun Robinson** – Pastor Rimun is the President of the Indonesian Baptist Theological Seminary in Semarang, the city where we have lived for over 18 years. I had the privilege of teaching pastors and evangelists from Indonesia for over 12 years. Back in 2019 Pastor Rimun challenged me to write a book based on our many years of experience in Indonesia. He said that the book would be beneficial to many new missionaries from not only the IMB but also many other sending agencies as well. Thank you so much Pastor Rimun for challenging me to do something that does not come natural for me nor easy, and that is write extensively.

To *Jeremy and Becca Simmons* – Jeremy and Becca were a Journeyman couple that was sent out by the International Mission Board to work with Students in Semarang. I can remember that is was Jeremy and Becca that gave me the challenge to start writing my book on March 17th, which was not long after the Corona Virus was declared a Pandemic by the Center of Disease Control. We were shuttered up in our houses for 4 months, which God sovereignly used to carve our time to harness my energies to write this book. Thanks to the Simmons for the challenge they issued to me on March 17th to start the long and tedious process of writing a book.

To **Shelly Bruckert**, my beloved wife of 41 years. Shelly gave me the gentle shoves and needed encouragement to persevere in writing this book. Not to mention the many meals and cups of coffee she helped prepare for me during the many months of writing. Thank you Shelly for being so patient with me during the time I know I was very preoccupied with the book but you always managed to exercise your spiritual gift of "encouragement" and apply it to my situation during times when I most needed it.

STRUGGLING WITH GOD IN THE DISTANT ISLANDS

Copyright © 2020 by Greg Bruckert

All rights reserved. This book is copyright; and so no part of it may be reproduced, stored in a retrieval system or transmitted in any form or by any means – electrical, mechanical, electrostatic, magnetic tape, photocopying, recording or otherwise – without the prior written permission of the author.

Riverstone Group Publishing
ISBN: 978-1-7346235-2-9

Printed in the United States

Unless otherwise indicated, all Scripture quotations are taken from the Holy Bible: New International Version®, NIV® Copyright © 1973, 1978, 1984 by the International Bible Society. Used by permission of Zondervan. All rights reserved.

CONTENTS

Foreword 11

Introduction 13

Chapter 1   Call to Salvation 35

Chapter 2   Call to Serve 43

Chapter 3   Call to Go 49

Chapter 4   Call to Wait 55

Chapter 5   Call to Persevere | Language School 63

Chapter 6   Call to Be a Learner | Solo, 1989–1996 73

Chapter 7   Call to Humble Myself | Kediri, 1997–2001 105

Chapter 8   Call to Train | Semarang and STBI, 2002–2014 ... 147

Chapter 9   Call to Suffer 169

Chapter 10 Call to Preach the Gospel 195

Chapter 11 Call to Stay | Volunteer Retirement Incentive 213

Chapter 12 Call to Finish Well 221

Endnotes 265

FOREWORD

Throughout human history, God has chosen to send seasons of His manifest presence to revive His church and awaken the lost. These moments of revival and awakening have brought necessary course corrections to nations—adjustments that could not have occurred otherwise. It is God's way of opening heaven and reminding us why we are here and what we are to be about. Jonathan Edwards said that in these seasons the work of God is accelerated. They are generationally necessary and extraordinary.

Greg Bruckert received his spiritual birth during one of these visitations from heaven. The Jesus Movement occurred in the United States during the late 1960's and early 1970's. Thousands of churches were revived, and record numbers of people came to Christ, particularly students. More students were baptized, records show, among Southern Baptist Churches than any time before or since.

I know about this movement because, like Greg, I owe much of my spiritual understanding to that period. My college campus received a burst of spiritual life during this time. Fifteen-minute student-led services lasted for hours, marked by confession, repentance, and many coming to Christ. My life was forever changed, as were thousands of others.

If you have ever tasted God's manifest presence, you long for it the rest of your life. You pray for such a visitation for yourself but also for your world. You realize, as one man said, that God can do more in five minutes of His manifest presence than 15 years of our best human effort.

Greg has carried this burden throughout his life. "Struggling with God in Distant Lands" gives us Greg's personal pursuit of revival and awakening. Filled with practical illustrations from his own life—his experiences of seasons of revival and his pursuit of revival for himself and those he has served in Indonesia—illustrate what it takes to be a catalyst for revival. The story of one missionary's life yields many truths that can help us all in our pursuit of God.

If you study the history of spiritual awakenings, you will notice that God always raises up voices—men who are called by God to sound a trumpet and prevail in extraordinary prayer for their nation. Greg describes this struggle well and is himself a voice to us, reminding us of how desperately we need nothing less than a Divine Invasion. And, we need it now.

As you read, make notes of the principles and truths that would help you become such a voice. And then let this good book put you on your knees until Jesus comes in power to your life, your family, your church, and your nation.

— *Bill Elliff*

INTRODUCTION

Struggling with God in Prayer for Revival and Spiritual Awakening

For the better part of the year preceding it, we had been getting ready for our big "Foundations" meeting to be held in Bangkok, Thailand, in mid-May of 2018. By "we," I mean all of the missionaries who, like me, worked for the International Mission Board. Together, we made up nine "affinity groups" spread across the planet to serve the people of the world. Over a thousand of us planned to gather in Bangkok to discuss the foundational document recently forged by some of our key leaders and now in the hands of all of us missionaries.

The document's purpose was not to spell out specific tactics and tools of missions work. Instead, it was to answer foundational questions about who we are and what we do and to explore some of the answers' implications for how we live and work around the world.

Basically, our new "Foundations" document had been made for our use in assessing and strengthening the goals, strategies, methods, and tools of our missions organization. It had been drafted and then edited and revised several times before copies were sent to employees of the International Mission Board. These employees, all in positions of leadership, were asked to read the document ahead of the Bangkok event. I started studying it some five months before the May meeting, in January. There was even a quiz to see how well we comprehended the new document.

As the time for the meeting was drawing closer, I had conversations, I remember, with certain IMB personnel about exactly what our meeting was expected to accomplish. What was the purpose of bringing us all together? Sometimes, this question was posed doubtfully. Didn't it seem like a big waste of company funds and time to bring us from the far corners of the world to a fancy hotel to study a document we were already reading and could easily discuss at our local levels? Some missionaries considered not attending the meeting (even though it was mandatory), since its purpose appeared to be nothing we couldn't achieve from home.

I considered something else, which I shared with a few of my colleagues. I can remember saying to several, "I am thinking *this*: All of our leadership from across our organization coming together for six or seven days, *what an opportunity for God to do something in our midst!*" I held out my optimism to my coworkers, little knowing what lay in store for our entire organization.

On the second day of the meeting in Bangkok, David Platt, president of the International Mission Board, brought a message on the book of Exodus, a sermon he titled "The Spirit of God, the Missionary Task, and the Glory of God." David's sermon brought up important questions as he made the case that the only hope for the success of us missionaries' work is the presence of God with us.

A question that struck me hard was "Are you working in dependence on yourself, or are you working with desperation for His Spirit?"[1] David explained through the example of Moses pleading with God not to withdraw His presence from the Israelites (Exodus 33:3). Earlier, Moses had pleaded with God to spare His people and not destroy them. And indeed, the destruction of the nation of Israel was averted through the intercessory prayer Moses offered.

In a later chapter of Exodus, however, God threatens a remedial judgement on Israel in the form of the withdrawal of His presence (Exodus 33:3). Then, in Verses 15–16, Moses says, "If your presence does not go with us, do not send us up from here. How will anyone know that you are pleased with me and with our people unless you go with us? What else will distinguish me and your people from all the other people on the face of the earth?" (Exodus 33: 15–16).

Were we—was I—desperate to have the presence of God in our lives and our ministries, as Moses had been desperate? My assembled colleagues and I, numbering over 1,500 missionaries, certainly should have felt desperate for the presence of God in our lives. Without His presence there, David reminded us, our ministries would be powerless and fruitless!

PYONGYANG REVIVAL

From Bangkok to Korea, now, the Korea of more than a century ago. There are some clear similarities between what we experienced in our five days in Bangkok and what went on during a revival over 100 years ago in (as unlikely as it now sounds) the present capital of North Korea. Around 1900, less than one percent of Korea's population was Christian. The "Pyongyang Revival" started changing that in 1907. This long-ago revival is sometimes called the Korean Pentecost. What was the Pyongyang Revival, exactly?

In January of 1907, a Bible conference had been planned that would bring together in Pyongyang a large number of Korean Christians as well as Christian missionaries from outside their country. In anticipation of this conference, pastors in Korea began pleading with God, praying prayers full of desperation. Korea was a struggling nation, and its churches were struggling. The pastors kept up their desperate prayers. The conference began, and during the preaching of the Word at one service, the pastors and the missionaries became overwhelmingly aware of their sinfulness and their need to repent. The conviction stirred first one, then others, then many of these leaders to publicly confess their sins, including sins they had "hidden," in vain of course, from God. They confessed bitterness harbored in their hearts against others in their circles. Before long, people in the audience were confessing their own sins, standing and crying out to God for mercy. The desperation was so powerful that the confessions did not wind down until hours after midnight.

The wave of soul-searching awareness that overwhelmed participants in the Pyongyang Bible conference resembles what I was going to see sweeping over the Baptist missionaries hearing Pastor Platt on the second day of our "Foundations" meeting. In Bangkok as in Pyongyang, those gathered were led to study God's Word, to confess sins, to utter audible collective prayers, and to cry out to God for mercy—the four marks of revival.

In Korea, since the 1907 revival, nothing short of a miracle has occurred. Its political history in the twentieth century may be one of turmoil, resulting first from the Japanese occupation and later from war that ultimately divided the country into South Korea and communist North Korea. But Korea's spiritual history 113 years after the Pyongyang Revival truly glorifies God.

Today, more than 10 million believers are found in South Korea (many descended from Christians who fled from the north after Korea's civil war). Today, only the United States sends more missionaries into the world than South Korea does, which is absolutely incredible given that its population is equal in size to the populations of California and Florida, merely two of our fifty states. In one century, an area in which less than one in a hundred citizens had been Christian became a leading center for mission work, offering the Gospel of Jesus Christ globally.

One has to ask, "How does this happen?" and only one answer makes sense: It happens only through the power of the desperate prayers that have been offered in Korea. Fruits began to flow when Korea's Christians realized that a desperate devotion to prayer was required. Moreover, one has to wonder, "When will this happen in other nations, like Indonesia, or in a place like Afghanistan, with a population still including less than one in a hundred Christian residents?"

The revival in Korea in 1907 exhibited all four required marks, or components, of revival. The four produce the fertile ground in which seeds of spiritual awakening can grow. Importantly, we can't pick and choose components. Although it is necessary, it isn't sufficient to study God's Word, no matter how well and how thoroughly. Also necessary is confession of sin, but it is rare that we encounter a hatred of sin like that unleashed during the Pyongyang Revival. After all, how many of us compare to Ezra, falling on his knees to pray desperately that the sins of the people would be forgiven—and his own sins as well (Ezra 9)? How many of us have even seen prayer like that? For me, the closest such experience occurred in Bangkok at that IMB "Foundations" meeting.

REVIVAL AMONG MISSIONARIES

After David gave his sermon, I remember, we took a break for refreshments. As we came back together, something very interesting happened. Two colleagues proposed to one of the event leaders that the Spirit of Christ had been moving in our session before we broke. They suggested giving an invitation for folks to respond to what God had said to us all. The group of event leaders concurred and asked David to extend an invitation, which he promptly did. That is when the Spirit of God started moving in a way that is hard to put in words.

People began by confessing their sins openly. I can remember seeing several leaders, including David Platt, prostrate on the stage, pouring their hearts out to God. Some asked to be forgiven for wrongs they had personally done to others. Eventually we had said what we had to say in that moment. But throughout the rest of that day, and sporadically over the rest of the weeklong meeting, we were moved again to confess and ask forgiveness. When this outpouring of God's Spirit came over us following the sermon and break, nothing strange or sensationalistic happened. It was just that we experienced together a deep awareness of the holiness of God and also an acute awareness of our own sinfulness.

Things got even sweeter as we met in the evenings in our affinity groups. We continued the time of public confession and repentance, and we frequently broke into spontaneous praise that lasted until midnight. One night, the East Asia affinity group overheard the group I belonged to, the Southeast Asia affinity group, singing in our meeting room. They wanted in on the unplanned worship and praise session we had begun. It was beautiful, this need to respond to God's manifested glory in our midst.

After many years of praying for revival and spiritual awaking, those days of the "Foundations" meeting were the closest thing to revival that I have ever been part of. They showed me what revival is: God's manifested presence among His people. Revival is God drawing near to those who are earnestly seeking His face. Every one of the missionaries attending that meeting had an experience that was going to influence their being and their ministries for the rest of their lives. No one isn't *somehow* changed upon being presented with God's manifest holiness and righteousness in such a demonstrable fashion. Moses was changed by it in Exodus 33: 17–23, where we read that it pleased God to manifest His glory to Moses because Moses's heart sought not just God's power, but His glorious presence. I am persuaded that God made his glory unforgettably known to the entire IMB leadership that week in Bangkok. I am persuaded that our experience there was a heaven-sent revival.

I shared my certainty with my Southeast Asia affinity group when we convened to discuss what God was doing in our midst: Our meeting was the scene of a real reviving. I also shared the story of my conversion experience dating from the Jesus Movement of the very early 1970s. I talked about how the movement saved the United States from coming apart at the seams, so divided was it politically, racially, and economically. There was 1968, for example, just over a dozen months—at most two dozen—before 1970. Writers for the History Channel described that year like this: "The year 1968 remains one of the most tumultuous single years in history, marked by historic achievements, shocking assassinations, a much-hated war and a spirit of rebellion that swept through countries all over the world."[2]

The Jesus Movement helped heal America's worst rifts of the era, those brought about by the Vietnam War, urban racial strife, and the 1968 loss of two beloved leaders to assassination. And I had been saved during that great spiritual awakening. I talked with my affinity group about my longing for another such movement of God, which was desperately needed not only in the USA but in each country our particular ministries served.

I wanted to see the heaven-sent revival that had graced our Bangkok meeting repeated in every area my colleagues and I served across Southeast Asia. And I knew it had happened before in Indonesia. It was not impossible; "with God all things are possible" (Matthew 19: 26). Avery Willis has written about this major movement of God among Javanese Muslims, in his book *Why Two Million Javanese* Came to Christ. Great spiritual awakening had already taken place in Indonesia when our missionaries there experienced revival. God had worked in the hearts of many Javanese Muslims, bringing them to Christ amidst the socioeconomic upheaval that followed an attempted coup d'etat and ensuing counter-coups in the mid-1960s, when Sukarno was in power. The missionaries were inspired by their own revival to pursue key changes to the Baptist mission in Indonesia. Collectively, the changes are called the *Tretes* Decision. That is because the missionaries carried out the work of strengthening their organization's goals, strategies, methods, and tools at *Tretes*, a resort in the mountains of East Java.

Not only could I imagine revival happening all over Southeast Asia, I could imagine it happening anywhere the International Mission Board had personnel around the world. Could God's reason for bringing all of us together in Bangkok for that meeting be a reason well in line with His purposes for the Nations? Was He spiritually preparing each one who had come to discuss that document and ended up in revival in His manifest presence, powering us to return home and share this vision with family, with our IMB teams, and most importantly with the believers we served?

Large numbers of the people attending the meeting could see this with me. Maybe, they agreed, that was just what God was doing. But shortly, there was pushback, too. Some people, although they were well-meaning, hesitated at the thought of sharing such an idea of revival. They feared it would cause jealousy and envy among colleagues not invited to the meeting—and also spiritual pride on the part of the missionaries who had been sent. I recognized such outcomes could very well occur. Still, I yearned inside to communicate the story of what we experienced, so that it would not just end in Bangkok. The need felt desperate.

BERGUMUL

It is hard to put in words exactly what I was feeling. For me, the sort of intense desire and struggle in prayer I experienced is best named with an

Indonesian word. In Indonesia, my brothers and sisters in Christ have often used this word to talk about times when to finally hear God in their prayers required them to struggle and strive and agonize to recognize His voice. The word is *bergumul*. I am most likely to hear it when someone is spending time in prayer in order to know God's will on a particular matter, like some change in one's role or a move to a new location with a challenging new ministry. Bergumul suggests struggle, a wrestling with God if you will, similar to what Jacob endured at the River Jabbok, in the strange passage that has him encountering an angel, or perhaps the preincarnate Jesus, Son of God Himself (Genesis 32: 22–32).

Jacob prays, and what he prays for is important: "I will not let you go until you bless me," he states. Now unfortunately, a distortion of biblical Christianity too intent on believers' great health and great wealth has come to warp the thinking of too many of our Christian brothers and sisters. Naïvely, they have been convinced that physical and material well-being alone constitute God's blessing. Such name-it-and-claim-it teachings represent a radical departure from biblical truth. David's sermon in Bangkok reminded us that what Moses wanted from God was God's most important blessing: His presence in Moses' life. God's presence is the ultimate blessing in any life, however much that life is touched by sorrow and trouble and suffering.

The top priority for us in life does not involve riches or success. Our top priority is to seek God's face, which we do when we place highest value on experiencing His presence in our lives. When he asked to be blessed, Jacob hoped simply to have God's presence in his life. Jesus also taught this lesson, directing us to seek God's kingdom and God's values above all things. For instance, Jesus said, "But seek first his Kingdom and his righteousness, and all these things will be given to you as well" (Matthew 6:33). To seek God with all of your heart, to seek Him *whole*heartedly, is to set your sights on His presence in your life.

Richard Owen Roberts talks about God's presence having three parts, the essential presence of God, the manifested presence of God, and the cultivated presence of God. That God's presence has an *essential* form means that God is omnipresent and omniscient: God is everywhere, always. This is the form of God's presence that Psalm 139: 7–10 talks about: "Where can I go from your Spirit? Where can I flee from your presence? If I go up to the heavens, you are there; if I make my bed in the depths, you are there. If I rise on the wings of the dawn, if I settle on the far side of the sea, even there your hand will guide me . . . ."

The *manifested* form of God's presence, in turn, is available in moments when we are fully aware that God is near. This is revival, when heaven draws near to Earth. God's manifested presence enables you to know yourself and sort out your offenses before Holy God. Outside that presence, if reminded of our sins, we can actually be casual about them and perhaps say, "Oh, well, so what?" Inside God's manifest presence, that becomes impossible due to the intense recognition there that His presence is sheer delight to us! Sinning against Almighty God seems undoable, undareable. *How could I?* His presence so delights us that we reject even fleeting desire to commit sin, even a sin that would never come to light in our home or community. When we seek for the delight contained in God, we are seeking God's manifest presence.

Finally, we can avail ourselves of the *cultivated* presence of God. While no man or woman can make revival happen, day by day each of us can cultivate God's presence and consciously acknowledge its value to be more precious than gold. We can cultivate our recognition that nothing is equal to God, who as we have seen is *essentially* present. Daily and weekly prayers and Bible study are how we commit ourselves to finding God in

His cultivated presence. This commitment is both an individual one and a corporate one, belonging as we do to our churches, where in worship services and prayer meetings we can diligently seek Him together.[3]

Returning to the concept of *bergumul*, at our big meeting in Thailand, what did I struggle with, specifically, as I prayed? My struggle was the contemplation of how our Indonesian National Partners could be led to experience the thing that we were experiencing during that May week in 2018, which was nothing less than God's manifested presence. I longed to help lead them, and so did most of the folks who came to spend the week studying and discussing our "Foundations" document. But how?

Too many of the churches we missionaries worked with made only lethargic efforts to carry out the Great Commission. Too many were spiritually asleep. Within the Indonesian Baptist Convention of Churches, some churches that we worked with had drifted from their concern for the lost. They lacked much interest even in reaching their very own nation's Unreached People Groups, which remained virtually untouched by the Gospel. If we wanted to go out from Bangkok to influence, initially, our own churches, and then the multitudes of lost people across the countries we served, making real impact on their cultures, then the first thing required was *churches come alive*. What I mean by that is all of our churches needed a fresh visitation of the Spirit of God in their midst. But again, how to facilitate that?

I wrote this book because I wanted to share the *bergumul* I have experienced in prayer (*bergumul*, remember, is the struggle to discern God's voice). This struggling or grappling or wrestling or contesting has been with me since I arrived on the mission field in 1986, but the "Foundations" meeting in Bangkok heightened my prayer struggle's urgency and desperation. As I see it, my missionary career was born in revival and is turning out to finish up in revival, too, a pleasing symmetry. But it saw its share of struggle, of the workaday-life variety and the *bergumul* variety as well. A runner who manages to break the tape and cross the finish line successfully does so through hard work—training that is daily and continual and rigorous, plus "the struggle" that goes into preparing to run the race. We can see the runner's *bergumul* or inner struggle as aching legs and lungs push toward the finish line. The struggle was also there well before the race. Rest assured that the struggle and its oddly simple goal—to win the prize—have accompanied the runner for a long time.

There are some parallels between foot races and the unfolding of a Christian's life, as the Apostle Paul mused in the first letter he wrote to the Corinthians: "Do you not know that in a race all the runners run, but only one gets the prize? Run in such a way as to get the prize. Everyone who competes in the games goes into strict training. They do it to get a crown that will not last; but we do it to get a crown that will last forever. Therefore I do not run like a man running aimlessly; I do not fight like a man beating the air. No, I beat my body and make it my slave so that after I have preached to others, I myself will not be disqualified for the prize" (1 Corinthians 9: 24–27).

GOD IS A COMMUNICATING GOD

The Christian faith is unique. Alone among all religions, Christians have a God that can be personally known, in and through the Son of God, Jesus Christ. Christians' God can be known intimately, since He wants a personal relationship with each one. When I first got saved, this is what excited me about Christian faith. I could speak to God and God, moreover, would hear me and answer me, my prayers rewarded with direction and guidance for living life.

Years on, I have served the Lord Jesus for over three decades among the largest Muslim population of any of the world's countries, and I've noticed something. Despite the regularity of their prayers, Muslims never talk about getting answers to their spiritual petitions. They value reciting prayers over and over, more so if the prayers are said in Arabic. Such recitation, in the view of Muslims, brings extra credit as they work to amass a pile of good works that might tip the scale on Judgement Day (*Kiamat*, in Arabic) and be enough to get them into heaven. But never have I heard any Muslim brag about how Allah heard a fervent prayer and answered, relieving distress or supplying comfort. That no doubt results from the fact that, while Muslims are taught that they can and should know the contents of their holy book, the Al-Quran, they are also taught the impossibility of personally knowing their God, Allah.

In contrast, many a former Muslim has talked to me of how God answered their prayers that had been prayed in Jesus' name. One was Bowo, a taxi driver who took me home from the airport in Semarang, where I live. He and I spoke on some general topics, after which I proceeded to share the Gospel with him. Bowo then described how his disabled wife had been prayed for in the name of Jesus at a 2002 crusade in Semarang and miraculously stood up from her wheelchair and started walking!

Christians' prayers are spiritual communication, and the God known in the person of Jesus Christ is a communicative God. Repeatedly He gives us a personal Word for our life. And, choosing to speak to *me* or to *you*, the Word He gives is not given to anyone else. It is this person's or that person's or yours or mine *personally* and reflects the circumstances of that one life. I worry that in North America, our churches are forgetting the important personal nature of God's Word to us. God wants to communicate to each individual the ideas that illustrate His perfect will for each life. I've met several one-time Muslims, though, who testified that they came to Christ when God spoke to them in a dream or a vision, and they subsequently confirmed His Word by reading Christianity's holy book, the *Injil*, or New Testament. They were drawn to Christ and His assurance that His followers' prayers get answers. They walked away from the religion in which they were raised to embrace a faith that promises personal answers and an actual dialog about what is happening in that life for which He indeed has a plan. Every life.

If we forget the personal nature of God's Word, we miss the heart of Christianity, which is the gift of living in intimate relationship with God in a way that is real and dynamic. North American churches these days are at risk of losing the concept of personal communication with the Divine that gives Christianity deep meaning and makes it unique and exciting. It may be that our society's overemphasis on *doing*, on *activity*, has led us to equate the good with the busy. But genuine spirituality, while it consumes both time and energy, is not generally perceived to be busy-ness. Or it may be that more-liberal churches' antisupernaturalism has colored evangelical churches' outlook. It seems rare anymore to find evangelical Christians really struggling to hear God's voice concerning a big decision to be made, whether in work or romance or other arenas. Rarely do today's Christians pray about things like this, instead seeking counsel from peers or friends or a search engine. Seldom is the Lord of Lords and King of Kings consulted.

Yet leaving God out of a decision means we have only our own limited understanding and vision to rely on. When we invite God to contribute His vital input, what we gain is the largest possible perspective. After all, He is the One to see the whole picture, being both omniscient and omnipresent. We have nothing to lose by relying on Him alone—whereas there is much to lose in relying only on ourselves: "Trust in the LORD with all your heart and lean not on your own understanding; in all your ways acknowledge him, and he will make your paths straight" (Proverbs 3: 5–6).

INTRODUCTION

One item God may contribute to the making of life decisions is His well-known "call." As a person in full-time ministry for approaching fifty years, I can say I have heard a whole lot of discussion about "the call to ministry" and the call to become a foreign missionary. A lot of different opinions can be found on what constitutes such a "call."

If you are like some others, you might consider it a call when you notice a need in a church or community and then notice that your spiritual gifts and the way God has shaped you seem strongly in line with serving that need. You conclude you have had a call from God to take up that "ministry." However, perceiving a call from God solely through such observations is an exercise in futility. All will be based on your inevitably limited perspective as you size up the need and assess your own talents or gifting.

If you are like yet others, you might think another person or an organization can decide what God's will for your life is. But you would be mistaken to turn to some church council or missions board, administrator or bishop to relay a call so thoroughly affecting your future. Certainly God can, sometimes, use His body to communicate with you. But an entirely new role, or a whole new direction in ministry, is a call you absolutely must hear in the form of God's personal Word to you yourself.

Authentic calls from God are described all through the Bible, in both the Old and New Testaments. When God was about to destroy the Earth with a flood, He spoke to Noah. The communication was a personal Word, given to Noah alone, directing him on the details of the ark (it turned out that the ark prefigured Jesus Christ, and all that are in Christ—like the people on the ark—are not condemned but are saved). When God spoke to Abram telling him to leave Mesopotamia for Canaan to the southwest, it was a *personal* Word and calling. God also said to Abram that God would make him the father of many Nations, with descendants outnumbering the grains of sand on all beaches combined and outnumbering the stars in the heavens. No other man would be that father. Again, a very personal Word.

God spoke to Hannah when Peninnah mocked her childlessness. He promised Hannah a child, whose name would be Samuel. Samuel would not be born to any other mother. Another personal Word. Samuel grew to become the first prophet, eventually anointing a shepherd boy with ruddy complexion as King of all Israel. The boy, David, had also received God's personal Word. As David was harassed and chased all over the Palestinian countryside, he clung fast to his Word from God, the only sign at all in his life thus far that he would rule Israel.

The New Testament tells of old Simeon and his contemporary, the elderly Anna. God's personal Word to Simeon was that one day, Simeon would see and hold the long-awaited Messiah. God spoke to Anna about her life and what His purpose for it had been.

Following his dramatic conversion on the Damascus Road, Saul of Tarsus received God's Word and calling directly from Jesus, whom Saul had been recently persecuting. *Personal Word.* Saul then knew to go to Damascus, to a street called Straight, and wait for further directions.

The Bible is full of this kind of story. There was the church at Antioch that prayed until God spoke a personal message to Paul and Barnabas. It was His call to begin the missionary endeavors that would bring the Gospel to Asia Minor and then Europe.

In stories, motive is often important. It seems natural to wonder why God gave us the Scriptures and prepared our salvation. Did He save us merely to go to heaven and avoid a burning hell? Clearly no. So what is, in fact, God's purpose for humankind? Are we here to hang around until Jesus comes the second time? Again, no. God's will for each life includes specific tasks, which are communicated personally through God's Word to the believer for whom the tasks are tailored. But the believer must hear, which means the believer must listen.

I want to be clear. God is a communicating God, wanting to communicate with you, with me. God speaks to His children and gives each a personal Word or calling. But what can explain God's emphasis on communicating individually with us?

First, such individual communication enlarges our faith. God wants us to grow in our understanding of His Person, His ways, His purposes. That growth comes through challenges in our walk with Him. These challenges include listening for and listening to His personal Word. In other words, discerning God's voice and heeding His personal Word can be difficult, requiring us to struggle toward understanding. In his book *Experiencing God*, Henry Blackaby explains that it is very common for a crisis of faith to occur in association with hearing God's call. This crisis of faith is experienced by so many Christians that Blackaby calls it a "reality" ("Reality 5" of a series of "realities" he writes about). "God's Calling brings us to a crisis of faith," according to Blackaby, "that requires of us faith and action." God personally communicates His will to us in order to strengthen our faith by requiring our action.

Second, God further wants us to grow in our capacity to be used by Him. Expect to be called to God-sized tasks! I was, when I heard God's call to learn another language and culture in the place with the world's largest Muslim population. A human charged with a God-sized task can only work at it and trust that God will pull it off. Where such tasks are concerned, God's will is achieved only through absolute dependence on Him to use us as is best.

May I just say to you, reader, that God has a purpose for your life. But it may well be something other than spending your next 35 years in a faraway place like Indonesia. It is very unlikely you will need to take the same steps that God's call to my wife, Shelly, and me required all those years ago. But whatever He calls you to do, it is certain He will enable and empower you to do it.

The first step in accomplishing something great for God is hearing Him on the subject of what He wants us to do. We simply don't know what to do until we hear His personal Word, the call. The call will tether us to the task He wills for us, keeping us going in tough times and dark days. The call holds our hands to the plough, continually engaging the heart in the task even when every outward indication (not to mention everyone we know) seems to urge, "Take the easy way out, go home, resign."

In the pages of this book, we will examine different facets and aspects of God's call. A number of chapters explore a specified kind of call experience that my family and I went through. If you'll join me in traveling again the route of my family's life journey to date, I will show you a selection of our victories and defeats, the mountain tops and valleys on view as the Savior challenged our walk with Him. I want you to be able to feel our *bergumul* with our Lord Jesus as we persistently sought His will, struggled for His will, on various matters.

Some things I will share still have the power to make me weep as I relive them on paper. And some of the experiences I have shared in the book will, I hope, strike you as humorous. Living in Indonesia gave our family plenty to laugh about, and most other people also seem amused, at points, as we tell certain stories aloud (as we do for churches in the United States and for our colleagues on the mission field, our National Partners, and folks encountered during stateside assignments and furloughs). The book looks over my family's missionary work beginning in 1983, when my call to the foreign mission field directed that I go and reach the Muslim men and women of Indonesia. It also includes some of my background and Shelly's that paved the way for our service overseas.

Importantly, I have tried always to highlight the struggle, the *bergumul*, we faced leading to each new phase of our journey. We sought our Lord's Will at every turn on the mission field. Deciding to serve in Indonesia, receiving that call from God, was only the beginning. Our walk with Christ has been a constant seeking of His face and of His leadership in our lives. Seeking God once, then being done with that, is not how it works. The called accept a lifelong quest, each day of which involves denying one's flesh in order to seek Christ's face and His Will. The prophet Azariah gave King Asa a similar lesson: "He went out to meet Asa and said to him, 'Listen to me, Asa and all Judah and Benjamin. The LORD is with you when you are with him. If you seek him, he will be found by you, but if you forsake him, he will forsake you.' But in their distress they turned to the LORD, the God of Israel, and sought him, and he was found by them" (2 Chronicles 15: 2–4).

I wanted this book to illustrate how, at the key transitions of our journey with God, He gave my family direction and guidance. In the valleys, God's presence helped us bear up under difficulty and heartbreak of a kind we had not imagined. At points of spiritual victory, too, God's presence came, and with it the awareness that His grace in our lives was precisely the thing securing victory. He blessed us because He was leading, and we could follow where He led because we worked so hard at seeking His face.

To lay the groundwork for an effective cross-cultural ministry overseas, choices must be made. None is equal in importance to seeking God and hearing from Him. To handle the multitude of challenges that accompany attempts to minister cross-culturally requires firm faith and concrete action. Faith grows more firm from hearing God's personal Word that specifies His call and His will for our lives.

In biblical accounts, whenever God is about to take action of some kind, He communicates this fact to His people. He spoke to Moses, to David and Samuel, and He speaks now to people living in the twenty-first century. Now as then, at times when important transitions loom, God's people wait for their God's call and take direction from it. The Bible makes clear that this is key to any decision's success. Do you remember, for example, when Joshua forgot to consult God before making a covenant with the Gibeonites? Notice how this played out: "The men of Israel sampled their provisions but did not inquire of the LORD. Then Joshua made a treaty of peace with them to let them live, and the leaders of the assembly ratified it by oath" (Joshua 9: 14–15). Quickly, however, Joshua discovered that he had made a mistake, erred gravely, committed a serious sin. *Not inquiring of the Lord* in such a weighty matter would haunt him over the rest of his career as a leader.

Joshua was a veteran strategist and knew enough to talk with God before leading troops in battle. But agreeing to a peace seemed innocent enough. So Joshua and his team rushed the decision and acted on their own. Leaving out God's perfect guidance soon found them dealing with angry people and an awkward alliance: "Three days after they made the treaty with the Gibeonites, the Israelites heard that they were neighbors, living near them. So the Israelites set out and on the third day came to their cities: Gibeon, Kephirah, Beeroth and Kiriath Jearim. But the Israelites did not attack them, because the leaders of the assembly had sworn an oath to them by the LORD, the God of Israel. The whole assembly grumbled against the leaders" (Joshua 9: 16–18).

For as long as they continued in the Promised Land, Joshua and the Israelites were greatly bothered by various ramifications of their agreement with the Gibeonites. Just by being there, the cunning, conniving tribe constantly reminded the Israelites of their unthinking transgression. . The story's inclusion in holy Scripture forever reminds us of the importance of seeking God's will and Word before making decisions that will prove meaningful in our lives.

CHAPTER 1

CALL TO SALVATION

⁶ About noon as I came near Damascus, suddenly a bright light from heaven flashed around me.

⁷ I fell to the ground and heard a voice say to me, "Saul! Saul! Why do you persecute me?"

⁸ "Who are you, Lord?" I asked. "I am Jesus of Nazareth, whom you are persecuting," he replied.

⁹ My companions saw the light, but they did not understand the voice of him who was speaking to me.

¹⁰ "What shall I do, Lord?" I asked. "Get up," the Lord said, "and go into Damascus. There you will be told all that you have been assigned to do."

– Acts 22: 6-10

JESUS MOVEMENT AND ASBURY REVIVAL

The evangelical Christian *Jesus Movement* began in the later 1960s on the West Coast of the United States. The movement spread through North America, Europe, and Central America, primarily, thriving for two decades before subsiding by the late 1980s. Members of the movement were called *Jesus people* or *Jesus freaks*. In another chapter I will share some details about the movement's influence on my ministry and my life.

During the time the Jesus Movement was catching hold in the United States, a remarkable event occurred on the campus of Asbury College in the small community of Wilmore, Kentucky, not far from Lexington. A scheduled fifty-minute worship service—one of the college's regular chapel services conducted in its Hughes Auditorium—broke out in revival that continued non-stop for *185 hours*, from Tuesday, February 3, to Tuesday, February 10, 1970. It was the "Asbury Revival" of 1970, and its influence, along with that of the Jesus Movement on the West Coast, proved to be a spiritual awakening of gigantic proportions. Surrounding the Asbury Revival and Jesus Movement, millions of young people came to faith in Christ. They were college students or they were hippies, and large numbers were people caught up fervently in protesting against the Vietnam War.

I came to faith in Jesus Christ in 1975, during that time of significant spiritual awakening. I see my own spiritual conversion to have taken place not in a spiritual vacuum, but as part of a very significant movement of God in the life of our nation (which was just a little more than a year away from celebrating its bicentennial). By 1974, signs of the power of the spiritual awakening were seen all across the American landscape. Most notable were the "coffeehouse" ministries known as Jesus Houses, which sprouted up everywhere and had the sole purpose of reaching out to the millions of students and other young people who felt "turned off" by the traditional church. The Jesus Houses sponsored by churches from the late 1960s to middle 1970s were where we could hear Christian music played by guitarists and other musicians whose beat was as contemporary as it gets. In the Jesus Houses, the work of artists like Second Chapter of Acts and the duo Larry Norman and Phil Keaggy took the place of the time-honored hymns of the old Broadman Hymnal. It was a significant movement of the Holy Spirit. It brought a Christian message to a kind of music that appealed to folks like me, people in youngest adulthood who loved music with a contemporary flavor.

Embarrassingly, I must admit I was three sheets to the wind when I had my first experience visiting a Jesus House. I was a first-semester university student in West Palm Beach, Florida. Fellow students invited me to go with them to the coffeehouse that had been opened by local pastor and evangelist Fenton Moorhead. More embarrassingly still, I must admit that I went along because the fellow students who invited me were two girls I thought were cute.

At the coffeehouse, I listened to the music briefly. But soon, I remember, I was under such heavy conviction by the Holy Spirit that I bolted for the door, deciding never to attend such a strange church meeting again! That was in the fall of 1974. And as that semester and year came to an end, I only became more rebellious. After my second semester at the university, I had earned "disciplinary probation" from university administrators when marijuana was found in my dorm room. In summer 1975, I went home to Louisville, Kentucky, for the break. My subsequent decision not to return to Palm Beach Atlantic University was an abrupt one that I blamed on others: I had had it with Baptist institutions always seeming to breed a bunch of Jesus freaks!

God had other plans, however. On an evening in early June, two friends dropped by, one of whom had been my gambling buddy during high school days in Louisville. Earlier that day, as it just so happened, I had been at Churchill Downs, the infamous racecourse, and had lost my proverbial shirt. Spending time at Churchill Downs had been a habit since my senior year of high school. But this appearance by my two friends, and what happened that evening, was going to change my life forever.

"Terry" I knew well, and he was spokesman during the guys' forty-five-minute visit that night. The Lord used Terry in a significant way. Terry told me first that Jesus Christ had transformed his life. He had turned from a path of gambling, drugs, and debauchery and promiscuity to a walk of faith in Jesus. He shared this passage out of Revelation: "I know your deeds, that you are neither cold nor hot. I wish you were either one or the other! So, because you are lukewarm—neither hot nor cold—I am about to spit you out of my mouth" (Revelation 3: 15–16). And honestly, I knew I was not hot; good grief, I wasn't even lukewarm! What's more, I was so under conviction that I welcomed what I thought would be the end of the guys' visit.

Then Terry, my buddy, offered me a pocket-sized New Testament and invited me to the local Jesus House later, where each Saturday night young people gathered to play and listen to music and to worship the Lord Jesus. I knew I'd find it uncomfortable and weird, but I agreed to go, probably just to get rid of the two. When my friends left, things got even stranger for me. I turned on the TV, thinking to block out the clutter in my mind by watching some show. I scanned the few channels we had back then; I found Billy Graham starting one of his crusades and in fact just beginning his sermon. As I listened to him preach the Gospel, it was as if his message was being delivered especially to me. By the time he finished, I was so convicted by the Spirit that I went out to the back porch and kneeled and prayed to receive Christ. Although I have no idea what the exact words were that I prayed, I am certain you could describe them as a "crying out to the Lord."

At the Louisville Jesus House two days later, I made a public profession of faith with Harold Beeler, an old Marine who led the outreach ministry of Rockford Lane Baptist Church. I could not overstate how influential that particular church's mission outreach was for me, and I'm sure I have company. Over the two-year heyday of Rockford Lane Baptist's Jesus House mission, over 300 young people came to faith and were delivered from sex addiction, drug and alcohol addiction, and as in my case, gambling addiction. I see the Rockford Lane Baptist Church outreach as something firmly linked to the Jesus Movement and Asbury Revival, even if those were winding down by 1975. I was saved through one church outreach in Louisville, Kentucky, that was part of God's casting of a magnificent broad net over the whole country during that time.

Obviously, the experience had a big impact on the way I viewed evangelism and Missions, such that after receiving Christ in June, by July I felt led to return to the university after all and change my major from business administration to biblical studies. Back on campus, when they learned of my conversion to Christ many who had known me the previous year came to view me, I think, in something like the way Ananias viewed Saul of Tarsus: "'Lord,' Ananias answered, 'I have heard many reports about this man and all the harm he has done to your saints in Jerusalem. And he has come here with authority from the chief priests to arrest all who call on your name'" (Acts 9: 13–14).

I greatly appreciate people that God raised up to help disciple and mentor me during those first few months after I became a believer. And I have great appreciation for the many people God led me to who have enriched my belief and challenged me to be a faithful follower of Jesus Christ. If it came to singling out one person, though, it would have to be Jerry Cadenhead, who also became a missionary with the International Mission Board. Jerry was just a couple years ahead of me in college, but I remember how he took me under his wing to disciple and to pour his life into me. As someone who followed Christ with abundant energy, Jerry provided a stirring model.

Jerry invited me to help out at a mission church located about an hour's drive from the Palm Beach Atlantic campus, in Delray Beach, Florida. This church, Grace Baptist Church, focused on outreach in Hispanic and African American neighborhoods. It was a challenging ministry in a tough area. Grace Baptist was one of many experiences I would soon have through which God shaped me for the mission field. I served with Grace Baptist Church for the next three years, as bus minister, youth director, and associate pastor. I even helped in opening a coffeehouse that, during my days at Grace Baptist, reached out to some rather tough hombres included among the neighborhood kids. One night, one associate minister, Ron Lentine, had to put his black-belt-karate skills to use to take down a thug who threatened him with a knife during the course of Ron's witness. Gradually, the community's ethnically and culturally diverse residents began to come in for performances of Christian music and also for testimonies. The Gospel's transforming power when people sing about it and witness to it at multiethnic, multicultural gatherings is such astonishing testimony of how God unifies all people in Christ!

PEAS OR CARROTS?

The thing for which I most wholeheartedly thank Ron and Jerry, my good friends, is the introduction they gave me to Susan Michele Smith, or Shelly, my future bride. We had encountered each other before. I will always remember her first words to me: "Peas or carrots?" You see, Shelly was a server in the university cafeteria. I was pushing my tray along through the lunch line, and suddenly a petite brunette with big brown eyes was offering me the day's choice of vegetable! Jerry and Ron were able to tell me that the attractive cafeteria worker with the sunny disposition was the daughter of their pastor in Delray Beach. Once I had served at their church a couple of months, I started noticing that the right chemistry seemed to exist between me and Shelly. I was attracted to her and also impressed that she was such a strong Christian. And her father's church was going to be my church home for the next three years as I pursued my degree in biblical studies. How blessed was I?

How very much the Lord blessed me *throughout* my time at Palm Beach Atlantic University. I had great opportunities for ministry. I had places to land on weekends, with members of a church that served Him by feeding and caring for me. But most importantly, He in His Sovereign plan brought me into contact with the love my life, Shelly Smith Bruckert, my wife for more than 40 years now. She has truly been a blessing, the perfect match and helpmate in life and ministry.

With a bachelor of arts degree in hand, in August 1978 I began seminary studies in Louisville, my birthplace. Concurrently, my home church at Rockford Lane called me to join its staff as a minister to the occupants of some apartment houses about four miles from the church. For Southern Baptists, an apartment house ministry was a pioneering effort, something new that very little had been done with. What a challenge! God had again called me to a kind of ministry that pushed the envelope. It remained my challenge until January 1981, when I completed my master of divinity degree at Southern Baptist Theological Seminary.

CHAPTER 2

CALL TO SERVE

"Then I heard the voice of the Lord saying,
'Whom shall I send? And who will go for us?'"
— *Isaiah 6: 8*

"If God calls you to be a minister, don't stoop to becoming a king."[1]
— *C. H. Spurgeon*

A large part of my understanding about a call to full-time ministry, I owe to Shelly's father, my father-in-law, Dr. James Stanley Smith. He was a robust version of the typical Fundamentalist Southern Baptist Preacher. And while on occasion my father-in-law and I didn't see eye to eye about things related to interpreting scripture, I clearly benefited, during my early years as a Christian, from reading texts he brought to my attention that presented conservative theological perspectives. All in all, I owe a lot to Brother Jim, as I called him.

I considered his views to be very scriptural. When we found ourselves toward the end of the decade of the 1970s, I really appreciated his understanding of the doctrine of the inerrancy of scripture, which was being hotly debated by evangelical churches, especially the leaders of the Southern Baptist Convention. Indeed, the inerrancy of scripture was the hot-button topic during my time as a graduate student at seminary. From about 1978 to 1981, Southern Baptist Theological Seminary was influenced greatly by a liberal and neo-orthodox theological position.

Many of its students were sucked into that left-wing persuasion. Thanks to the theological foundation given to me by my father-in-law, I knew something about the theological right, which students heard very little about on campus at Southern. (An unquestionable exception to that quietness was Dr. Lewis Drummond, professor of evangelism, who labeled himself the seminary's "resident fundamentalist.")

Well before my time at seminary, Brother Jim—my future father-in-law, Dr. James Stanley Smith—had placed the theological underpinnings that would hold me fast and keep my feet solidly on scriptural ground during my time at Southern. They had done the same at Palm Beach Atlantic, where the prevailing theological winds had similarly blown from the direction of a liberal perspective. After I began working weekends under his supervision at Grace Baptist in Delray Beach, Brother Jim initially challenged me about my call to ministry. He said that if I had genuinely been called by God to full-time ministry, then I should be able to match my experience to the experience of a character in Holy Scripture. If no story could be found to match my experience, then he simply doubted the call. Honestly, I was offended at first that he had questioned God's call to me. As it turned out, however, what he said reiterated an invaluable lesson. It is this: When God speaks to us He speaks through the Bible, the inspired, inerrant Word of God. So I prayed. "Lord," I asked, "speak to me through your Word if you are really calling me to ministry. Please, Lord, speak to me through the scripture."

It would be my first experience of *bergumul*, or struggling with the Lord and the call experience, and it set the tone for many such wrestling matches to come, as I sought to hear His voice and get direction. The effort required great focus and mental strength, taking lots of my energy and effort to become certain about the call and to get from God that undeniably clear direction for my life and ministry. I did not know the word **bergumul**, of course. As this book's introduction notes, the Indonesian language includes this word I would learn years later, which encompasses the idea of just such an inner wrestling match as my praying set off, following Brother Jim's challenge. Its general sense is *intense struggle*, frequently of an internal kind, the kind endured in order to clearly hear God's voice. In some real-life examples in later chapters, I'll continue to turn to this word to describe what had to be done not only in my own life as a missionary from the West, but in the lives of several Indonesian brothers and sisters in Christ.

How blessed I had been as a college student to get that input from Brother Jim each weekend as I served the church he pastored. Still, I remained open to guidance from others I trusted. Not long after my first real experience of *bergumul*, or struggle in prayer, a ministerial fellowship I had joined on campus was gathering to hear remarks from a well-known speaker, Dr. Bill Billingsley, who was pastor at Sheridan Hills Baptist Church in Hollywood, Florida. Dr. Billingsley spoke on Isaiah, Chapter 6, in which Isaiah experiences the thrice Holy God in the temple, after King Uziah has died. God issues a call to Isaiah, who hears that call: "Then I heard the voice of the Lord saying, 'Whom shall I send? And who will go for us?' And I said, 'Here am I. Send me!'" (Isaiah 6: 8).

In time, God would use the very same passage to call me to the foreign mission field, and to me that fact is terribly interesting. But there is a much larger point to Isaiah's account, which is this: The key to a call from God is not what you think or what others think, nor is it how promising some job offer is, how generous the salary and retirement plan. Instead, the key is to *struggle* to an understanding that God wills a particular path for your feet. It is often in times of potential major transition in our lives that God desires to speak to us. We need to be

Here is a picture of Dr. James Stanley Smith, the family patriarch, sitting down for a meal with us in April 1986, just before we left for the mission field. Miss you, Brother Jim!

listening carefully then, when He wants us to seek His face and hear His voice above every other thing.

My father-in-law taught (as usual, right on target!) that for me to be called (for anyone to be called) the ears had to be tuned to God's frequency. And Brother Jim knew that almost without exception, tuning in is a result of studying one's Bible. When God calls, He will be coming to us through His written Word that becomes His *Rhema Word* for each one personally.

Studying in Louisville, I began an intense engagement with Henry Blackaby's book *Experiencing God*. In it, he insists that God still communicates with His children right now, in our own day and time. Like thousands and thousands of others who read Blackaby's book, I found it extremely helpful. Followers of Jesus need to know, as Blackaby lays out so clearly, that God speaks to them primarily in five ways: by the Holy Spirit, through the Bible, in prayer, in the circumstances of everyday life, and through His body, the church. Very possibly, He will speak the same Word through several of these. When God speaks to you through the church, Christ's body, your communication from the church will line up with communications delivered by the other means. After studying Blackaby, I prayed and listened to Christ's body and searched Holy Scripture for the Rhema Word just for me. Through a series of experiences, God spoke my call and confirmed my call. He had communicated it initially, I thought, through the church body. It began to be affirmed in the other ways, and I obtained firm evidence backed up by the Word found in Isaiah 6. God was certainly calling me to full-time Christian service.

When I get to heaven, I want to come to my father-in-law, James Stanley "Brother Jim" Smith, and thank him specially for insisting it was so important to be sure we heard correctly what God said to us. For insisting it had to square with the written Word of God. And he advised that I might not immediately see how the call and the written Word squared. I might indeed have to wrestle with that. It was indirectly rather than directly, but I was being offered lessons about *bergumul* even that early in my ministry—although Brother Jim was unlikely to have ever encountered the term itself.

CHAPTER 3

CALL TO GO

"It takes the same spiritual elements to bring revival on the mission field as anywhere. Prayer for revival should top our prayer list. No spiritual victory is easily won." [1]

— *Avery Willis*

In January 1981, I accepted the call to pastor the Mill Creek Baptist Church in Bardstown, Kentucky, an hour's drive south of Louisville. Shelly and I moved into the pastorium right beside the church, a typical rural Kentucky church atop a hill, with a splendid view of rolling hills in the central part of the state. (Recently, Shelly and I were given two burial plots next to the church in Bardstown, so that may be our future resting place!) It's amazing to think that Mill Creek Baptist Church dates way back to 1792—about the same time Mozart was writing some of his famous symphonies.

Our firstborn, Jennifer, arrived while we were living in the Mill Creek parsonage. I remember bringing her home from the hospital two days after her birthday, Thanksgiving Day of 1983. We were such proud young parents! About that time, I dropped a bombshell on Shelly. I had no other choice. I had been continuing to struggle with a call to foreign missions that, to be honest, had dogged me since the early 1980s. That call was beginning to crystalize. God was even giving me direction on where Shelly and I should go: Southeast Asia, tending particularly toward Indonesia. I was to reach the Muslims of Indonesia, the fifth most populous country in the world at the time. God began placing on me this burden for reaching Indonesia's Muslims following an opportunity I had (a conference on world missions our association held) to meet a former missionary. Her name was Catherine Walker.

Not long after I met Miss Walker, God really touched my heart through a book I picked up that had been written by former missionary to Indonesia Avery Willis. (Later he would serve as president of the Sunday School Board, now called LifeWay.) The book had begun as his doctoral dissertation. It described a revival that took place in Indonesia between 1966 and 1971, an astounding spiritual awakening against the backdrop of a Communist coup attempted in 1965 by the PKI, or Indonesian Communist Party. One particular point covered in Willis's *The Indonesian Revival: Why Two Million Muslims Came to Christ* especially intrigued me. It was that such a huge number of the followers of Islam could come to Christ in such a relatively short time. That kind of movement of God among Muslims had been unheard of to that point. But even before I had read a paragraph, considering the book's title I could think only of how much I would love to be a part of something like that! While I read, I became convinced that revival like that could happen again. Clearly, the subject of missions and revival has long colored my thinking.

I decided I would have to meet the author of this book. Not long after I began to feel called to Indonesia, Shelly and I drove to Nashville. We went to Opryland and then met Avery Willis and his wife, Shirley, for lunch. They wanted to share with us the home movies they had made in Indonesia, so they invited us to their home. I really admired Avery and Shirley and looked up to them right away. I was hooked! As I watched the 35-mm films from their ministry, I could picture myself giving my life to reaching Muslims in that country.

But I faced two problems concerning being appointed to Indonesia.

The first was obvious. Just when we started to inquire about Indonesia, it "closed" due to tensions between our missionaries and the National Baptist Convention of Indonesia. The candidate consultant we had just been put in touch with described the impossibility of any appointment in the near future and encouraged us to consider another, similar place. Malaysia was suggested. We prayed about it but just didn't have a peace about working with Chinese in Malaysia.

After much *bergumul* in prayer, we decided to wait on Indonesia to open back up. Our consultant may have had misgivings about that, but not more than ten days later, appointments to serve in Indonesia were on the table again.

The first problem appeared solved, but the second problem was promising to pose an even greater obstacle than acquiring visas for Indonesia. It was getting my wife, Shelly, on the same page as me about this call to missions. Listen to the testimonies of missionary couples about how God called them to missions. A recurring plotline involves how at first just one of the two, husband or wife, runs to the call—in our case, me, with my call similar to that of the prophet Isaiah. But the other spouse initially wishes to run away from the call. Resisting a call is not uncommon, but from the couples' testimonies it also seems, thankfully, that few would-be missionaries respond as hastily as Jonah, hopping a ship for any other port only to end up in the mess that is a whale's belly.

Remember that when I told her about my belief that God was calling us to foreign missions—Indonesia, specifically—sweet Shelly had given birth to Jennifer just three days earlier. On Thanksgiving Day, no less. Talk about postpartum blues! Forced to contemplate her infant in a distant country with a strange culture and unknown language, the brand-new mother at that point saw foreign missions—Indonesia, specifically—as not her idea of a good time. I can remember telling her, "Well, pray about it, see if God is saying the same thing to you as He's saying to me. Because if He truly called me, it makes sense He would want you to hear the same call. Right?"

Shelly started praying. Something as important as a "Call to Foreign Missions" deserved some serious prayer, and *bergumul* in prayer, although we still didn't know the word. Shelly is "wired" in such a way as to take more time to confront and grapple with change than I take. Time would help her entertain the idea of pulling up stakes and settling ten thousand miles away to minister in a wholly different society while raising her baby daughter. Just a *little* time! But I also recognized that Shelly's fear of God was strong, passed down to her from her father and mother alike. I could be relaxed about the struggle she faced, because I knew how high a priority it was to my wife to hear God's Word for her life. I was confident she would hear what I had been hearing.

Problem was, the timing did not pan out like I thought it should. The morning after she started praying and seeking God's voice for her individually, I asked her, I remember, "Well, did you hear anything from the Lord yet?" "Nope, not yet," was the answer. I didn't think that was too unexpected after only one night. But her praying went on longer than I had anticipated, and I became surprised by it, though I tried always to treat it lightly. I would jokingly tell others, gesturing in Shelly's direction, that whenever I prayed about my call I always let the Lord know that *there* was His "problem." Now, however, I think I know that the real problem was Shelly's impatient husband!

What Shelly needed, to be able to really hear from God, was some time away (and not just from her pesky husband). We decided a visit to her parents in Oklahoma City would be helpful, and off she went. The time frame is a little fuzzy, but we are sure it wasn't long after I unloaded on Shelly about my call to missions, and the largest Muslim country, that she decided to spend the time with her parents, trying to get on the Lord's frequency, to tune in His Word about the whole thing. I don't remember exactly how long my wife and little daughter stayed in Oklahoma City, but it was enough time for the Lord to confirm to Shelly's heart that He was indeed calling both of us to the foreign mission field.

For Shelly and her parents, the culmination of the stay was a walk Shelly took up the aisle of her dad's church as Jim made the announcement that his daughter and her husband were being called to the mission field. He asked the congregation at West Riverside Baptist Church to pray for Shelly, and he asked Shelly's mother, my sweet mother-in-law, Sue, to join Shelly at the front for the congregation's prayer. Sue refused. It was her way to demonstrate her disagreement with this decision. She would have felt like a hypocrite had she stood with Shelly and prayed along with the people of the church.

Getting pushback or subtler resistance from family is a common denominator among couples whom God calls to foreign missions. You would think families would be overjoyed by the decision to go to the field. On the other hand, I can understand that it can be sometimes difficult to love Jesus more than family. In the Gospel of Matthew, we see that Jesus in fact spoke to this difficulty: "Anyone who loves his father or mother more than me is not worthy of me; anyone who loves his son or daughter more than me is not worthy of me" (Matthew 10: 37). As His disciples, we must strive to be worthy of Him.

My mom-in-law is sweet. I say it straightforwardly with not a touch of sarcasm, and I mean it. Sue and I have a long-running joke that, upon seeing me for the first time, she quickly urged Shelly to marry me. I too joke about how I fell in love with Shelly's mom before I fell in love with Shelly. Point being, we have always gotten along and still do! And she is 90 years old now.

My family responded much as Sue did when we explained to them that God was calling us to Indonesia. By then, our second child had been born. My parents didn't understand choosing to raise one's children in any foreign culture, let alone a Muslim one in Southeast Asia. My father felt that there, "They do not value life." I imagine he was thinking of the Killing Fields in Cambodia or the slaughter so many Americans experienced in Vietnam during the war.

Their expressing opposition to our decision was understandable, especially since my parents at best were nominal Christians. After all, Shelly's mother, who deeply objected, and Shelly's father, who although fairly supportive was maybe not jubilant, were *committed* Christians and a pastoring couple besides! They had been for decades. Shelly's mom, Sue, really never stopped questioning the wisdom of relocating our young family to a land we had never set foot in. It didn't make sense to her, didn't add up. That's where faith comes in, though.

At the time Shelly did not receive a whole lot of affirmation from her parents about going to the mission field—affirmation she had assumed she would get. So while she was in Oklahoma City, she was forced to press in harder listening for God's voice. Her parents' cool reception of our news made Shelly's ears more sensitive to the Lord's voice. She heard Him at last. God put Shelly on the same page as her impetuous, impulsive husband, *called to Indonesia!*

CHAPTER 4

CALL TO WAIT

> "Impatience tempts you to make rash counter moves against the obstacles in your way. It tempts you to be impetuous, or hasty, or impulsive, or reckless."[1]
>
> —John Piper

We were appointed by the Foreign Missions Board in December 1985, and we left for the field in April 1986. There would be, however, a slight delay before we could actually enter Indonesia, the country God had clearly called us to and in which we would begin our language study. No one could say with certainty how long the "slight delay" would last. I asked Bill Wakefield, who was the area director for Southeast Asia at the time, whether our visas might be ready for us by the time we finished that round of language study, at the International Learning Center. He replied, "It's possible, but it's not probable." He knew to be realistic, coming from Missouri!

It proved to be quite a challenge, getting even semi-permanent visas for Indonesia. Today, it is standard to bring people appointed to Indonesia to the country immediately, on student visas that allow them to study the language for one year. That usually provides plenty of time to acquire the more permanent visa, for example the KITAS (which must be renewed annually). But the student-visa option was not available when I was appointed, unfortunately. What missionaries had to do then was take a temporary assignment that lasted until the KITAS came through.

Some folks bound for Indonesia served in India while they waited on the paperwork, like Dr. John Clement and his family did for a year or so. His visa came through earlier than mine, since he applied through the Indonesian national department of health and I applied through the national department of religion, in order to serve as a theological teacher. It is normal for visas like mine to take much longer to obtain. As I waited out the expected delay in obtaining my visa, I busied myself in a temporary assignment in the Philippines, pastoring the International Baptist Church in Metro Manila. Initially, I was delighted with this work. It gave me the opportunity to roll up my sleeves and get busy in mission work immediately. This period in Manila provided an advantage, as I learned hands-on about mission work while communicating with the people in English. I loved it!

At the same time, from the moment we arrived in April 1986, the country was very unstable politically. Just weeks earlier, in February 1986, the Philippines' infamous People Power Revolution had occurred. Ferdinand Marcos had been forced from power and replaced by Cory Aquino, widow of iconic leader Benigno "Ninoy" Aquino, Jr., who in August 1983 had been gunned down by an assassin as he stepped off a plane at the Manila airport. While the people of the Philippines were excited that their efforts had managed to avoid a bloody revolution, their country was very precariously situated and volatile. The political and governmental chaos was not improving. Over the months, several coups d'etat would be attempted against Cory Aquino, who was perceived as a weak leader. In fact, six such plots failed while we were living in the Philippines for 20 months during 1986–1987 (we moved on in December of 1987). Various members of the Filipino armed forces were involved in trying to overthrow Mrs. Aquino. Adding to the tension and uncertainty was the murderous activity of communist militants in the nation's rural areas. Participants in the so-called New People's Army roamed the countryside robbing and terrorizing and killing those who opposed them. In addition, the Islamic militants organized as *Abu Sayaff*, as well as the Moro Islamic Liberation Front (MILF), terrorized the public, kidnapping people all over Mindanao, the Philippines' southernmost island.

Were we scared? We sure were, although probably not as scared as we should have been! What kept me focused, though, was Manila's incredible openness to the Gospel of Jesus Christ, an openness I had not seen, frankly, since the revival days of the Jesus movement in the early 1970s. It made me feel right at home, truthfully, despite what else was happening. I could share the Gospel anywhere, in the subway, on planes, on buses—and then there were all the Bible studies. All over the Makati, Manila's business district, Bible studies were conducted in almost every building, almost every office. It was great!

I remember Bob Nash's remark during an early visit to our apartment at the Philippine Baptist Mission guest house in Metro Manila's Pasay City district. Bob was the FMB's associate area director for Southeast Asia and a gregarious person. He asked us, "So Greg and Shelly, isn't it great to be here in the Philippines? It's so open that you can start a church here almost accidentally!" He laughed, so I knew he meant to joke, but I took his words as a challenge.

The first time I responded to this challenge, I was walking in Makati, the shopping district, in a mall. I was carrying my son, Jonathan, who was about nine months old. I was strolling past the stores when somehow I locked eyes with a Filipino father carrying his son, who seemed to me to be Jonathan's age and size. We stopped and talked, and later I shared the Gospel with him. His name was Alex. I remember him well because he was the very first person I led to faith on foreign soil. For me, it was a stellar moment. And I learned that Alex and his family lived only a block from our apartment at the guest house. That day Alex and I would also lead a friend of his to faith. The experience led me to consult with Floy Smith, a single missionary serving as assistant treasurer for the Philippine Mission and occupying the apartment two doors down from ours, to ask if she would like to help us open a church.

After praying about the possibility, Floy expressed her strong interest in opening a church. She asked a Filipino lay pastor and his wife to help us start one in her garage at the guest house. That little church continued to meet in the garage until we left the Philippines, in December 1987. It would later become Good Samaritan Baptist Church, after the church members acquired land to build on in the Pasay City neighborhood. Bob Nash's joke had more truth in it than he dreamed. You can indeed "accidentally" start a new church in Manila!

CULTURE SHOCK

Driving to work one morning at the International Baptist Church, where my office was, I took note of a group of people waiting to cross the street. I was nearing the church. Suddenly, one of the persons in the group stepped in front of me, and the next thing I knew, a young lady was on the hood of my car. I had been trained in what to do. Every missionary completes training (during his or her International Learning Center experience) on how to handle situations that could become dangerous, situations like the accident I had had. We were taught that, if ever our car hit someone, rather than stop at the scene, we should go immediately to a police station to bring an officer back to the site. If that sounds callous and insensitive, it isn't meant to be. It's just that IMB's leaders know how quickly a random group of strangers can become an angry mob. And a mob is a volatile and potentially violent phenomenon. Our training wisely taught us we should ignore our deepest instinct, namely to get out and help the injured person. We should rein in that impulse in order to avoid unintentionally endangering ourselves and any family members or others with us in the car.

I did not exit the car after I hit the young lady. I must confess, however, that I did not stick to my mission training, either. While I sat there trying to figure out what came next, a man from the crowd flung open a back door and put the lady in my car. He ordered me to the nearest hospital, giving me directions. I sped as fast as I could to the hospital, where we checked the lady in at the emergency room. As Shelly, who had joined me at the hospital, and I waited to hear about her condition, I remember asking someone for permission to go back and pray at her side. Permission was given, and I prayed. Then, we notified our leadership about the accident and, finally, found a police station.

Here is an interesting thing: The man who had enabled me to bring the injured lady to the hospital just up and disappeared in the rush of arriving at the ER. I searched for him. I asked hospital staff about him, and they raised their eyebrows. When we had arrived, they said, there had been no Filipino man along. Had the staff been so preoccupied they overlooked him? Maybe so. But we knew that man had played the lead role. Lord, was he your guardian angel, for our comfort and the young lady's? Whether or not an angel was present to us that morning, we were grateful for the Lord's protection. We would be grateful too, eventually, that our insurance would cover treatment of the injury to the lady's hip—and that the injury would fully heal.

DOUBTS ARISE

I had worked at the International Baptist Church in Manila for about a year when I started having doubts. Not about being on the mission field or about doing the job as a church planter and evangelist. I was very certain I had found my niche, because this role had been such a good fit for me. No, the doubts I began struggling with were related to the fact that I was almost half-way through my first term but still had not studied at *all* the language I so wanted to learn.

I knew the Clement family had received their visas, so why was mine being held up? What was the big delay over mine (even if I wasn't a medical doctor like John Clement)? I worried that since my visa had to be processed by Indonesia's department of religion, it wouldn't arrive for . . . I didn't like to think about it. What if we were stuck waiting for the better part of my first term, which would be just four years? How on earth could I learn my language with only an abbreviated time to study it? Making the visa delay still more worrisome, I was hearing rumors that missionaries in Indonesia were experiencing problems in keeping visas they needed in order to stay there.

I wondered what I should do. Shelly and I prayed, but it appeared that my impatience was going to win out. Despite having felt so early on that strong call to Indonesia, I asked if we couldn't just go ahead and transfer to the Philippines. On the island called Mindanao, we could start studying the Cebuano language. I met with the executive committee of the Philippine Baptist Mission, which gave me—somewhat reluctantly—the okay to seek a transfer.

Soon, it was official. We moved to Iligan City, on the north coast of Mindanao, and we started studying the *Cebuano* language, using the "Barefoot Language Learning" method. (Under the "Barefoot" method, students work with language tutors but no formal language school system is used.) We encountered a series of problems. *Cebuano* was much more complicated than we had anticipated. Worse, Shelly got dengue fever. But we pressed on, my progress with the language moving ahead of Shelly's as she recuperated from dengue *and* went through the first half of her pregnancy with our daughter Jamie during that time.

Then came an interesting development in Indonesia. Over half of the people IMB employed there had been denied their visa renewals. This became known as the "Indonesian Exodus." Not long after it had occurred, we heard personally from Dr. Jerry Rankin, a former missionary to Indonesia and the new area director with IMB. He came to our house and pled with us to reconsider our decision to settle for Mindanao. We could well understand his passion and burden for Indonesia; Jerry and Bobbye, his wife, had had a truly fruitful ministry in East Java. But I did really love the openness to the Gospel that I had found in the Philippines. When Jerry challenged me to reconsider our original call to Indonesia, asking if we would at least pray about it, I told him we would. As Shelly and I prayed together, we couldn't escape this fact: I chose our transfer amidst doubt and confusion that got the best of me because I was impatient and having to wait and wait and wait some more for our visas; yet before *any* of that, God had called us specifically to Indonesia. That I had an impetuous, impulsive streak had been illustrated by my gambling days, when I played the horses. But the blatant impatience I showed when our visas were delayed was honestly a form of unbelief. You can learn a lesson from the mistake I made in neglecting God's choice for me, which from the beginning was, absolutely, service in Indonesia. The psalmist also taught it: "Wait for the LORD; be strong and take heart and wait for the LORD" (27: 14).

I saw how our IMB work force in Indonesia was depleted. I understood the value of the semi-permanent visa I had in hand. And I came to agree with Dr. Rankin, it only made sense for us to follow through with our original calling to Indonesia. I really praise the Lord for folks like Jerry and Bobbye Rankin, and also Ed and Jaletta Sanders, for encouraging me to rethink that transfer. Once we had prayed sufficiently about it, it just felt right to pull up stakes once more and move to Indonesia. It was definitely the right decision.

CHAPTER 5

CALL TO PERSEVERE

"What does running a marathon have to do with learning a foreign language? I'd say they are close to the same thing when it comes to the brutal, punishing amount of pure 'road work' required for both endeavors."[1]

– Brian Nelson, Major,
Washington National Guard

On December 30, 1987, Shelly and I and our children (Jennifer, who was four, and Jonathan, who was two) arrived in Jakarta, Indonesia. I had finally arrived in the land God had called me to. How good it felt to see this place God had spoken to us about so clearly, this place where we would serve Him. We were picked up at the airport by Gerald Pinkston and his wife, Florence, veteran missionaries with the International Mission Board. We stayed one night with the Pinkstons and then off we went to Bandung, by *kereta api* (train).

I was amazed by the beauty of our new home as we travelled through West Java's lush, green, enchanting countryside. Eventually we made our way up the steep mountains to Bandung. Not just mountains, but active volcanoes as well, in some places. What else stood out to me, along with the natural beauty of this corner of Indonesia, was how crowded it was. Jakarta had been *crowded*, and so, it seemed, was every city that our train took us through on our three-hour ride to Bandung.

More than 18,000 islands make up Indonesia; it is the world's largest archipelago nation. The most heavily populated island is Java, which crowds more than 140 million people into a space no bigger than the state of Alabama. Java is the hub of the nation's commerce, political power, and social influence. If it is going to happen in Indonesia, it is going to happen in Java—and drive human activity on all the other islands. This was going to be our home for the next thirty-five or so years!

At the train station in Bandung, we unloaded our baggage. I was amazed at how helpful the porters were. I wasn't sure how much to pay them for their work, but I sure was grateful to them and knew that the folks picking us up at the station would know what was proper. That couple, Michael and Patty Hampton, got us to our house on *Jl.* (the abbreviation for *jalan*, or *street*) Cisangkuay. We would live next to the government building that is familiarly called the *Gedung Sate* (because its main pinnacle looks something like the beloved Indonesian food known as *satay*). The oversize building would help us newcomers find our house on those early occasions when we got lost, because everyone knew where the Gedung Sate was.

READY FOR THE RACE

Language school was to start for us the very next Monday, and we were eager for the challenge that lay ahead. Our language course at the Indonesian Language Acquisition Center consisted of nine units of study that were spread out over a year. The best way I know of to describe our year of language study is to say it was like running a race with hurdles that had to be cleared cleanly in order to advance and finish the event. We learned not to worry in advance about the hurdles waiting for us toward the race's end. We had to focus on clearing the particular hurdle that was immediately before us, in order to win the opportunity to attempt whatever hurdle came immediately after *it*. A stumble over any preliminary hurdle meant disqualification and a requirement to start again, at the beginning.

INTERNAL CHALLENGES

Shelly and I started in on Unit One, studying Bahasa Indonesia (the Indonesian language) together. I quickly figured out that many challenges were ahead for us. For me, the biggest was perhaps what was going on inside while I worked to learn how to talk again. In my view, *Bahasa* was a strange language that sounded stranger yet as I tried speaking it! But I was flying high as we went through the first unit, full of excitement and ready to learn. By Unit Two, just a month later, the adrenaline had mostly worn off. I felt defeated when my verbal efforts brought me only humiliation and frustration; I was used to receiving mostly affirmation and praise for them—when they involved the English language. Not that I hadn't been warned of what would happen during language school. But reading cultural adaptation books (or listening to long-time missionaries reflect on their experiences) is one thing, while repeatedly being hammered by critical if well-meaning *pelatih* (language coaches) is another. It just didn't set well. I'm afraid that on many occasions I was short with the *pelatih*—and could at times even be condescending or rude to these Indonesians. I didn't plan it that way. But the intense study of another language was like culture shock, and when you're in shock, what is in your heart comes out. There's that metaphor about a person being a lot like a tube of toothpaste: When it's squeezed, what's inside comes out.

So we are unlikely to be our best selves when we're under too much stress. Struggling to communicate. Driving *crowded* streets on the "wrong" side of the road, so many cars and motorcycles weaving in and out and around. Did I mention there are lots of motorcycles?! (The late humorist Erma Bombeck may have described Indonesian traffic better than anyone, in telling about a vacation she and her husband took there. Here is a link to her reporting, if you are in need of a laugh: https://www.expat.or.id/info/ermabombeck.html) To drive in a developing country, especially one in

Asia, is to do battle with the traffic. And also with your anger, an emotion that takes you nowhere fast in those circumstances. Even after thirty-five years, I still find driving in Indonesia to be a struggle.

EXTERNAL CHALLENGES

When we had finally gotten to language school in Bandung, Shelly was five months pregnant with our third child, Jamie Marie. We faced two decisions. The first concerned where this baby would be born. Horror stories were what we knew about health care in Indonesia, so we were reluctant to have the baby in Bandung. Our hesitancy was reinforced by a visit to the doctor that was not at all what we had hoped for. The seasoned missionaries we knew encouraged us to go to one of two Baptist hospitals in Indonesia. These, however, were very far away. The one in Kediri in East Java was the oldest Baptist hospital in Indonesia, and there was a second one on the island of Sumatra, in the city of Lampung. We chose the latter, Imanual Hospital, because we knew of a very experienced Southern Baptist missionary doctor who served there as an ob-gyn, Dr. Oliver Gilliland.

During the disappointing doctor visit in Bandung, we had been told that the baby was in a breach position (*sumsang*, to the local doctor), which meant Shelly would need to consult with the ob-gyn at Imanual Hospital. "Dr. Gill" and his wife, Peggy, invited Shelly to stay with them for a time before the delivery, to obtain the needed consult, rest, and prepare. It was soon settled that I would take the role of Mr. Mom in Bandung, caring for Jennifer, now five years old, and Jonathan, now three, and Shelly would fly to Lampung to stay with Dr. Gill and Peggy. Shelly ended up staying four weeks in Lampung awaiting the delivery. We made a success of it, with the help of prayer! (Although being Mr. Mom was not very conducive to formal language learning.) At last, on May 27, 1988, Jamie was born. A few days later, I traveled to Sumatra to bring her and her mother home. Thank the Lord for the missionary family that helped us by giving Shelly a wonderful place to stay while awaiting Jamie's birth. Thank the Lord, too, for those who cared for the older kids as Dad escorted Mom and baby sister home.

FINDING A MENTOR

When we were new missionaries, the folks at the International Learning Center in Richmond, Virginia (which at the time was called the Missionary Learning Center), explained to us how important it would be to find a good mentor in whatever place we got assigned to. In Bandung, it didn't take me long to find that person. His name was John Smith—a common name, maybe, but quite a unique human being. I did not ask John to mentor me, nor did the leaders of our Baptist mission assign me to him. Still, he became my mentor along the way.

I had noticed some things in John's style and ministry that I liked and wanted to emulate. In addition, I was drawn to John by his taste for classical music. He especially liked Mozart (good choice!). He gave me some cassette tapes with some of Mozart's most famous symphonies; the Jupiter and Prague symphonies became favorites of mine. I'm still quite a fan of classical music, and to a large degree I can blame that on John Smith. Learning about music from him made me want to learn from him in general.

Perhaps what I most admired about John Smith was the way he shared the Gospel. He was so passionate to share it, and his reputation preceded him. Several of my colleagues had mentioned folks John had won to Christ in Yogyakarta, in the heart of Javanese culture. John had been an evangelist with a student ministry during the time of the Indonesian Revival (1966–1971). So many people came to faith then, a portion of them directly through John's ministry and witness in Yogyakarta (along with that of his wife, Nell). I liked that; it was inspiring. I wanted to be an evangelist like John. I liked the spontaneous way that John started new churches. I asked him once, "John, how did you start the churches you started in Yogyakarta and Bandung?" I remember he shrugged his shoulders, then threw up his hands. "I don't know exactly!" he said. "We just started sharing the Gospel with a bunch of people, and suddenly there was a small church that started gathering weekly, and we just started calling it a Pos PI or Mission point." It wasn't a complicated strategy, but it was effective. And I believed I could emulate it.

In Bandung, it seemed to me, the response to evangelism was more modest than it had been in Yogyakarta, in central Java. But of course John's passion for the Sundanese (the Unreached People Group which, for the most part, populates West Java's Bandung area) did not diminish in return. The Sundanese were the largest UPG, numbering over thirty-three million people, of whom less than one percent were Christian. John gave it his all as he shared the Gospel, and he had such a knack for sharing it. Some would say of him, "John's language isn't the best, but he communicates with Indonesians well and knows how to quickly get to the Gospel." That gave me hope of one day being a successful evangelist, since I myself had been described by one of our leaders in Indonesia as a guy who "wasn't exactly knocking the top off the language."

The Lord led me to two more vitally helpful people who knew Indonesia's culture and language well and were especially effective in ministry. They were Clarence and Ruth Griffin. I met them when I was in language school. I made a special trip to Semarang to meet the Griffins and spend some days with Clarence to see how he did things. It was time well spent. Clarence's love for the Indonesian people and his ability to just have fun in ministry rubbed off on me.

CHAPTER FIVE | CALL TO PERSEVERE

Clarence and Ruth Griffin, our mentors in Solo. Both loved Indonesia and Indonesians; Clarence had a rare sense of humor.

THE SUMAMPAU FAMILY

John Smith made many notable achievements as a missionary. Among the greatest, surely, was leading to Christ the family that owns the three "Taman Safari" theme parks in Indonesia. One is located in Cisarua, West Java, and is the oldest. Another is in Prigin, in East Java, and the third is found in Bali, the famed tourist destination. All three were patterned after the "Lion Country Safari" enterprises in the United States and Australia. Before the parks were opened, the family (three brothers and their wives) traveled around Indonesia presenting the "Oriental Circus." In 1977, John Smith led the entire family to Christ. Even more amazing, he led almost every one of the employees of the traveling circus to faith in Jesus, more than 70 people in all. Ten years later, about a year before we came to Indonesia, the first Taman Safari park, the one in Cisarua, opened and was immediately successful. People from all over the world visited and stayed at the affiliated hotel. They rode through the grounds gazing in wonder at the assortment of animals living in the park. Posing with albino tigers, feeding carrots to giraffes outside one's car window, and basically having a grand time made for warm memories and ensured the safari owners' financial success (each brother was a one-third owner).

John Smith and I visited the park in Cisarua in late October 1988. I drove us from Bandung in his car. We enjoyed listening to the trumpet concerto by Mozart on the way, and John also told the story of leading the Taman Safari family to faith in Jesus when their circus had come to Yogyakarta for a few weeks. That was the door that the Lord opened that no man could shut:

> [7] To the angel of the church in Philadelphia write: These are the words of him who is holy and true, who holds the key of David. What he opens no one can shut, and what he shuts no one can open.
>
> [8] I know your deeds. See, I have placed before you an open door that no one can shut. I know that you have little strength, yet you have kept my word and have not denied my name.
> *– Revelation 3: 7-8*

God had opened the door and John Smith had made himself available to God to serve Him, as he saw God working in this family and among their employees. When we reached the park in Cisarua, John introduced me to one of the owner-brothers and his wife, Tony and Yanny Sumampau. In that moment, I could not know that I would forge a deep friendship with this family years later. And that's a story for another chapter.

Shelly and I had come to Bandung to learn the language. Our time there was drawing to a close. My thoughts had turned to the question of where we would go from Bandung, or alternatively, what first Indonesian assignment we would receive. There were two basic options, as it turned out. I was allowed a preference, but the final decision would belong to the National Baptist Convention of Indonesia. The convention provided all missionary visas at that time (the 1980s until 1997), because it was the organization that sponsored all IMB missionaries in Indonesia.

CHAPTER FIVE | CALL TO PERSEVERE

It made sense that the National Baptist Convention of Indonesia, which secured every single visa our missionaries received, would want input concerning new placements. A great deal of input. (Things have completely changed now, largely because available means of obtaining visas and sponsorships of IMB personnel have multiplied. Back at the start of the twenty-first century, we decided we didn't want all of our eggs in one basket, so we began to turn for visas to universities, English centers, even travel agencies. Doing so greatly reduced the number of personnel tied to National Baptist Convention visas, giving us more say-so about missionaries' placements.) At any rate, I was told we could stay on Java—something I had felt led to do from before the beginning, almost—in one of two ways, as follows. Did I prefer to serve in little Wonosobo, in the mountains of central Java, with its lone Baptist church? Wonosobo had been less responsive than other places in central Java. Or did I prefer to serve in Solo, a large city also in central Java?

Among Baptists the work in Solo, located in the middle of central Java with Yogyakarta to its south and Semarang to its north, was fairly well developed. An Association of Baptist Churches there covered an area that was home to ten million people. On the surface, Wonosobo would seem like the place to go, since the work there was far less developed. The percentage of believers in Wonosobo was far lower than was found in and around the city of Solo (a location sometimes called Surakarta). But I didn't know which location to choose, not at first. So we prayed. "Which direction should we go, Lord?" Were we meant for a more developed work or for an area that remained something of a "pioneer" area. We prayed and we thought about it, and we sought a lot of input about where we should go. We very carefully weighed all of these opinions—some of which were rather strong—and we gave much prayer and thought to it.

One particular way the Lord helped me reach a decision to move to Solo was a certain conversation over some *ayam goreng* (fried chicken) with my IMB colleague Harry Bush. As we talked about my options, he said something that stuck with me: "If it were me making the decision, I would definitely go to Solo, where I could work with those little Javanese pastors there that know how to evangelize and plant churches in the Javanese culture." Harry's words had the ring of truth. After all, I was coming from the United States, and I had never once planted a church (yet). Sure, I had evangelized and won a fair number of people to faith and then discipled them. But gathering people into local churches that would multiply would be novel to me. I felt that Harry was offering wise counsel. I should go as a learner for my first term, not so much as a person in the know. I was aware I had come to Indonesia with ultimate Truth entrusted and imparted to me by the Lord. The Gospel was what I was to share, and I knew how to do that in one culture and language. Doing it in a new, vastly different culture using a language I was still learning would be doing it as a learner.

As we prayed some more about the decision, Shelly and I both felt that, heading into our first assignment, we certainly had things to teach and to impart to the Javanese pastors and believers—but only from a position of being people who were still learning. This proved to be a good idea. Thanks, Brother Harry Bush, for your words of wisdom!

CHAPTER 6

CALL TO LEARN: SOLO, CENTRAL JAVA 1989–1996

> **Be a learner not a knower. Be a server not a master. Be a listener not a speaker. Go with only the expectations that you are open to God's plan and you want to be used in any way he wants to use you. Go with the heart that you have been sent by God. Act like a diplomat of God's kingdom, because you are.[1]**
> *– Annette Adams*

The advice from a colleague to go to the city of Solo as a "learner" was very helpful. We ended up spending three terms, or eight years, there. That was a long time to be in learner mode, but the Lord taught us some valuable lessons in central Java, among them the following:

1. We are often most useful to God when we are least aware of being useful.

2. We are most productive when we work with Nationals to accomplish things.

3. We must never stop seeking after God's voice.

4. We as missionaries need a biblical approach to spiritual warfare.

5. We as missionaries need a clear pattern of teaching the principles and practices of revival and spiritual awakening.

In this chapter, I want to recount how staying in learner mode during our first three terms in Solo brought invaluable discoveries that helped me throughout the remainder of my ministry in Indonesia.

LESSON # 1 — We are often most useful to God when we are least aware of being useful.

I came to my ministry in Solo understanding what I understood from God, yet as a learner. I quickly realized, however, that the Association of Baptists in my location heartily wanted a knower. Actually, what the association asked me to do I had been doing in the USA, during my time as pastor at Mill Creek Baptist Church, namely, leading my church in witness training, using *Continued Witness Training* (CWT) materials. CWT was basically the Southern Baptist version of James Kennedy's Evangelism Explosion curriculum that various evangelical denominations in the United States were then using. Southern Baptists made some changes to fit the curriculum to specific needs and began to produce the adapted material on our own. Our CWT materials consisted of about twelve weekly lessons. Each corresponded to a required weekly meeting, during which two kinds of work went on. First, we studied core information from the week's "model presentation." Memorizing that information was encouraged. Next, we actually went out each week and witnessed to others. The heart of CWT—and its strength—was this joining of study in the classroom with evangelism in the community, spreading the messages we had memorized. Signing up for the twelve-week CWT program was a commitment to attend each weekly session, to do the homework corresponding to each part of model presentation, and most importantly to make visits to lost people living in or near our community.

It turned out that, over the coming two years or so, the Association of Baptist Churches in Solo wanted to see me implement CWT in their region. They would have me travel around to the forty churches in the Solo association, providing CWT evangelistic training for each one. Well, sir, I rolled up my sleeves to get busy; I was raring to go! The calendar said I had just a year and a half to go before our first furlough (today, furloughs are called *stateside assignments*). We would be going home for a while beginning in April 1990. This was typical for first-term missionaries, a full four-year term on the field followed by the first furlough. In the time I had, I taught CWT in just about every Solo association church. Those I couldn't squeeze in to the schedule I promised to accommodate when we returned to Solo for our second term, which would start early in 1991.

A MEMORABLE VISIT

Our CWT trainees made lots of memorable visits, and we engaged lots of people with the Gospel. Many rejected it, but we did give them a chance to hear the Good News. One particular visit stands out in my memory. We were in the town outside of Solo called Delanggu. A man lived there who was so ill as to be bedridden, and while his children were believers, he was not. We shared the Gospel with him, completing the entire CWT model presentation. But the man did not accept Christ. So what made the visit so memorable? It wasn't actually the events of the visit themselves, at least the events I was aware of *then*. But about 16 years later, in Jakarta during an anniversary celebration we attended commemorating the founding of the Indonesian Baptist Convention, a young mother walked up to Shelly and introduced herself. She was a pastor's wife. She and her husband served a church in Jakarta. She wanted to thank Shelly and me for taking the time to share the Gospel with her mom and dad back in the early 1990s. No one had been aware of it at the time, but as I had shared the full length of the CWT model presentation with the bedridden father, this pastor's wife, then a girl about twelve years old, was listening from another room to the Gospel presentation.

She was under such conviction while hearing the Good News, that she accepted Christ into her heart that very night. Only thing, she didn't tell her parents about this until days afterwards. And Shelly and I didn't hear about it for sixteen years!

I do honestly think that some of my best experiences in ministry were ones that happened when I had no idea the Lord was using me in some significant way. Typically, when I have really been used by God, I don't find out about it for days, months, or as in this case, years. On the other hand, if I preach a sermon that, I conclude, was definitely effective—that knocked it out of the park—I'm likely to find out later that its results were not so good as I thought. Do you ever wonder why God does things that way? My guess is that He knows our hearts better than we do and sees how prone we are to becoming puffed up and haughty when we do something for Him that unduly impresses us or others. When I find myself feeling relatively more self-congratulating and relatively less in awe of God, my head tends to swell. It was a humbling experience to learn, after years, that someone was saved when you shared the Gospel with her father—while you remained utterly in the dark about her own attentive, if invisible, participation.

A similar thing happened in 2019, at Christmas, when I was speaking in Palembang on the island of Sumatra. A lady came up to me to share a story about a former assistant pastor at First Baptist Church, who was called Pastor Lukas. As a boy and member of the church youth group, Pastor Lukas had been challenged by me during a revival service I led. The lady said that Pastor Lukas remembered my approaching him during that revival service and saying over him, "In just a little while, the Lord is going to call you into full-time ministry to serve Him." She said that Lukas told her he had never forgotten these *exact* words I spoke that challenged him into ministry. Frankly, I don't remember it; I don't even remember Lukas. Memory isn't so reliable after a couple decades go by. I know I led a revival in Palembang, but my recall ends there. And here again, God's Ways are not our ways! And God is good! He uses us on many occasions when we are unaware of His design. When we never even see ourselves being put to use for His purposes, we avoid the inflated egos that can get in the way of serving and glorifying Him. God's Ways are not our ways.

LESSON #2 — **We are most productive when we work with Nationals to accomplish things.**

Again, I was seeking God's will about where we would go after our first furlough/stateside assignment/StAs was over. As we prayed about it, Shelly and I sensed that God was leading us to return to Solo for a second term. After talking with Pastor Markus, who was serving as director of missions for the Baptist Association of Churches in Solo, as well as Pastor Timothy Kabul, its head of evangelism, it seemed to me we had hammered out a clear enough understanding of my responsibilities to them if I returned to Indonesia. Pastor Kabul had been very helpful in helping me plan out a second term in Solo. One project he wanted my help with was starting a new church in the city's eastern portion, an area called Palur.

PALUR, MY FIRST CHURCH PLANT IN INDONESIA

So, following our first stateside assignment, we came back to Solo in central Java in January 1991. One of the first things I did then was meet with Pastor Kabul, who in addition to leading evangelism within the association also pastored the Bangunharjo Baptist Church, which my family belonged to when we served in Solo. I had already agreed to his request for help planting the Palur church. Several inaugural members were on board even then, including some residents of Palur's *perumnas* (residential areas on the city's edge) who had Baptist backgrounds. It was decided to meet at Mr. Sumento's house every Monday night. I would lead the group in inductive Bible studies, using some of the discipleship materials Jerry Rankin had written while serving as an IMB missionary to Indonesia. For good measure, I would supplement those materials with concepts from the *Pemuridan* curriculum (better known as Master Life).

I appreciated the way Bangunharjo Baptist Church worked with me on planting this new church and showed support for me and the members. Someone from the mother church was always with me when I visited people who might attend and when I shared the Gospel with the faithful at Mr. Sumento's house. I had good partners among the Nationals; in fact, this successful church plant could not have happened without them. I appreciated, too, the way the Solo area Association of Baptist Churches wanted from the start to make this church plant a joint effort. There was not so much as a hint of interest in protecting church "turf" or competing against other churches. There was a feeling of genuine cooperation for the purpose of seeing God glorified in this area not currently being reached for Christ.

Across the five years it took to arrive at a place in our development from which we could call a pastor, our little church led several people to faith in Christ. One was named Paiman, and he is active in the church at Palur to this day (so is his family). We also helped the church find land to buy in the community, for a very reasonable price. When Palur's Baptist mission point called its first pastor in 1995, he was a new graduate of the flagship Baptist seminary in Semarang. His name was Pastor Stephanus Ngatiman. By 1997, Pastor Ngatiman had helped the mission point folks build and occupy a brand new building. This gave me such a feeling of achievement, to have with God's leadership helped plant and cultivate—

in my first such experience in Indonesia—a new and thriving Baptist church.

PASTOR ELEANOR

During my second term in Solo, the pastor I worked most closely with was Pastor Eleanor Gunardi. But hold on, wait a minute, I do not at all mean a woman pastor! Pastor Gunardi was one hundred percent male (*laki-laki* in the Indonesian language). Why then did his parents name him Eleanor? Well, actually, Eleanor was the name he received at his baptism. Since many of them come out of Islam, baptized Indonesians often choose biblical names—Samuel, David, Jonathan, Mark, or the like—testifying to becoming a follower of Jesus Christ and an official Christian according to the compulsory "resident identity card" (*kartu tanda penduduk*, or more commonly, KTP). But then why in the world would a man take a woman's name at his baptism? If neither Samuel, David, Jonathan, nor Mark would do, there are still Paul, Matthew, and Abraham! Noah, Seth, and Jonah! Adam, Saul, and Isaac! Aaron, Benjamin . . . it's quite a long list, actually. I asked Pastor Gunardi the question. He told me that his name honored the Baptist missionary Eleanor Pennell, who had served for the IMB in Solo years before Shelly and I arrived. Eleanor Pennell had been Pastor Gunardi's piano teacher, and he had deeply admired and appreciated her. Personally, I could wish that Pastor Gunardi had taken the name Paul or Stephen (or even Wayne, Eleanor's husband's name). It would have spared him people's occasionally embarrassing assumptions.

But, hey, some Indonesians have chosen even less likely names! John Ingouf, who served as an IMB missionary to Indonesia, once told me about a man from John's assignment in Surabaya. After he was dunked, the man was told to choose a baptism name. He did as he was told, and the chosen name was, of all things, Cinderella. Someone asked "Why?"

and "Wouldn't a biblical name be nice?" The man answered simply, "I have always liked the name Cinderella." Living in Indonesia can give you lots to chuckle over.

I must say that Pastor Gunardi was proactive in seeking out lost people. What's more, he helped me start three Baptist mission points during my second term in Solo (1991–1993), the congregations at Selo Katon, Kedungombo, and Sumber Lawang.

FERNANDEZ PAIMAN, MY "TIMOTHY"

A very interesting story developed out of the church start in the village of Selo Katon, on Solo's northern outskirts. We started this church plant with meetings at the house of Mr. Agus, who had several children. One of his sons had just returned to Java from some time at his job on the island of Sumatra. His name was Fernandez Paiman. While he was working for the Enim Oil Company not far from Palembang, Sumatra, Fernandez had narrowly escaped death in an accident. It had happened about three months before his return to Selo Katon and Solo. During his time with the oil company, many of his fellow workers had shared the Gospel with him. He had always resisted these co-workers' and friends' invitations, hardening his heart to the Good News of Jesus. But that was going to change quickly as a result of the accident.

Their work having taken them into a very deep forest, an Enim crew that included Fernandez and three friends of his had made camp at the end of the work day. As they slept on adjacent mats in the middle of the forest, a tree suddenly crashed down without warning in three a.m. darkness. One man was killed instantly. Another was critically hurt. Fernandez sustained a leg injury and was hospitalized. Reflecting on the incident, he knew if he hadn't happened to change his position from the one he had fallen asleep in around midnight, the falling tree would have crushed his head. Such a minor choice had spared him, and similarly minor choices had forever affected his co-workers.

He realized gradually that he was afraid of death. He also slowly saw that his life was without purpose or meaning. I met Fernandez in the home of his father, Mr. Agus, which, again, was being used for church services. We became acquainted over the course of numerous conversations. Somewhere along the line, Fernandez said to me, "I began to think about what my friends had said, about how I needed a Savior and that Jesus could forgive my sins if I would ask Him to come into my life and reign." When he had returned home, Fernandez discovered that several members of his family had received Christ and joined a Baptist church. It was through evangelical work assigned to Pastor Gunardi and me that the Gospel had been shared where Fernandez's relatives could hear it, in the little village just outside Solo. Fernandez too had finally heard the message. He surrendered his heart to the Lord and was baptized on March 8, 1992, at Penumping Baptist Church.

I discipled Fernandez for a period, and then I challenged him about whether God was calling him to preach and serve full-time as a minister. By April, he had made it known that God was indeed calling him and that he would enter the Baptist seminary in Semarang as soon as possible. Successful application for a place at the seminary would require two years of service for the Lord at a Baptist church, which Fernandez completed. Then, Nusukan Baptist Church, the mother church behind the church plant in Selo Katon village (Mr. Agus's house) gave Fernandez the letter of recommendation he needed to enter the seminary.

EATING DOG FOR THE GLORY OF GOD

Indonesians are accustomed to using a ceremony of some kind to make nearly anything they plan to do or anything they have just done "official."

It is ingrained in the culture, a belief held deep in their hearts and minds, integral to their way of thinking and their view of the world. Everything that happens, if it is to be official, or *sah*, must be initiated through a ceremony. In order to officially plant a church, then, we had to start off with an *upacara pembukaan*, an opening ceremony. Fernandez was the guy in charge of the *upacara pembukaan* for the new church at Selo Katon. He wanted to make everything perfect for it. He made sure all the invitations were sent out and that the simple Javanese house where the ceremony would be hosted was appropriately decorated for the austere occasion.

Most importantly, an occasion of such importance required preparing special food for the guests. It was this way for the opening of any new business, or any new office or agency, or any new building—and any newly planted church. Mr. Fernandez was sure to take care of this detail. He arranged for a main course of *daging RW*, barbeque dog, to be served following the ceremony. I hadn't known of the menu. But I had noticed not hearing the dog that would typically wander back and forth outside barking during our meetings. And I was faced with a dilemma. As an American, could I say thanks but no thanks to the evening's entree? Or would that risk offending our guests and, worse, the people I hoped to reach with the Gospel? I decided I could not decline the meal altogether. But maybe I could kind of bury the *daging RW*, putting a little in my bowl and covering it up with rice. I concluded that wouldn't work either, when I was handed what looked like a thick black soup with dog meat swimming in it.

My only alternative was to grin and bear it and dive into the "delicious" bowl. When you come to the mission field, you know days like this are in store. Maybe you can get away with avoiding the food of the country you are in, if your mission trip is short or if you have a genuine food allergy.

(We once had to shadow a guy for the whole time he visited Indonesia, because he was allergic to peanuts. One peanut and he would have been a goner!) Rarely, there is an accepted reason for not eating what is served. But I didn't have such a reason that evening. So, I didn't allow myself to hesitate, I just dug in. It wasn't nearly as bad as I had anticipated, thanks to the quantities of black pepper and other spices prevailing over any flavor of dog meat that I might have discerned. I was very thankful for the cuisine's heat and spice that covered up any distinct taste of the pooch.

Indonesians like to talk about the aftereffects of eating special foods like durian (the notorious stinky fruit) or dog. They say specifically that if you eat either one of those, your body gets hot, as if you had been rubbed down with Ben Gay from the inside out. I ate dog that evening of the ceremony, and Indonesians and Americans alike have since asked me how I felt afterward. I simply say that after I got home from Fernandez's big event, Shelly couldn't sleep because, apparently, I howled all night. And it took me a month to break the nasty habit of chasing cars!

LESSON # 3 — We must never stop seeking after God's voice.

My first year on the mission field was spent in Manila, Philippines. Chapter 4, "Call to Wait," described my first experience with cross-cultural church planting, which came in Manila, where about ten million people lived then. It was hot, dirty, and crowded, and the traffic jams were ridiculous. But I found myself loving the challenge of reaching a large city. There was a mystique to it, to getting around and seeking to find where the Father was working. To me it was an incredible adventure! And the people were so responsive. Something I didn't mention in Chapter 5, "Call to Persevere," was my wish to serve in Jakarta, if possible, which is the capital of Indonesia and its largest city. I asked for that assignment when we initially arrived in Indonesia. Our Baptist mission's leadership let me know it was not an option, because leaders of the National Baptist Convention felt there were enough sufficiently staffed Baptist churches in Jakarta already.

URBAN EVANGELISM

So I was turned down, but I never fully got over my burden for reaching the large urban areas of Southeast Asia for Christ. In 1992, I had the opportunity to attend a seminar on urban evangelism and church planting led by David Hesselgrave, an expert on both cross-cultural evangelism and urban strategy. My colleague from Bandung, Don Dent, attended the seminar with me, in Hong Kong. We ate a lot of great Chinese food, and I spoke at an Indonesian church in Macao. I came home with a renewed passion to reach Indonesia's large cities. Jakarta still was not a possibility, but it seemed we might have the option to serve in Indonesia's third largest city, Medan, located in northern Sumatra. We began to correspond with a missionary couple serving there, eventually exploring whether we could and should move there. As we prayed about it and talked it over with our mission's executive committee, we felt a negative response from all directions.

We prayed some more, seeking the Lord's Face and seeking to hear His voice and have His opinion on the matter. Once we had prayed about it thoroughly, relocating just did not seem the Lord's Will for us at that time. Out of all options open to us, continued service in Solo seemed best. The Lord had, it was obvious, been blessing our efforts there. As we prayed it over, we concluded that the Lord wasn't finished with us yet in Solo. Once again, Dr. Jerry Rankin played a role in our decision. Our good friend and the area director for Southeast Asia and Pacific (SEAP) in those days, Dr. Rankin met us for lunch during the time we were deciding. We met at the Taman Safari hotel in Cisarua, West Java. We explained to him our enthusiasm for the mega-city experience and how my passion to serve God in the urban centers of SEAP had done nothing but grow after I attended the urban evangelism seminar in Hong Kong. At one point, Dr. Rankin pointedly reminded me, "Solo is also considered an urban area, you know, Greg." Very good point, Dr Rankin. We stayed another term in Solo.

GOD'S WILL ABOUT WHERE NOT TO GO

What better time to address the vital topic of knowing God's will for where one should serve—and where one should not. As I've said before, we must rely on His leadership and guidance to help us whenever we are making such decisions. This is even more true, if such a thing is possible, when the decision concerns some place we think He may be calling us to or, *equally likely*, away from. The classic passage most helpful here is Acts 16: 6–10:

> **6 Paul and his companions traveled throughout the region of Phrygia and Galatia, having been kept by the Holy Spirit from preaching the word in the province of Asia.**
>
> **7 When they came to the border of Mysia, they tried to enter Bithynia, but the Spirit of Jesus would not allow them to.**
>
> **8 So they passed by Mysia and went down to Troas.**
>
> **9 During the night Paul had a vision of a man of Macedonia standing and begging him, "Come over to Macedonia and help us."**
>
> **10 After Paul had seen the vision, we got ready at once to leave for Macedonia, concluding that God had called us to preach the gospel to them.**

Verse 6 tells us that the Holy Spirit kept Paul and Silas from entering

Asia. But it does not tell us how the Holy Spirit gave Paul and his apostolic team the understanding that they should not enter Asia. Maybe they met with a prophet like Agabus (Acts 11: 28, Acts 21: 10), who had the spiritual gift of foretelling future events. Or maybe they were sent a vision, like that they eventually received in Troas, calling them to Macedonia. Or maybe some inner voice gave birth to a strong conviction that helped show Paul that Asia and Bithynia were not the places he was to go. The passage teaches us that knowing God's will may not involve hearing God's audible voice. He leads in many different ways. When it came to weighing a move to Medan, it helped me to ask for advice from more experienced missionaries. They had wisdom I lacked. They knew the terrain and knew Medan's culture, which is a combative one compared to Javanese culture, which values the indirect and refined. To be advised by fellow believers is to hear from the Body of Christ. That is a help when you struggle to determine God's will about your next move.

I have compiled some useful guidelines for seeking God's will, which follow below:

1) **Let the Word of God be the final Authority for your decision.** Ask yourself whether others' feedback, along with what you are hearing from the Spirit in prayer, *and* your "reading" of your circumstances, line up with the Word of God. They need to. The classic example comes from the story of the pastor who told his congregation that God was leading him to divorce his wife and marry his secretary. Whatever he was hearing was by no means from God, that's a no-brainer. We know this because the Scriptures repeatedly oppose the kind of foolish action the pastor claimed was urged on him by God in prayer!

2) **Ask mature Christians for advice.** When the executive committee of our Baptist mission was interviewing me for the job in Solo, I noted

how it was made up of mature and very experienced men of God. I respected their input and advice. As I reflected on what they had said, comparing it to what Shelly and I were hearing from God through prayer, I understood God was directing us to remain in Solo for the time being and not relocate to Medan at that point.

3) **Check your own motives.** Are you seeking what God wants for your life, or are you really seeking to do what you want to do? Answering this question requires a keen self-awareness and familiarity with your inclinations gleaned from your past decisions and their outcomes. I learned more deeply about my own inclinations through the mistake I made in the Philippines. To learn, I was forced to humble myself and acknowledge my tendency to be impetuous and impulsive when making decisions. I needed to admit that that tendency came from my flesh and my old nature: I had used to decide issues based on what I wanted to do, rather than on what God had called me to do. But I knew better now.

4) **Pray for God to open and close doors as He desires.** By this I am not suggesting you should move haphazardly through your days, shuffled here and there by circumstances. Instead, strive to develop a keen spiritual eye that can see God at work around you, that can discern a closed door or an open one that He may have placed in your path. Paul prayed asking for this very thing in Colossians: "And pray for us, too, that God may open a door for our message, so that we may proclaim the mystery of Christ, for which I am in chains" (Colossians 4: 3). In Revelation, our Lord himself mentions an open door in relationship to the church at Philadelphia:

> **⁷ To the angel of the church in Philadelphia write: These are the words of him who is holy and true, who holds the key of David. What he opens no one can shut, and**

> what he shuts no one can open.
>
> ⁸ I know your deeds. See, I have placed before you an open door that no one can shut. I know that you have little strength, yet you have kept my word and have not denied my name (Revelation 3: 7-8).

I find it interesting that the Lord closed the door for Paul in Acts 16: 6–7, prompting Paul to wonder aloud to himself which direction he was now to take in his effort to spread the Gospel. Maybe you have sometimes wondered in a similar vein: Where on earth is God leading me? Why do I keep bumping into closed doors? Is this all really as futile as it seems to me? Wondering in this way, being unsure or even confused, isn't pleasant, but it can sometimes create the acoustics that, at long last, make God's Word sound crystal clear. Paul's vision in Acts 16: 9 is an example. The apostle was given a vision that showed God's definite direction for Paul's ministry. When the vision passed, he set his compass due west toward Macedonia, and his act would yield the historic moment when the Gospel was introduced in Europe!

Here is an important conclusion based on the verses from Acts 16: *The Spirit of Christ guides us to the right places.* When we are seeking His will and daily seeking His face in accordance with Holy Scripture, we can bank on it, the Lord will bring us where He wants us. A second takeaway from this important passage: *The spirit of Christ guides us away from the wrong places.* In my family's case, Medan was a wrong place, a place not within God's will for us then. I'm still not quite sure of His reasons, but I can fully trust that He led and guided us during that time. Seeking God's will entails knowing what God wants us to do and where God wants us to do it. Equally important, it also entails knowing what God does *not* want us to do and where God does *not* want us to be. In my case, God was clearly leading us to not move to Sumatra.

Praise Him for His Sovereign grace and plans for our life.

CONTEMPLATING A MOVE

In fall 1996, we were finishing up our third term in the city of Solo. We had been contemplating a move to Kediri, a smaller city in East Java with a large Muslim population. Kediri is the site of the oldest of Indonesia's three Baptist hospitals. The hospital's legacy is significant, largely due to the scores of IMB missionary doctors who have served there since its 1953 opening as a clinic. Moving to Kediri would be a huge change for us. In Solo, we had worked without any other missionaries, basically. The Buckners had been there when we arrived, but visa complications led to their departure, and although they came back to Indonesia, they came back not to Solo, but to Jakarta. If we went to Kediri to serve, we would definitely work with other missionaries; there were four units, all medical doctors who were serving at Kediri Baptist Hospital. In fact, my job in Kediri would involve living in the doctors' compound and being team leader for all IMB personnel affiliated with the hospital. It would also involve work with the Association of Baptist Churches in Kediri and with the hospital's own evangelism department.

We felt drawn to Kediri. We had good friends among the doctors there and their spouses. We also knew something of the hospital's history and its far-reaching impacts on the community. We knew how much that hospital mattered. Every time I had visited Kediri, it had been impossible to miss how much respect missionaries got from workers at the hospital, from the community, and even from churches around the area. Clearly, we would ride on the shoulders of those who had preceded us. Later missionaries to Kediri inherited the very early IMB medical personnel's rapport not only with hospital administrators and staff, but with Baptists generally, throughout the area. It would be a comfortable position from which to work, I thought.

Don Dent, who formerly headed SEAP, has wished for someone to write a dissertation or book about the Baptist hospital's impact around Kediri, where the population and culture are largely Muslim. Don was spot on in observing that the hospital's influence for Christ around the city of Kediri has been "nothing short of remarkable." Personally, I would call it a modern-day miracle from the Lord and one of God's mightiest works in the history of reaching Muslims for Christ. In all of Christian mission history, has there ever been any other institution remotely like the Kediri Baptist Hospital, one leaving such a huge footprint on a predominantly Muslim culture? Little wonder we felt a significant pull to serve there. And the healthcare that we knew we would enjoy should we go to Kediri was admittedly a plus. We were preparing for a stateside assignment coming up in 1996. Our prayers seemed to show us the Lord was leading us to Kediri once that stateside time was up. We told Dr. Charles Cole, our mission chairman, about the decision taking shape, and it was obvious he agreed with our interpretation and was excited for us.

A ROADBLOCK RISES

All seemed just about in place for a move to Kediri when our stateside assignment wrapped up in 1997. One thing, though, remained to do before our mission could give us formal permission to relocate. While we had already gotten the green light from Dr. Cole and the rest of the executive committee of the Indonesian Baptist Mission, we also needed approval from the head of the Indonesian Baptist Convention. His name was Pastor Sentot Sadono; we called him *Pak* Sentot or Mr. Sentot. He hailed from near Solo, and he served a growing church in Jakarta. We knew *Pak* Sentot very well, from working with him on a number of projects, for instance the translation and promotion of the *Experiencing God* workbooks used then by Cell Groups all around Indonesia. We really had a good relationship with *Pak* Sentot, yet we knew he could be strong-willed and even unbending at times.

We had to have Pak Sentot's approval, so Shelly and I drove to the house he owned in nearby Boyoali. We were nervous about how he might respond to our request. Inside his home, we tried to explain to him, through many tears, our sense of call. Our gifts were well matched to the work that the Kediri Association of Churches and the Baptist churches were calling us to do. More important, we had prayed about it and come away believing this to be the right move for us. Mr. Sentot agreed to the idea, albeit very reluctantly. As I reflect on it now, I think he was probably propelled by our established relationship to give his okay that day. I would guess he respected the personal bonds existing between us. Yet Shelly and I both remember how he remarked that Americans were all alike in using a *God called me* card to get their way (this is paraphrasing, since we have no record of his exact words). Mr. Sentot was probably right, many Christians do use this phrase as a means of securing their choices. They expect the words to peg them as being terribly spiritual, when too often their real bottom line is merely having things their way. Truly, such was not the case with Shelly and me. Together, we had sought God's will; alike, we believed we had heard Him direct us to Kediri.

Pak Sentot's mild display of resentment might have resulted from fear of setting an unhappy precedent, one that could free future missionaries to insist on their own way and that could follow the proverbial slippery slope to a point where every last bit of authority over placing missionary personnel was removed from the Indonesian Baptist Convention's hands. It was certainly not our intention to wrest such control from the convention. Even so, by the year 2000 we were seeing more and more placement decisions made by IMB personnel than by our Baptist convention. It seems *Pak* Sentot was not wrong if he suspected that a precedent could readily be set concerning placement of missionaries.

LESSON #4 — We as missionaries need a biblical approach to spiritual warfare.

The area of the mission field in which most missionaries, perhaps, feel least prepared or equipped to serve is that called *spiritual warfare*. A few very helpful books on the subject have appeared since I came to the field (for example, Jerry Rankin's *Spiritual Warfare* and Chuck Lawless's *Spiritual Warfare* as well as his *Putting on the Armor*). Such books were not available when I was in seminary, nor were such books required reading for any training I completed through the International Learning Center. Which is by way of saying that when I got to Solo, I knew far too little about the kind of satanic attacks that soon would be launched on my family and me. We were going to be tested and tried by the evil one. We would wonder if his purpose was to get us out of Indonesia, to make us go crazy, or both!

SATANIC ATTACKS IN THE MIDDLE OF THE NIGHT

Prior to entering Indonesia, we had studied about its people's animistic world view. That animistic stance affects how every Indonesian deals with fear that crops up in his or her life. Experiencing a fear of some kind, a typical Indonesian would consider seeking power from the spirit world in order to feel safe again. Among Indonesians, knowledge of such occultic powers is widespread, because they've dabbled in animism for hundreds of years.

The introduction of Dr. Rankin's *Spiritual Warfare* recounts an experience he had while visiting a missionary's house when he was the president of the IMB. "As he visited the family," the text reads, "an Indonesian young man dropped by for a visit and we seized the opportunity to share the Gospel with Adi. As Dr. Rankin shared, he offered him a Bible and told him to read a portion out of the Roman Road to Salvation. As Adi opened the pages of the Bible, he said that there were no words in the book. Funny, as we examined it, all the pages of the Bible were intact with all the words clearly printed. But Adi couldn't see them."[2]

One way that animistic Muslims deal with Christians who try to share the Gospel is by attempting to strengthen their power to resist the Good News. The attempt may involve reciting an incantation or a mantra, or carrying or handling a *jimat*, or charm, which is often just a piece of cloth believed to bring power. Having repeated the words or remembered the *jimat*, an animistic Muslim someone is evangelizing claims to be unable to see any print on any page of Scripture or in any gospel tract or the like. This seems to be what happened to our friend Adi when Dr. Rankin tried to evangelize him.

I have our own tale to tell about something that happened in our Solo home late one night. We had been in the process of parting with one of the household helpers we employed and welcoming a new one to replace him. The old employee wanted to return from Solo to his hometown in East Java; that had opened up the new employee's job. It is a custom in Indonesia to give a person who helped you get your job a little money, as a token of appreciation. We had learned that. But we little knew what was going on behind the scene during these employees' transitioning. Apparently, our new employee violated the custom, refusing to offer any money to the old employee. The old employee wanted revenge, and not so much on the new employee as on the ones responsible for hiring him—Shelly and me. His revenge was a *guna-guna*, or hex, on the household the new employee would serve. That would be us.

In Java, particularly, putting a *guna-guna* on an enemy to demonstrate one's superior power is common practice. Someone feeling angry with a boss, a friend, even a spouse consults the local *dukun*, to use his special witch-doctor powers against whomever caused the angry feeling. A payment is made to the *dukun*, who then casts a spell on the offender. In the middle of exactly this kind of squabble between two animistic Javanese was where we found ourselves. It was not an enviable place to be! Our former household helper reportedly connected with a powerful *dukun* in Ponorogo, a city well known for occultic and demonic practices. Word was he had paid one and a half million *rupiah* to the *dukun*, for a purpose that he stated plainly. A curse was to be directed at Shelly that would make her so sick or so insane that she and her family would return to America.

A DEMON FACE TO FACE

This part isn't easy to write down. It seems like a scene in a horror film. Suffice to say for now that God gave Shelly and our family the victory. I was asleep in the back room at about midnight. Shelly was still awake and watching television in the front room when she saw a demon manifest itself. This demonic imp said, "Either you and your family leave Indonesia or I will take one of your children." Shelly responded boldly, "By the power in the Name of Jesus Christ and His shed blood on the cross of Calvary, you must leave my house and my family right now! You have no power over us." The demonic manifestation disappeared.

Just at that moment, Shelly heard Jamie, who had been sleeping in her bedroom, gasp loudly for air, as if she had been struggling to breathe. Shelly was still shaking with fear as she woke me to tell me what had happened. As soon as we could, Shelly and I asked our pastor, Timothy Kabul, what all this was about. Pastor Kabul said we had witnessed an attack from the demonic spirit world, something that is not uncommon in Indonesia. We asked him then why he thought the attack happened. I will always remember what he said. "It is important," he told us both, "for you to understand what Javanese [that is, Indonesian] people deal with on a daily basis. You have experienced it, and Jesus gave you victory over it so you can help Javanese that are involved in it on a consistent basis. You got to see your enemy face to face, *Ibu* Shelly [Mrs. Shelly]." Shelly marveled that she had been so bold in the face of it, taking that unshakeable stand on the authority that is ours in Jesus' name and through His blood. Her courage that night still amazes us. But after all, she had received the boldness of the Lord as she was equipped with the armor of God:

> [10] **Finally, be strong in the Lord and in his mighty power.**
>
> [11] **Put on the full armor of God so that you can take your stand against the devil's schemes.**
>
> [12] **For our struggle is not against flesh and blood, but against the rulers, against the authorities, against the powers of this dark world and against the spiritual forces of evil in the heavenly realms.**
>
> [13] **Therefore put on the full armor of God, so that when the day of evil comes, you may be able to stand your ground, and after you have done everything, to stand.**
>
> [14] **Stand firm then, with the belt of truth buckled around your waist, with the breastplate of righteousness in place,**
>
> [15] **and with your feet fitted with the readiness that comes from the gospel of peace.**
>
> [16] **In addition to all this, take up the shield of faith, with which you can extinguish all the flaming arrows of the evil one.**
>
> [17] **Take the helmet of salvation and the sword of the Spirit, which is the word of God.**
>
> [18] **And pray in the Spirit on all occasions with all kinds**

of prayers and requests. With this in mind, be alert and always keep on praying for all the saints.

— Ephesians 6: 10-18

Shelly and I both understand that she herself did not win victory over that manifestation of the demonic world Indonesia is so steeped in. That night she learned firsthand of how victory is won by the power and authority that is ours in Jesus.

LESSON #5 — We as missionaries need a clear pattern of teaching the principles and practices of revival and spiritual awakening.

During our second stateside assignment, in 1993, I was introduced to Henry Blackaby's *Experiencing God* materials. I remember taking my brother Mark and my nephew Terry through these materials while my family was staying in a missionary residence belonging to Beechmont Baptist Church in Louisville, Kentucky. Mark and Terry would come to the house once a week, and we would study the "seven realities" made famous by Dr. Blackaby. How much those seven realities and twelve chapters (and twelve cassette tapes) would come to mean to my life! Once we were back in Solo, I remember, I listened to Dr. Blackaby's book on tape, using a Sony Walkman and walking around and around our own house. I listened to him explain and expound on the crucial truths embedded in the seven realities. Listening to my *Experiencing God* tapes again and again, I became burdened with seeing them translated into *Bahasa Indonesia*, one of the country's languages.

FRESH ENCOUNTER WITH SPIRITUAL AWAKENING STRATEGIES

In time, I went to work with a steering committee formed to produce just such a translation. By 1995, we had acquired all the materials we needed

CHAPTER SIX | CALL TO BE A LEARNER

and were ready to teach Dr. Blackaby's *Experiencing God* to our Cell Groups, as the Indonesian National Baptist Convention Department of Evangelism had planned. Fairly soon afterward, I came across another course written and produced by Henry Blackaby, *Fresh Encounter*. Dr. Blackaby wrote *Fresh Encounter* especially for churches, associations of churches, and conventions wanting to lead their people in preparing for revival and wanting to train them to pray for their nation's spiritual awakening. We had a stateside assignment beginning in 1996, and I was lucky enough to obtain the *Fresh Encounter* materials then, to bring with us back to Indonesia. This time, we could all listen to *and watch* the tapes of Dr. Blackaby's seminars. They had been recorded and reproduced on VHS tapes. We could view them to our hearts' content!

It was an unexpected thrill to find that Avery Willis (the missionary and writer on the 1960s Indonesian Revival whose home in Nashville Shelly and I had visited) appears in the videos with Henry. In them, Avery talks about revivals in church history, laying the groundwork for Henry's discussions of the "cycle of revival and spiritual awakening" found in the Old Testament and New Testament. I was personally very inspired by Avery's insights into the Indonesian Revival, which saw two million people come to faith in Jesus in the largest Muslim country in existence. My heart would leap out of my chest when he talked about revival here. Had the church in Indonesia been ready, he explained, many more individuals could have been won and discipled.

From the first time I heard that, I interpreted Avery's words as a challenge to me to pray for revival in the United States and also for another mighty movement of God in Indonesia. I knew I must pray that, once again, God's manifested presence would come among his people—especially among the people of the two Baptist conventions we worked with as IMB missionaries. I needed to pray, Avery indicated, that God's Word would spread rapidly, becoming a mighty river rushing across the islands of Indonesia and bringing thousands, maybe millions, of lost people into His Kingdom.

BORN AGAIN IN THE JESUS MOVEMENT

At this book's beginning, I told about being born again during the Jesus movement, but only after its peak. I think of the movement as having started with the Asbury Revival, in 1970. Pastor Greg Laurie, however, the senior pastor at Harvest Christian Fellowship in Riverside, California, says that the Jesus movement began in Southern California *before* that date. I identify with Greg. He comes out the same spiritual awakening I did. He was saved on the West Coast in the late 1960s, through the influence of Calvary Chapel and Pastor Chuck Smith, while I was saved in the Southeast U.S., influenced by the Asbury Revival that occurred in 1970. (Whatever the start date of the Jesus movement—at times an Indonesian-style "officialness ceremony" would really come in handy, wouldn't it?—ultimately, the Asbury Revival joined hands with what was already going on along the West Coast, primarily. This generated an impetus and force that has moved revival experts to call the movement a "nationwide" spiritual awakening.)

Laurie's book *Jesus Revolution: How God Transformed an Unlikely Generation and How He Can Do It Again* Today tells the extraordinary story of the Jesus movement, that unusual time of revival, renewal, and reconciliation. Brilliantly, Laurie draws parallels between the turbulent, tumultuous 1960s and the times today, when there is so much apathy and indifference in the church and so much hostility expressed toward the church by a society getting more and more secular each day. Like Laurie, I believe God can still transform unlikely generations, whether millennials, Gen-Xers, Gen-Yers, or Gen-Zers. Experts on church growth have reported the proportion of millennials who are cross-carrying disciples to be under four percent. But God can bring the rest into His Kingdom, too, with a movement not unlike the old Jesus movement. The Gen-Yers sporting tattoos and body piercings now have the same need that the hippies sporting bell bottoms and tie-dye had then. All need that heart change and transformation that takes place only in a personal encounter with the Lord Jesus.

Pastor Michael Catt of Sherwood Baptist Church in Albany, Georgia, was like me, saved during the 1970s Jesus movement. He wrote, "I was part of a movement of God in my teenage years. And I want to be part of another one before I go home to glory." He went on, furthermore, to challenge readers: "But if I'm going to see it happen, I need to be right with God. Then I need to find ways to connect with this generation before they are so jaded that they reject the church, the message, and the messenger. They are probably not going to read this book, but you are. You could join me in making a difference".[3]

Like Pastor Catt, for some time I have had a burden to see God move in a mighty way that brings about a spiritual awakening ushering multitudes into the Kingdom in just a short time. What would this require? On the morning I am drafting this paragraph, I also joined the OneCry community on a Skype call allowing many hundreds to join their hearts in prayer for a worldwide spiritual awakening in the midst of the Covid-19 pandemic. Shelly was among those callers, too. Untold numbers of people are praying and crying out all over the world right now, crying out for revival in the desperate days we face. Those leading OneCry in this morning's prayer included Pastor Catt. He prayed for spiritual awakening to spread like a mighty river and bring millions to faith in Jesus.

The host of the OneCry prayer meeting, Bill Elliff, asked Pastor Catt to tell us how he interpreted what we all had seen happen in the recent dark days. What did he think God might be saying to His church? The pastor's short response was sobering: "The Lord is showing us that we have built altars to the gods of fame, fortune, and pleasure. And in a matter of weeks He has taken all these away from us by closing all sporting events in addition to allowing the stock market and economy to collapse in a way that this generation has never seen the likes of. Everything that we have leaned on to bring us joy and pleasure He has taken away from us in a matter of just a few days. Through demonic pressure, people of faith have been marginalized and pushed out to the fringes. We as the church have been guilty of spiritual adultery."[4]

Timely words from a true man of God. I have never met him, but I sensed a oneness with him as he led our prayer for revival and spiritual awakening in our nation and our world. Pastor Catt's response to Bill Elliff was a stinging indictment. But notice his words are not directed to the mass media, the academic community, or the government in power. They are instead directed to the church in America, which is spiritually sick. I agree with Michael Catt that the solution is found in Hosea: "Sow for yourselves righteousness, reap the fruit of unfailing love, and break up your unplowed ground; for it is time to seek the LORD, until he comes and showers righteousness on you" (10: 12).

Revival and spiritual awakening were topics in a class I took with Lewis Drummond in 1979 at Southern Baptist Theological Seminary in Louisville, Kentucky. "Principles and Practices of Spiritual Awakenings" was honestly the best course I had during my entire seminary experience. A definite highlight of the class was hearing Bertha Smith give a testimony, at the request of our teacher, Dr. Drummond. As all of us preachers filed out one by one afterwards, we each shook her hand and were told by Miss Bertha to "Confess your sins . . . confess your sins . . . confess your sins." It was a pretty pointed message; indeed it has "stuck" with me. And

CHAPTER SIX | CALL TO BE A LEARNER

not one of those preacher boys argued with Miss Bertha that day.

In Dr. Drummond's book *The Awakening that Must Come*, he shared his concern for the moral blight visible across the United States. He made an argument that was essentially a warning: "If a Spiritual Awakening does not occur by the end of this century, we will lose the freedom we enjoy at this time." He went on to predict something else: "In addition to losing our religious liberty this nation will become morally corrupt to the degree that we will no longer recognize the America we once knew."[5] Such sadly prophetic words. Forty years later, the attack from the left, especially from those pushing the LGBTQ agenda, bluntly threatens religious liberty in the United States. Millions of Americans would prefer that the church be silenced, or eliminated. We desperately need revival once again.

I am typing up this chapter in my office in Indonesia, "social distancing" in light of the coronavirus by staying indoors for at least the two weeks ahead. It feels absolutely unreal. Who could even have imagined such a vicious pandemic infectious disease? And not just the disease, but ensuing economic devastation that is potentially the worst since the Great Depression of the 1930s and the most globally far-flung since the era of World War II. Everything is closed and people are sequestered in their homes, probably for weeks. No church, no school, businesses and restaurants closed, half the work force off work! But I have found some comfort in the book I'm reading by Bill Elliff, titled *One Cry*. In it, Elliff observes, importantly, that "In the first 150 years of American history, God sent such awakenings every thirty to sixty years: the First Great Awakening (1730–1740), the Second Great Awakening (1790–1830), the Prayer Revival of 1857–1858, and the Welsh Revival of 1904–1906, which expanded during the next few years to impact the US and many countries around the world."[11] Elliff continues, "All served to provide dramatic course corrections, bringing Christ front and center to our consciousness and worship."[6] You probably noticed that Elliff does not place the Jesus movement among major spiritual awakenings that have shaken the USA periodically over its two hundred forty-four years of existence. He excludes that significant movement of God's Spirit from his list. Nor does Dr. Richard Owen Roberts, the most thoroughgoing expert on revival still alive, include the Jesus movement with the greatest spiritual awakenings of our national history. I highly respect, these two scholars, but I humbly disagree with them here.

What's the take-away, you may ask. It is this. Assuming that God sends revival and spiritual awakening about once every fifty to sixty years—as a look at the history of revival and spiritual awakening in America shows—we are clearly due a major movement of God *if* the Jesus movement of the late 1960s and early 1970s is counted as a great spiritual awakening (and as you know, I do count it!). Now, I am not a prophet, I do not predict what will happen. But I can puzzle out a pattern God has worked in humanity's past, and observing our present situation reminds me of 2 Chronicles: "When I shut up the heavens so that there is no rain, or command locusts to devour the land or send a plague among my people, if my people, who are called by my name, will humble themselves and pray and seek my face and turn from their wicked ways, then will I hear from heaven and will forgive their sin and will heal their land" (7: 13–14). I know that most who read these words are very familiar with 2 Chronicles 7: 14. With high hopes of again seeing revival, it has been taken as the theme of protracted meetings in our churches all over the United States and even in Indonesia. Most people are aware of the promises in Verse 14. But have you noted the context surrounding the verse? As you read the verses preceding Verse 14, give close attention to the fact that Solomon alludes to those times when a nation or a group of people experiences some calamity or natural disaster. Would a novel coronavirus count as one of those? In my opinion it would.

We're anxious beings, so we may worry now that God seems to have abdicated His throne, but He has not. We have to remember that God is in sovereign control of our world. Is He controlling these events we face? Yes, He is. Is the world right now like a top spinning out of control? No, it is not, although too many believe that way. They would tell you our world is heading to its ultimate destruction at a fast clip. But God's Word tells you He is still in control.

There is a parallel between our times and the times surrounding the Prayer Revival of 1857–1858. That revival was accelerated by an economic crisis dating to October 10, 1857. That October 10 date was about two weeks after Jeremy Lanphier began convening his lunchtime prayer meetings on Broad Street in Manhattan. That October 10, the stock market crashed without warning, banks closed, and scores of workers were laid off from jobs. Suddenly people were flocking to the Broad Street prayer meeting, and others. Within six months, ten thousand people were gathering daily for prayer in New York City alone. Other cities also experienced renewed interest in prayer. In Chicago, the Metropolitan Theater was filled every day with two thousand praying people. In Louisville each morning, several thousand came to the Masonic Temple for prayer. Two thousand assembled for daily prayer in Cleveland, and St. Louis churches were filled for months at a time. In many places, tents were set up for prayer meetings. The newly formed YMCA played an important part organizing prayer meetings and spreading the revival throughout the country.

There is, again, a parallel between what is happening to us today and what happened surrounding the 1857–1858 Prayer Revival. As Shelly and I called in to Skype to join that OneCry prayer meeting, I was greatly encouraged. The OneCry ministry unites people like us in prayer with luminaries like Bill Elliff, Byron Paulus, Dave Butts, Bob Bakke, and

John Avant. We were among hundreds of people in America and in far-off countries like Indonesia, all met together (if electronically) to pray. Together, we asked God to send another spiritual awakening akin to that Prayer Revival during which so many people joined in heartfelt, desperate prayer that God honored their petition. Just how meaningful was the Prayer Revival of 1857–1858, in terms of its results? As one website summarized,

> One Million Saved—With little human planning, a nationwide revival broke out among God's people in "union prayer meetings" beginning in 1857. In the awakening that followed, nearly 1,000,000 people accepted Christ and became involved in churches in a two-year period. Based on percentages of converts to the general population, a similar move of God in our day would result in 8–9 million people turning to Christ.[7]

What if even one-thirtieth of today's U.S. population of 327 million would come to Christ? It is hard to imagine (and not solely due to the math!). Yet God is working. He might be moving right this minute to prepare the final casting of His net and the last catch of souls saved in time.

CHAPTER 7

CALL TO HUMBLE MYSELF

Humility is not thinking less of yourself but thinking of yourself less.[1]
— C. S. Lewis

Is there a difference between being humiliated and being humbled? Yes, a significant one. I have heard before that humiliation results when a proud person is brought low by circumstances beyond his control. (But God is sovereign, and nothing escapes His control or attention or providential watch care over our lives. Furthermore, each person responds or reacts to circumstances, as well as to God, in his own way.) Being humbled is different. We come away humbled when we no longer compare ourselves to others. Such comparison leaves us with either an overinflated opinion of self or with a sense of inferiority—depending on whom we compare ourselves to. To truly be humble, or in other words to demonstrate true humility, requires ceasing to compare ourselves to anyone other than Jesus Christ. Like John the Baptist, we will gain proper understanding of self and of relationship with God by acknowledging how we stack up in comparison with Jesus: "John answered, saying unto them all, I indeed baptize you with water; but one mightier than I cometh, the latchet of whose shoes I am not worthy to unloose: he shall baptize you with the Holy Ghost and with fire" (Luke 3: 16, KJV).

Jim Halla distinguishes humiliation and being humbled using this explanation:

Consider the contrast of the two men who went up to the temple to pray: the tax collector and the Pharisee (Luke 18: 9–14). Both men approached God with statements about themselves. The Pharisee, with eyes focused on himself, prayed assuming God heard and approved of his self-litany. The tax collector had a different view of himself and God. He remembered the Levitical system of sacrifice. He prayed for mercy, which was a direct reference to the mercy seat and atonement cover in the Holy of Holies. He was God-dependent, and as a result a humble man. He had a proper view of himself and God."[2]

This chapter is focused on events in the period 1997–2002, when my family and I were in the city of Kediri, in East Java. Some were significant. God shaped me with those, rendering my character more appropriate to my tasks. As God so often does, He used circumstances to remind us that we are not in control. Grasping that is essential if we want to free ourselves from self-dependence and self-centeredness. Between 1997 and 2002, God humbled me in four ways. He humbled me through failing health. He humbled me through the work and example of extremely capable colleagues. He humbled me through a new relationship with an Indonesia National Partner who was serious about hearing God's voice. And he humbled me through the destabilizing of Indonesia politically and otherwise.

As we have seen, our move to Kediri and a new assignment involved a vigorous inner struggle to discern, hear, and obey the call of God. Our Indonesian term *bergumul* is, again, helpful for writing about an effort to, in a prayerful way, discern and hear the voice of God. *Bergumul* means struggling in prayer in order to break through to the genuine, heard voice of God that will direct one's course. *Bergumul* indicates struggle-in-prayer that is so almost physically intense that the term is sometimes translated as *wrestling with God*. In the first chapter of the Book of Habakkuk, the prophet wrestles with God, suggesting that he is struggling inwardly with what he sees around him. (The meaning of the name Habakkuk is to *embrace*, a word with roots meaning "two arms," easily bringing wrestling to mind.) Habakkuk is driven to confront God this way by all of the injustice surrounding him. In his prayer meeting with God, the prophet complains to God at length, pouring out his heart. It is the very picture of one experiencing *bergumul* with the Lord over some burden, in this case, "The burden which Habakkuk the prophet did see" (Habakkuk 1: 1, KJV).

Jacob had a similar encounter, described in the Book of Genesis. By the river Jabbok, he met the preincarnate Christ:

> **22 That night Jacob got up and took his two wives, his two maidservants and his eleven sons and crossed the ford of the Jabbok.**
>
> **23 After he had sent them across the stream, he sent over all his possessions.**
>
> **24 So Jacob was left alone, and a man wrestled with him till daybreak.**
>
> **25 When the man saw that he could not overpower him, he touched the socket of Jacob's hip so that his hip was wrenched as he wrestled with the man.**
>
> **26 Then the man said, "Let me go, for it is daybreak." But Jacob replied, "I will not let you go unless you bless me."**
>
> **27 The man asked him, "What is your name?" "Jacob," he answered.**

> ²⁸ Then the man said, "Your name will no longer be Jacob, but Israel, because you have struggled with God and with men and have overcome."
>
> ²⁹ Jacob said, "Please tell me your name." But he replied, "Why do you ask my name?" Then he blessed him there.
>
> ³⁰ So Jacob called the place Peniel, saying, "It is because I saw God face to face, and yet my life was spared."
>
> ³¹ The sun rose above him as he passed Peniel, and he was limping because of his hip.
>
> ³² Therefore to this day the Israelites do not eat the tendon attached to the socket of the hip, because the socket of Jacob's hip was touched near the tendon.
>
> —Genesis 32: 22-32

In this strange passage of scripture, Jacob's wrestling match continues all night, as he seeks to receive a blessing from the preincarnate Christ. Jacob did not just want to hear God's voice, he wanted to lay hold of the blessing of God.

When we endure *bergumul*, when we are wrestling with God, it's usually related to a change of location or a change of work. As we seek His leadership about where to serve, we yearn to know if God will red-light or green-light the ministry we are considering. Make no mistake, *any* time we seek His will concerning our future, what we want is the blessing of God on our ministry. We want to identify and secure the position from which God can most effectively use us, so we become proactive in reaching for God's anointing of the potential new ministry we are weighing. Thus, we wrestle with God. And we shouldn't wonder why we feel so drained from *bergumul* with God. Just laying hold of His voice can use up all the mental, emotional, physical, and spiritual energy we can generate.

We know that hearing His voice, or receiving His Rhema Word, assures us of future blessings in ministry. I do not mean physical blessings, although sometimes those present themselves. What I mean are the twin blessings of an anointed ministry and a ministry filled with God's presence. This is what authentic wrestling with God can secure. It is what those of us at that 2018 "Foundations" meeting (described in the introduction) sought more than anything else: to wrestle God for His presence.

Jacob was persistent when it came to his wish to lay hold of God's blessing. Persistence is paramount when we are trying to hear from God. God requires us to show persistence in all areas of life, and especially in the spiritual realm. Each and every experience seeking God in order to know and do His will develops the aptitude for hearing His voice the next time we listen for Him. Peter Lord has told the story of an entomologist who belongs to his church in Titusville, Florida. The man wrote his doctoral dissertation about different kinds of crickets that exist in God's creation. The entomologist visited Peter Lord's home one night, and at one point they stood together outside, talking. The bushes surrounding the home were evidently filled with crickets, because the sounds of crickets emanated from the darkness all around. The entomologist told Peter that no less than ten kinds of crickets were audible there. Peter wondered how the man could tell one cricket's sounds from another's. The man explained that he had trained his ear to discern distinct sounds from various species. He was not the average person, able only to say, "I hear a bunch of crickets."

Hearing God is like that. The ability doesn't come automatically or naturally, because there are just too many distractions, too many other voices, around us. But the spiritual ear can be trained to be sensitive to the Master's voice, to be able to tune in His wavelength. With persistent training, the voice of God can be distinguished from the many voices we hear daily. When in life do we need more persistence than when we are trying to hear from that Good Shepherd who would lead us by still waters and restore our souls? When your struggle is a prayerful one, struggling through the tough times in life does more than build character. God blesses you for taking on *bergumul*, the prayerful struggle, the interior wrestling with God.

Isn't it interesting that Jacob, after wrestling with God, changed his name from Jacob, which means trickster, to Israel, which means *one who struggles with God*? A new name signified that God had changed Jacob's life, as he had changed others' lives, who subsequently changed their names (Peter, Sarah, Abraham). Becoming Israel pointed to the former Jacob's changed character. No longer the ambitious deceiver, Israel is now the one who struggles with God and overcomes! Once Jacob had wrestled with God, his utterly changed character propelled him to humble himself. Perhaps fear had something to do with this. He would now have to face his twin, Esau, whom he had hoodwinked many times as they were growing up. But fear would have been infinitely less important than the holy encounter with the preincarnate Savior by the river Jabbok. Jacob's wrestling match had truly humbled him, which had immediate repercussions in his life, including some for his dealings with Esau.

FAILING HEALTH AND A HUMBLING STATESIDE ASSIGNMENT

We had a stateside assignment beginning in 1997 that would become a very humbling experience. I would get about as close to death as you can get, short of actually dying. I had been making a whirlwind trip across the Southeast region of the United States, stopping briefly here and there to speak at churches and missions conferences. I wasn't doing much healthy eating, but I was doing a whole lot of eating. We missionaries can be kind of good at that. Getting to eat things you've had to go without for

CHAPTER SEVEN | CALL TO HUMBLE MYSELF

years on end is one very nice thing about stateside assignments. But my travel schedule had me eating late at night, many times, and then going immediately to bed. That's a problem for a person with a hiatal hernia and acid reflux disease; if only I had known I had those conditions! Over a three-week period of back-to-back speaking engagements in multiple states, the problem got serious.

It was time to drive home to Elizabethtown, Kentucky, from a missions conference in Champaign, Illinois. I felt okay. I remember that I even stopped for a couple of White Castle hamburgers. But soon after I pulled into the driveway that night, I started feeling very strange. I thought a shower might help me fall asleep despite the strange feeling. But then I passed out in the shower. Shelly came to revive me and was helping me to the bedroom of the mission house when I began to throw up blood uncontrollably. I passed out again, but Shelly fortunately kept her cool. She calmly called 911 and waited. I came to again and got dressed. We waited together then, for a few minutes, but the ambulance driver couldn't find the house, which was outside the city limits, in the boondocks. Shelly, we decided, would need to drive me to E-town's North Hardin Memorial Hospital.

I walked into the emergency room on my own but soon collapsed a third time. As the staff were examining me, they asked all kinds of things about a possible cause of the internal bleeding they diagnosed. Had I been stabbed? Had a recent automobile accident? I vomited again mid-interview, blood that looked black and projected with a force rivaling that in the scene from the movie "The Exorcist," with Linda Blair. (Sorry folks, but that is how I remember it.) In time the doctors stabilized me, and it looked as if I wouldn't need an anticipated blood transfusion, for which I was very grateful. Still, I had just six liters of blood remaining, the least you can have without needing a transfusion. I worried because the hospital was close to

Fort Knox, and blood products I might be given could well come from Fort Knox soldiers, whose blood might be tainted with HIV.

Despite my worry, the road to recovery beckoned. I was diagnosed with esophagitis, an irritation of the esophagus so severe it causes bleeding. The esophagitis resulted from the acid reflux and hiatal hernia conditions. Those conditions were triggered by overeating and then going to bed right afterward. Overeating at bedtime, of course, resulted from the actions of a person. And that would be me. I was put on Prilosec, which I have taken daily ever since. Prilosec controls the acid reflux that got me into the initial, frightening trouble. With this medication, I can live with and manage my condition. But the experience of being so ill humbled me. I was reminded that earthly life is fragile and short—and we are never sure how short it will be. In our pride and selfish ambition, we assume we can pursue our goals and keep going without any interruptions of the schedule or challenges to the agenda. I was forced to admit I was not indestructible. Except for God's Grace, I might easily have died during that horrifying experience. My family had been terrified witnessing the bloody scenes at home and in the emergency room. For their sakes and my own, it was time to take a break from the schedule and reflect on the meaning of my life and ministry. In that sense, my esophagitis was a bad thing that God turned to good use. It was also a kind of preparation, because as it turned out, my near future would hold a series of similar humbling experiences surrounding our move to our new assignment in the East Java city of Kediri.

A HUMBLING ROLE

In October 1997 we moved into our house on Mauni Steet in Kediri. We were greeted by all the American doctors serving at Kediri Baptist Hospital. Don and Sarah Duvall lived next door. Both came from the Lexington, Kentucky, area. Don was an avid University of Kentucky

CHAPTER SEVEN | CALL TO HUMBLE MYSELF

basketball fan. How great, a fellow member of the Big Blue Nation was my closest neighbor! Don was a veteran missionary and a surgeon, Sarah an ob-gyn. Don was also a gifted administrator and quite a people person. He and Sarah both had great relationships with the local churches and especially with the people who worked at the hospital.

Also living in our cul-de-sac were Dr. John Clement and his wife, Martha. Martha and Shelly had been close friends for some time, and Martha may have been the one who initiated the effort to bring us from Solo to Kediri. John was a gifted oncologist. Although he was quite cerebral, we used to talk a lot about basketball (he was an LSU fan from Louisiana). John had compassion and a heart for people. He worked seemingly nonstop at the hospital throughout our four-year-long ministry in Kediri.

Another doctor's family lived right beside the hospital in a house on the compound. Dr. Phil Wakefield was a dermatologist who, with his wife, Jeanne, had only recently arrived on the mission field in Kediri. Their four beautiful children accompanied them. Phil really had a heart for ministry. He helped me as I worked to start a new church in a city called Jombang. At the time, this church plant conducted services in a house it had purchased in a Jombang housing development. Phil and I took turns leading those Sunday services, bringing with us each time a group of supporters from the mother church. Phil and Jeanne Wakefield were two of the most humble people I have ever met.

Dr. Ken Hinton rounded out our little community. Ken was a pediatrician who had been serving the Kediri hospital since the early 1980s. A scholar through and through, Ken spent a good bit of time studying how to witness to Muslims. He helped me in many ways, over the months, for instance with evangelizing; he had an unusual knack for reaching youth and young adults. In a conversation we had, Ken pointed out that the sermon Peter preached to the gathering of family and friends at Cornelius's house (the sermon cited in Acts 10) is one of Scripture's most concise, most contextual presentations of the Gospel. He thought the sermon could be a useful evangelistic tool (it certainly was), and he had cards printed with the text of Peter's sermon. Honestly, Ken carried out more evangelism during his hospital ministry than many full-time church planters and evangelists carried out.

Ken Hinton, the Duvalls, the Clements, and the Wakefields were the missionaries I had come to serve as team leader. Just before my family moved to Kediri, our mission had adopted its "New Paradigm." This plan entailed many changes, one of the most significant being the grouping of all personnel in Indonesia into location-based "teams." (It is an approach that for the most part has made a positive impact on our ministry in Indonesia.) The Kediri Baptist Hospital team of doctors had asked me to become its first team leader. Receiving their invitation had been very humbling. I wanted to succeed; I knew it was an honor to serve among these people of God, and I felt they deserved my absolute best effort. Their long hospital shifts claimed the largest part of the doctors' time. I so respected them for their commitment to giving Indonesians what I suspect was the best health care available in the nation.

When we arrived in Kediri, Dr. Hinton was transitioning out of his role at the hospital. Within the year, he began preparing to move away; he would become a teacher in a medical college in Surabaya, East Java. In the short time we worked together, Ken inspired me with his way of reaching, evangelizing, and discipling young Indonesians. He felt such compassion for the lost. He had a gift for evangelism as well as for apologetics, always able to offer Muslim seekers very reasonable explanations of the Christian faith.

Among my first tasks in Kediri that fall of 1997 was to help with a survey in Ngawi, East Java. The survey would bring in information we needed to begin planting a Baptist church in that city two hours west of Kediri. The Baptist Association of Kediri had targeted Ngawi as its top priority for a church plant. Activities with this new church got under way in March 1998. I began making the drive to Ngawi every Thursday, to conduct services for and visit with the handful of folks who were helping us start the church. The new church met at the house of Mr. and Mrs. Supomo. Mr. Supomo was a government worker who had moved to Ngawi from Surabaya and was committed to getting our Ngawi church up and running. Once we started meeting on Thursdays, it wasn't too long before we had enough people to think of screening properties for the location of the new church building.

HUMBLED BY ANOTHER'S SERIOUSNESS CONCERNING GOD'S VOICE

In 1999, I left Indonesia for a short time to go to my father's funeral. Just after I came back, the convention's Department of Evangelism stepped up and helped find someone to live in Ngawi and become the church start's full-time pastor. I was glad the folks of Ngawi Baptist Church would soon have their own pastor. He was Pastor Eko Kurniadi, and he was a godsend for certain. Between 1999 and 2001, the church at Ngawi tripled in size, under Eko's solid leadership. Eko and his wife, Hendi, are among my and Shelly's closest friends, and I am enjoying the fact that they now pastor the Candi Baptist Church in Semarang, the city where I am also working. About a year into his new pastorate, Eko is doing a great job. In fact, everywhere Pastor Eko has served he has worked wonders. When it was time for him to move on from Ngawi, in 2007, Eko received an invitation from Courtney Street, a strategy coordinator for the Mid-Americas and Caribbean. Mr. Street is an African American IMB missionary whom I met at a 2006 conference for strategy coordinators in Bangkok, Thailand. At the conference, Mr.

Street asked Mike Shipman and me if we could suggest a good person to go plant churches among the 70,000 or so Javanese living in Suriname, the country on the northern coast of South America. I will never forget how Courtney Street described what kind of person he was looking for: "We want somebody who's willing to jump out of a plane without a parachute." Well, that certainly narrows the field. But Pastor Eko came to mind, and quickly. I felt he could be a great fit in Suriname. Back in Indonesia, I wasted no time approaching Eko about it. I asked if he would be willing to pray about going to Suriname for a two-year term. I can remember him laughing hard when I mentioned how Courtney Street was looking for a guy who was ready to jump out of an airplane without a parachute!

CASE STUDY: AN INDONESIAN PASTOR AND *BERGUMUL*

Because we have worked so closely with Pastor Eko for such a long time, I want to make him a case study illustrating how a pastor or missionary who is not from America understands God's call. Specifically, how did they hear the Voice that sent them to seminary or to the field? And afterward, had they depended on that Voice to make decisions about new ministries, in new locations?

Or maybe such decisions came out of organizational systems in which an employee deferred to those in higher positions concerning changes in assignments or placements? This latter arrangement is basically how Methodist and Presbyterian churches in the U.S. move pastors from placement to placement. Pastors and missionaries don't go to the Lord to determine if God is speaking to them about such changes. Rather, they receive direction from a bishop or council that makes those decisions. While I don't want to sound overly spiritual, that kind of arrangement differs crucially from our Baptist approach. As believers who emphasize *soul competency* or the *priesthood of all believers*, the practice of seeking God's voice is extremely important in Baptists' lives; we take pride in our need to hear directly from the Lord.

Thus each local Baptist church is autonomous and has authority to call pastors to serve. There is no requirement to consult a synod or other hierarchy concerning placement of pastors. While we find our approach to be the more biblical—the Bible is full of accounts of people seeking God's voice in order to hear personally and individually from Him about where and how to serve Him—our system can, we realize, include certain flaws, or be misused. Maybe you've heard the funny story about the Baptist pastor who got an invitation from a church much larger and better-paying than his own church. Right after hanging up the phone with the pulpit committee's head, the pastor turned to his wife and said, "You go pray about the move, and I'll go pack." Funny, yes, but each time we skip the search for God's voice concerning a decision, we run a risk of circumventing God's plan for our lives. We all need to study the concept of learning God's will for one's life by listening to God. In studying it, it's impossible to escape the fact that hearing from God is tied very closely to struggling with God in prayer.

Over the years, I have heard more than a few of our own missionaries lamenting the way the Indonesian National Baptist Convention's ecclesiology resembles too closely the ecclesiology associated with Methodist and Presbyterian churches. Overseas, the leaders of Baptist conventions and even the leaders of local associations have far greater say than most Baptists in the United States would feel comfortable with. I suppose most Indonesians would say their church polity is congregational, at least in theory. In practice, however, in my opinion it is rather presbyterian.

According to Wikipedia, "Presbyterian polity was developed as a rejection of governance by hierarchies of single bishops (episcopal polity), but also differs from the congregationalist polity in which each congregation is independent. In contrast to the other two forms, authority in the presbyterian polity flows both from the top down (as higher assemblies exercise limited but important authority over individual congregations, e.g., only the presbytery can ordain ministers, install pastors, and start up, close, and approve relocating a congregation) and from the bottom up (e.g., the moderator and officers are not appointed from above but are rather elected by and from among the members of the assembly)."[3] And therein lies the rub, notably when a decision one makes clearly goes against what those in a higher position would choose. We experienced something similar to this as we prayed through a potential move to Kediri. Our Baptist Convention's leader, Mr. Sentot, opposed such a move. In prayer, however, we learned it was very likely the right decision for us; we could feel very plainly the Lord's leadership in the matter.

Which returns us to the question of how pastors and missionaries from outside American culture come to understand God's call. Do Indonesian Baptist pastors, evangelists, and missionaries often face the kind of tension we ourselves have felt between seeking God's voice and functioning in the hierarchy? Does the leadership tend toward telling them what they should or, worse yet, must do? If their leadership should oppose some change they find themselves called to, are they bold enough to act on God's voice rather than the organization's voice? Or are they somehow convinced that to simply "cave" is all they can do in the position they occupy—despite what they have heard from God? We can start on some answers by studying Pastor Eko's experiences with a series of decisions affecting his role and the direction of his ministry.

EKO'S CALL TO KARANGANYAR GUNUNG CHURCH

When Eko was studying at the Baptist seminary in Semarang, following a period of *bergumul* in prayer he felt led of the Lord to become associate pastor, not senior pastor, at a church expressing interest in hiring him. He had chosen to go where the Lord led but was being criticized by pastor friends and fellow students for thinking of "settling" for the associate pastorship. They preferred to see him as the senior pastor. Eko wrestled some more with the Lord in prayer, and found again that the voice of God directed him to the associate pastorship, a learner role, and what's more, to a time of mentorship under the church's established senior pastor. Eko had been wanting to sign on with a church to study how the pastor worked with the deacons, other leadership, and in truth the whole congregation. He was curious about teamwork's role in the work of a church and about how understanding teamwork might be useful to a pastor. His idea—which, he was being told by God's voice, was more than his idea, it was indeed God's will—was not the idea his superiors in the hierarchy liked. They wanted him installed as sole pastor in charge, even if the church were small. They wanted him to learn by having all the responsibility. But Eko was hearing from the Lord about a different way to learn.

The story of Samuel tells how he was groomed or mentored by the high priest Eli. From Eli, the young boy learns how important it is to recognize God's voice in the throng of voices, if he wants to hear from God (see I Samuel 3: 1–21). Verse 7 is significant: "Now Samuel did not yet know the Lord: The word of the Lord had not yet been revealed to him." Thus hearing that Voice was a turning point in Samuel's life. Now despite being a bit of a slacker, Eli did possess the spiritual maturity to recognize that God had spoken to young Samuel. Eli also understood the great opportunity presented to him to help Samuel sharpen his spiritual ears and hear the voice of God more readily (see 1 Samuel 3: 8–10).

You see, in Samuel and Eli's time, during the rule of the Judges, the audible Word of God became unusual. In the past, God had been given to speaking audibly, notably with Moses and Joshua. Then for three centuries, God was quiet and hearing God's Word aloud was rare. (There is a simple explanation. Eli had two sons who were priests, but the two were scoundrels. They refused to listen to God, letting greed get in the way of hearing from Him. And slacker Eli definitely didn't know how to correct his wicked sons effectually! As a remedial judgement on Eli, his sons, and Israel, God chose to be silent during this prolonged period.) It is vital to our relationship with God that we listen for and respond to His voice. While God communicates only sparingly using the sound of a human voice, He nevertheless speaks clearly.

What does Samuel's story say to us? Simply put, it says we should always be listening for the voice of God and we should always be ready to act when God speaks to us. Samuel was listening and prepared to act. Once Samuel learned it was God's voice he'd heard, he listened and received the message he needed to deliver. Through the Lord's spoken instruction, Samuel discovered an important truth about prophets' and preachers' weighty task. Many times, the message we are given that we are directed to share with others is not a message that will make them happy. (See Verse 18, for instance.) The task of the preacher or man of God is to both hear from God and to faithfully communicate what God says to others. The message for his mentor that Samuel had to pass along was an unpleasant one, but the experience taught Samuel early on that after hearing from the Lord, it is a believer's duty to act on what the Lord said.

Like Samuel, Eko acted on God's Word to him. His peers and the leadership talked at him, but he also heard God's word, and he acted on that. He became associate pastor at Karanganyar Gunung Baptist Church and would serve its people for seven years. I admired Eko then, and I admire him still, for following through with the work he believed God was leading him to do.

Pastor Eko at the church plant in Ngawi, in 1999.

EKO'S CALL TO NGAWI

When Eko answered Pastor Sartono's telephone call in 1999, the Baptist convention's head of evangelism invited Eko to pastor our church start in Ngawi in East Java. I had belonged to the evangelism team from the Kediri association that had planted the church in 1997. Two years on, the need for a full-time pastor there was desperate. Once again Eko found himself *bergumul* in prayer, struggling to hear God's voice about His will for the proposed move. As Eko prayed, he began to feel God leading him to accept the challenge in Ngawi. Yet once again, he also contended with other voices. Many sought to prevent him from accepting because Ngawi's was just a small, relatively unestablished church. One seminary teacher told Eko to decline the invitation because serving that church would be like "raising a church that had already died." (That is how we learned that years before, Ngawi had been the site of a different Baptist church that had had to disband.) Others thought he should stay in Semarang to pursue a master's degree at the seminary. All of this could have distracted

Eko. But he knew enough to go back to the Lord to confirm, one more time, what he believed he had heard in God's own voice. He got his confirmation and knew he could ignore the surrounding noise. The advice from his friends and others had been well-intentioned, Eko knew, but the bottom line was the need to act on what the Lord said to him.

A strange story from I Kings helpfully reminds us to stay true to what God has told us when we begin hearing from others who might directly contradict what He is saying. In the story, a prophet had heard the voice of God. It instructed him, "Do not eat or drink anything while on your mission" (13: 7–32), but this man of God chose to listen to someone other than God. If he had ignored the other advice and instead followed God's clear Word, he would not have died. This story illustrates the principle that Eko was learning. Listen for and obey God's Rhema Word, not what someone else is telling you to do. While in another context the seminary teacher's counsel might have proved wise, Eko knew he must be guided by what he felt God had repeatedly said to him. That was a good call, Eko!

When Eko was still *bergumul* in prayer, trying to pin down God's word for him about the Ngawi church, a man who worked as a janitor at the church he helped pastor at Karanganyar Gunug came up to him and started to speak in tongues. This was strange for two reasons. First, Eko knew him as a member of the church and knew he hadn't spoken in tongues before. (Eko doesn't remember him ever speaking in tongues again.) Second, because Eko could not understand him when the man was speaking in tongues, Eko told him to stop, that they wouldn't get anywhere trying to communicate that way. Right away, the man switched to Indonesian, which obviously Eko understood: "It's God's will that you go to Ngawi and pastor that church," the janitor said. "God will be with you and bless you." Eko moved to Ngawi in May 1999.

EKO'S CALL TO SURINAME

You know already that a time came when I thought Eko might be the right person to go to work in Suriname, where Courtney Street needed someone extraordinary. Allow me to share in greater depth about Eko's grappling with that call to move his family to another country and become involved in cross-cultural missions. You probably weren't aware that a large community of people of Indonesian descent is established in a northern region of South America along the continent's Caribbean Sea coast, in the nation of Suriname. Suriname is a former Dutch colony and a vibrant place with people of several cultures. Over 70,000 Javanese make up the Indonesian community I mention. These Javanese families have lived in Suriname for several generations, but they often continue to identify as Javanese—despite the fact that few have ever visited the island of Java or have ongoing family connections there. The Javanese in Suriname speak a creolized version of the Javanese language, but nevertheless their culture (notably its cuisine) has made a mark on their Caribbean nation's larger culture, and Javanese names crop up at all levels of society.

Eko was invited to pray through whether God was calling him to a foreign mission in this interesting transplanted Indonesian community some ten thousand miles from home. While pastoring in Ngawi, many offers had been extended to Eko to change churches, but he felt unusually drawn to this possibility of mission work so far away. In his life to this point, Eko had enjoyed no "connections" making it even remotely possible that he might serve overseas. Now he did. Was this his confirmation that God was calling him and his family to Suriname? Once again came the voices aimed at discouraging Eko from going. Some said it made no sense to go so far for just one year. So the leadership extended the proposed time, encouraging Eko and his family to spend two years in Suriname. And Pastor Eko made the commitment to the Lord to go. He let the appropriate leaders in Indonesia and Suriname know. And then he encountered a couple of problems.

First, while off doing some outreach in Tuban, a city near Ngawi, Eko was involved in a motorcycle wreck and broke his collar bone. It caused a lot of pain and seemed like a setback that could delay or even cancel his plans in Suriname. He hesitated to tell Mr. Street, for fear he might reject someone who had sustained such an injury. Eko's next obstacle was a flood that took place in Ngawi in early 2008. So many members of his church had lost a home or been otherwise affected that Eko and Hendi felt it would be wrong to leave just then. There was much they felt they should do to help their parishioners who were in such pain. They wouldn't be able to do it from another continent. But they prayed over the additional, possibly inevitable delay of their Suriname call. Eventually, in February of 2008, Eko and Hendi and their son Joash boarded a flight to Suriname. During the flight, Hendi became very sick. She was much better, fortunately, by the time the plane landed in Paramibo, the national capital. They say God healed Hendi en route to Suriname!

Something that struck Eko as rather humorous happened to the family as they changed planes in the Netherlands. The three had seats by the emergency exit, and the emergency door wasn't functioning properly. Flight attendants were working on it but couldn't quite get it to close. Eko's family was offered seats on a different flight to Suriname, or they could also continue on where they were, after waiting for maintenance technicians to come fix the door. They chose not to change flights, although they did switch seats, ending up in the very back part of the plane. When maintenance arrived, they proceeded to weld the emergency door shut! The flight attendant later commented to Eko and Hendi that it was a good thing the door problem was discovered before take-off. Otherwise, the occupant of the seat next to the emergency exit would have been in danger of being pulled out of the plane had the malfunctioning door been jarred open in flight. Of course, Eko thought immediately of Courtney Street's preferred job candidate, the one willing to jump out of an airplane without a parachute. This incident too he saw as God's confirmation, albeit lighthearted, of Eko and family's call to Suriname. The family settled in (away from that emergency door) for the long flight, Eko weeping happily and praising the Lord for his protection!

Pastor Eko, Hendi, and Joash with Courtney Street and his wife, Arleen, in Suriname in December 2008.

CALL TO BECOME THE EVANGELISM COORDINATOR

About two years later, early in 2010, Pastor Eko and the family departed Suriname for Indonesia. They got home just in time for the national "Congress" convened by the Baptist convention every five years. I attended it too, and it was the first time I had seen Eko since he left for Suriname. During the gathering, Eko was recognized and given the opportunity to share with those assembled concerning his ministry to Suriname's Javanese community. We were riveted by his presentation on the planting of house churches there, and by his larger message. At some point, Eko and I talked about an invitation he had gotten from the Baptist seminary in Jakarta to become a teacher of theology. The seminary even proposed that Eko study at Mid-America Baptist Seminary in Memphis, Tennessee, on a scholarship he could be awarded if he promised to join the faculty in Jakarta once he graduated. As he had prayed about this, Eko had realized God wanted him to remain in ministry, not take time out for the seminary. Before the Congress (which took place in Lembang, West Java, in March of 2010), Eko had heard from Pastor Timothy Kabul, head of the Baptist convention. Pastor Kabul had asked him to take the position of the Convention's coordinator of evangelism, effective immediately. Eko knew he was young yet and relatively inexperienced. But the more he prayed about it, the more the job seemed to be a good fit for him.

It didn't take long, however, for voices other than the Lord's to interject. It had happened to Eko before concerning his life and ministry. (It actually happens to all of us, this recurring pattern of well-meaning others trying to "speak over" God.) Seminary leaders and many of Eko's friends believed turning down this opportunity to study in America and then teach would be a mistake. Men's opinions—which, weighed against the clear Word of God in your spiritual ear, should be unconvincing. Eko was not convinced. He continued to pray and came to see even more clearly that being coordinator of evangelism would truly fit him. He knew he would love the challenge of strengthening the program of evangelism. He knew what he was hearing from the Lord. He went with it and completed two five-year terms with the convention. As early as 2017, however—three years before his second term as coordinator of evangelism would end—churches began to contact Eko about pastoring for them. Two of these churches were outside Indonesia. Eko began asking God something along these lines: "Lord, why am I getting all these offers to take a job as a pastor? What is it you are trying to say to me?" And thus began a months-long struggle, a difficult *bergumul* in prayer, as Eko wrestled with the Lord for his guiding Word.

One church that approached Eko and Hendi about pastoring them was Candi Baptist Church in Semarang. Hendi came from Semarang, but it was no place they had wanted to serve. However, interestingly, a day came when it appeared that all the other churches that had approached Pastor Eko had "moved on." Only the invitation from the Candi Baptist Church in Semarang remained open. His way had certainly narrowed, but even that would not spare Eko from the kind of rumors that regularly swirl through the conversations of pastors and Baptist convention leaders. Such voices seem part of the process of working through whether or not God is calling us. The voices are distracting, so we have to be determined to focus and keep listening for the still small voice within us. When everybody has an opinion for you about your future course, just appreciate their good intentions and ignore them, if they seem indifferent to what you have heard from God's own voice.

At times, the opinions can also be simply discouraging. Eko dealt with discouraging comments from colleagues and others who believed he was not a pastor. They had seen nothing that showed Eko to have the gifting to pastor, apparently. They were sure his lack of pastoring experience would undermine his work in the church in Semarang. Paul had dealt with discouraging voices among the people of his country and religion. It frustrated and upset him when his countrymen rejected the Gospel:

> **5 When Silas and Timothy came from Macedonia, Paul devoted himself exclusively to preaching, testifying to the Jews that Jesus was the Christ.**
>
> **6 But when the Jews opposed Paul and became abusive, he shook out his clothes in protest and said to them, "Your blood be on your own heads! I am clear of my responsibility. From now on I will go to the Gentiles"** (Acts 18: 5-6).

Paul endured rejection and hard-heartedness from his own not once but on many occasions. In these verses, he has had enough, even though he had a heart for the Jewish people, his own flesh and blood. If they would not see that Jesus was the Messiah, he could do nothing further for them. That hurt, that was discouraging. But in the midst of Paul's feelings of discouragement and futility and aloneness, God speaks to him again. God offers Paul nothing less than a personal Rhema Word: "One night the Lord spoke to Paul in a vision: 'Do not be afraid; keep on speaking, do not be silent. For I am with you, and no one is going to attack and harm you, because I have many people in this city.' So Paul stayed for a year and a half, teaching them the word of God" (Acts 18: 9-11).

Paul was told not to leave the city, even though a good percentage of the challenges he was up against involved the city itself, Corinth. It was a pagan and immoral place. But perhaps the internal problems of the church seemed even more challenging to Paul. The Church at Corinth was far from a healthy church (as a glance at the "Foundations" document and its ideals, hammered out in Bangkok in 2018, reveals). Its internal problems were enough to drive anyone to a new place of ministry: immorality the likes of which wasn't seen even in wicked Corinth city (a church member having relations with his stepmother); believers taking each other to court; factions within the church fighting about which leader was best. Absolutely the most discouraging thing to Paul was the Jews' rejection not just of his ministry but of Jesus as their Messiah. This was the context for God's spoken message to His apostle. The message was threefold. Paul was not to be afraid, he was to continue speaking the Gospel, and he was not to be silent. What an encouragement! I love the last part, "Because I have many people in this city." R. Kent Hughes has commented on this passage from Acts:

God assured his apostle, "I have many people in this city." Those were encouraging words. Paul's work would not be fruitless. Some of the Corinthians were tired of Tinsel Town. The fleshly pleasures had lost their attraction. Some were suffering deep guilt and an awful emptiness of soul. They were ready to receive Christ. These people, according to Paul's other writings, included Erastus, Gaius, Stephanos, Fortunatus, and Achaicus.

According to Acts 18: 11-18, Paul stayed in Corinth for eighteen months. For him that was like putting down roots! It was not long before there were many believers, perhaps hundreds. Persecution did come, just as Paul had expected, when the Jews took him before the proconsul Gallio (the famous Seneca's brother) and charged him with introducing an illicit religion. However, that opposition backfired, and for a time Paul and his followers enjoyed more freedom than before.

There is in this a great example of the power of a personal Rhema Word from God. The Word for Paul was uncomplicated: Don't leave, stay where you're at and put down roots. No need to fret over the challenges of ministering in a megacity like Corinth. God's call to stay put proved to be a game changer in Paul's ministry in Corinth. Growing numbers of residents would soon come to Christ. Among them were Phoebe (Romans 16: 1), Tertius (Romans 16: 22), Erastus (Romans 16: 23), Quartus (Romans 16: 23), Chloe (I Corinthians 1: 11), Gaius (I Corinthians 1: 14), Stephanas and his household (I Corinthians 16: 15), Fortunatus (I Corinthians 16: 17), and Achaicus (I Corinthians 16: 17). These are just a few who came to faith because Paul heard and obeyed the Word that God spoke to him.

So, Eko needed to stand firm against discouragement, which he did. There remained one other obstacle to overcome before he could have an official okay from his supervisor. He would have to find out if Pastor Wartono, our Baptist convention's new leader, approved of the plan. Eko was in basically the same spot I had been in in 1996, when Shelly and I visited *Pak* Sentot to seek his approval of our plan. We had known *Pak* Sentot, and we knew Wartono. He was a friend from Cola Madu Baptist Church days in Solo. Cola Madu Baptist had already produced over 60 preacher boys for the Gospel ministry. Wartono and *Pak* Sentot had differing leadership styles. Take official discussions. In typical Javanese fashion, Wartono would state his position; then listen to others' feedback, opinions, and lines of reasoning; and then come up with some consensus or compromise, termed *mushawara* in Indonesian. Eko must have gone to Pastor Wartono and explained his call to Semarang, after which I am pretty sure the pastor gave his opinion and listened to Eko's response, and so forth until they gradually negotiated a settlement. Its terms allowed Eko to move in May 2019, yet hold onto his position as evangelism coordinator until the following March, when the next five-year Congress was scheduled. Eko was ready to move to Semarang.

A group of five pastors and their wives, including Eko and Hendi and Shelly and me, once studied Bill Elliff's book *The Presence Centered Church*. Eko was asked to summarize what the book taught him about hearing from God. He said two points seemed particularly helpful for understanding the mechanism at work in hearing God's voice. First, Elliff had emphasized what Eko called *sikap*, roughly meaning attitude. To hear God's voice, people needed to develop an attitude of confidence in their own intuition or inner voice (or "still small voice"), as well as confidence that God would speak, that He would never force them to depend solely on the opinions of people. The second of Elliff's points that Eko found especially valuable was that the Lord's voice is to be found in the printed

Word of God. As we read and study the Bible, we can hear His voice and His individualized Rhema Word for us. Eko saw that one implication of Elliff's point is the need to pray that God would sharpen our spiritual hearing, like Phillip's (Acts 8: 26), making us better at catching what He says to us. What amazes me in the passage about Phillip is his ability to hear God's voice even in the midst of all the activities leading into that revival up in Samaria. Phillip was enjoying great success in preaching to large crowds (Acts 8: 5–8). Still, once he had heard God's Rhema Word for his life, he didn't ask for details, he merely obeyed the Word God had given him. Because he obeyed, Ethiopia was opened up to hear the Gospel.

In the course of discussing Elliff's book, Eko also shared that he needed to improve his prayer life, as leader of Candi Baptist Church. Once, he said, when a family member on his wife's side was sick in the hospital, that relative had tried phoning him one evening. The call didn't connect because Eko's cell phone battery was too low and he had turned the phone off. The relative phoned at 8:30, and at that very time Eko had felt directed by the Holy Spirit to go to the hospital. But he had ignored that prodding of the Spirit, had not visited the hospital, and had missed a chance to minister to that whole family. Eko felt convicted of being more in tune with what the cell phone was telling him than with the voice of God trying to enlighten him. Eko said that *The Presence Centered Church* helped him listen better *for* God and to God, meaning he became more successful at obeying God's voice. That was most important. Imagine if Phillip had heard from God about the road to the south that led to Gaza, and then did . . . nothing. Like Eko, Phillip would have missed an opportunity. But in Phillip's case, he would have missed the opportunity of a lifetime, helping bring the Gospel to an entire nation and being an agent of change reshaping an entire culture. In knowing and doing God's will, hearing is important and obeying is absolutely essential.

HUMBLED BY DETERIORATING PEACE AND ORDER

In 1996 our Indonesian Baptist Mission asked me to add another assignment to my role as church planter for Kediri, serving as the mission's coordinator of evangelism. This new role would not require a move to a new location, but it would mean quite a bit of travel on my part. Mission chairman Dr. Charles Cole wanted me to work on some projects planned by some larger Baptist churches located off the island of Java. I would work with Pastor Sartono, who headed our Baptist Convention's evangelism department and also pastored Ngesrep Baptist Church in Semarang.

REBAPTIZED WHILE ARRIVING AT KELUK BALI VILLAGE

As evangelism coordinator for our mission, one trip I made frequently was that to Central Kalimantan, the Indonesian island you may know as Borneo. I visited regularly to see the progress on work that Immanuel Baptist Church and our mission were involved in in Palangka Raya and another village. While commercial flights were available to Palangka Raya via Surabaya, getting to the second village, Keluk Bali, was not so easy. Keluk Bali sat at the edge of one of Kalimantan's many rivers. To get to it, we could take a *klotok* (small motor boat) up the river, but that trip took the better part of a day. And since there were no roads to Keluk Bali, driving was out of the question. So, we looked for alternative transportation. We learned that a six-passenger plane could be rented and we could be flown to Keluk Bali by a Missionary Aviation Fellowship pilot. The plane would land on and take off from the river right in front of the village we were going to, and our flight would reach the destination in a matter of 45 minutes—amazing! We decided to rent the plane. I remember that we landed just about right in front of the church, which was located along water. The whole village had gotten word of our visit from the church pastor, Jeremiah. Everyone was waiting on the riverbank at a makeshift dock built of logs. I stepped out of the plane onto the dock, which was so slippery that my feet went out from under me and I went under the water of the Kahayan River! Maybe the villagers interpreted it as my being rebaptized, *baptisan ulang*!

About a year later, in April 1999, Pastor Sartono and I returned to Central Kalimantan and Keluk Bali on the same plane. We were joined by Kyle and Jill Leach, IMB personnel who hoped to survey the Central Kalimantan area and explore the possibility of moving there. It fell to Kyle, during that trip, to give me word that my father had had a stroke and was near death. My good friend Pastor Sartono said later he could hear me crying in the next room at our hotel in Palangka Raya after I had received the news. The next day, our little six-seater to Keluk Bali landed on the river just like it had the previous year. Looking out the window as we approached, I noticed the crowd of greeters was more than double the last year's. Perhaps they remembered my great sermon from back then and were enthusiastic that the American was here to worship with them again. I quickly found out otherwise, though. When our visit was announced, a question had apparently begun circulating in the village: Would the white missionary fall into the Kahayan River again this year? I wonder if they possibly laid odds on such a fall! I'd guess I was probably a 6-to-5 favorite for repeating my klutzy move. I didn't disappoint. As soon as my toe touched that log dock, I knew I was a goner. It was one small *slippery* step for mankind and, hopefully, a giant step for the Kingdom of God.

With my father so ill, I needed to get to the United States as soon as possible, to tend to family needs. Before I could go, Pastor Sartono and I needed to visit the city of Sampit, where we were starting a new church on behalf of the Department of Evangelism of the Indonesian National Baptist Convention. We had made an initial survey trip in 1999 and were ready to start a new work. An Indonesian from near Sampit was married to a Javanese young lady, and they would move to Sampit to contribute their work to this new church. He was named Lewi, or Levi. He was a *Dayak*, a member of Kalimantan's predominant tribe. Like Keluk Bali, Sampit was built along a river. It was close to the port of South Kalimantan, from where the river soon flowed into the South China Sea. We had officially started a new work in Central Kalimantan, but as it turned out, it wouldn't last long.

DAYAK AGAINST MADURESE IN CIVIL WAR

It wouldn't last, because civil war came to Indonesia. This is a part of the past that I'd much rather not write about, but it affected our church plant, so it will be included. The conflict was between the indigenous Dayak people and the migrant Madurese, who came from the island of Madura, off Java. The brutal war's beginning traces to February 18, 2001, when two Madurese were attacked by a number of Dayaks. The conflict resulted in more than five hundred deaths, with over a hundred thousand Madurese displaced from their homes. In an article I found online, "Identity Politics, Citizenship and the Soft State," the war and its brutality and horror are easily explained: "In this 'horizontal conflict' particular ethnic characteristics ('Madurese are violent', 'Dayak are head hunters') seemed to be sufficient to explain the violence".[5]

Dayak warrior involved in ethnic war in Central Kalimantan in 2000.

In general, I want to focus on what war did to our fledgling church in the city of Sampit. Remember our Pastor Lewi's wife was Javanese. Javanese are in appearance fairly similar to Madurese. During the Civil War, Dayaks were indiscriminately killing Madurese, and they located their victims through the Madurese's body scent. Dayaks used their keen sense of smell to actually sniff out these "prey," hunting them like a hunter does wild game. Then, often, they stuck their Madurese victims' decapitated heads on fences, like trophies symbolizing the savagery of the Dayak tribe. Naturally, Mrs. Lewi was scared for her life and her family's life. The Dayaks' violence terrorized her, and her husband as well, and she couldn't take that for long (I'm not sure many people could). Pastor Lewi's family returned from Kalimantan to Central Java and Semarang, the city Mrs. Lewi was from. The new church obviously folded.

SECOND YEAR OF LIVING DANGEROUSLY

The Year of Living Dangerously is an Australian romantic drama starring Mel Gibson and released in 1982. It is about a love affair that unfolds in Indonesia just after President Sukarno was overthrown. The movie title seemed appropriate for this section's heading, since the section will involve the very unstable times—both socially and politically—that characterized Indonesia after a coup d'etat was attempted in 1965 but ultimately failed. I discuss this failed coup, too, in an earlier chapter, because it was the backdrop of the Indonesian Revival of 1966–1971.

Living in Indonesia in the year 1998 was every bit as dangerous as living there in 1965 had been (and 1966). In 1998, President Suharto had been in power for thirty-one years. Suharto is described by Wikipedia as an Indonesian military leader and politician who became the nation's second president after Sukarno was finally ousted in 1967. Many foreign observers viewed Suharto as a dictator, although the legacy of his rule continues to be debated.[6] Pressure on Suharto to resign began to mount steeply in 1998, but the longtime president had no intention to willingly step down. When he wouldn't, protests broke out all over Indonesia.

Wikipedia describes a decisive time of student protest:

> At the start of May 1998, students were holding peaceful demonstrations on university campuses across the country. They were protesting against massive price rises for fuel and energy, and they were demanding that President Suharto should step down.
>
> On 12 May, as students at Jakarta's *Trisakti University* were returning to campus in the late afternoon after demonstrating near the parliament building, men in mobile police uniforms appeared on the flyover overlooking Trisakti. They shot and killed four students and wounded two more.[7]

On that day, May 12, I was with Sutoyo Sigar, who at the time was directing evangelism for the Baptist convention. Despite increasing incidents of unrest in Indonesia, Mr. Sigar and I had been leading seminars and revivals for churches all over Sumatra. We had just finished several seminars in the Lampung area, assisted by Pastor Timotius Kabul, and taken a train to Palembang for our next seminar. Spending the night of May 12 in a Palembang hotel, I remember we watched on television the widespread rioting that followed the Trisakti event.

We conducted our seminar the next morning, and when we got back to our hotel in the afternoon, we saw that its front windows had been broken out. We were glad to have tickets to fly out that very evening for Batam Island. We presented our seminars on Batam without any problem, but we learned that elsewhere, things had gotten dangerously out of control. We had a flight scheduled to Medan to present a seminar there the next day, but as Wikipedia confirms, Medan, along with Solo

CHAPTER SEVEN | **CALL TO HUMBLE MYSELF**

and Jakarta, were at that very moment running amok—especially the latter, the national capital:

> On 13 and 14 May, rioting across Jakarta destroyed many commercial centres and over a thousand died. Ethnic Chinese were targeted. The riots were allegedly instigated by Indonesian military members who were out of uniform. Homes were attacked and women were raped by gangs of men who wore ordinary clothing. The US State Department and a government fact-finding team found that "elements of the military had been involved in the riots, some of which were deliberately provoked". However, most of the deaths suffered when Chinese-owned supermarkets in Jakarta were targeted for looting from 13–15 May were not Chinese, but Javanese looters who were burnt to death by the hundreds when a fire broke out.
>
> Over a thousand and as many as five thousand people died during these riots in Jakarta and other cities such as Surakarta. Many victims died in burning malls and supermarkets, but some were shot or beaten to death. The riots destroyed thirteen markets, 2,479 shop-houses, 40 malls, 1,604 shops, 45 garages, 383 private offices, nine filling stations, eight public buses and minivans, 1,119 cars, 821 motorcycles, and 1,026 houses.[8]

Before our trip to Batam, I had not really realized how dangerous Indonesia had become. Sutoyo Sigar and I had been so busy with seminars that, although we had watched the televised reaction to the shootings at Trisakti University, the "sudden" chaos now was something of a surprise.

Then came a phone call from Shelly. She was noticeably shaken and asked me to come home right away. The riots had been steadily moving closer to Salatiga, where Jennifer and Jonathan attended school, boarding in the dorms. They were scared that rioters would soon reach their location, and Shelly even feared that the kids and their school might in fact be targeted. I started praying. I felt fairly sure that canceling our journey's next leg and going home to Kediri was a no-brainer. And then Dr. Cole, our mission chairman, told me in no uncertain terms to go home, and now! I can be pretty hardheaded, but the word from Shelly and the word from Charles, once I prayed over it, convinced me we must abort the trip to Medan, where the situation was reportedly becoming just as bad as the situations in Solo and Jakarta.

Sutoyo Sigar, however, my partner in ministry, didn't see it like that. We were close to completing our mission; Medan was the last seminar site, and Mr. Sigar felt we should continue on to that city regardless of the violence there. I told him that as for myself, I was buying a new ticket for Kediri. I would have to pass through Jakarta and Surabaya and then make the four-hour drive home, but I felt the Lord leading me to do it. The scene at the Jakarta airport when I arrived was surreal. Chinese from all over the city were camped out in this airport and others, waiting and waiting for space on flights to Singapore, Thailand, Malaysia—anywhere far enough away from Jakarta. They were afraid to return to their homes in Jakarta or West Java. Some had to sleep in the airport overnight more than once before a flight became available. It was complete and total chaos. Witnessing all of it, I was very surprised to actually make my connection in Jakarta for the afternoon flight to Surabaya. Arriving in Surabaya, I was again surprised, and happy, when a driver from our hospital greeted me, all set for the longish drive to Kediri. Traffic was heavy but we got there without incident, somewhat late that night. Praise you, Lord, for that safe trip.

Now I had to figure out the best plan for picking up Jennifer and Jonathan from Mountain View Christian School in Salatiga. A six-hour drive would be necessary, in each direction. Rioting relatively near the school was ongoing. We made a plan to use a car with an emblem on each side reading *Rumah Sakit Kediri,* or Kediri Baptist Hospital. I would accompany the car's driver to Salatiga. This plan went off without a hitch. I don't remember exactly how long we had to keep the kids home, but they probably got a windfall of about two weeks' unanticipated vacation.

REFUGEES FROM TIMOR TIMUR, OR EAST TIMOR

In August 1999 the tiny island of Timor was seeking to become politically independent from Indonesia. As they sought their independence, the island's inhabitants knew that their struggle would create an economic vacuum that would spell disaster for those who remained in the capital city of Dili. Many chose to become refugees, running over the border to Kupang, a city in West Timor (in Indonesian, *Timor Barat*). A camp had been set up there to deal with the thousands pouring in from East Timor. Before long, our missionary personnel were being asked to come to Kupang to help people in the camp. A first wave of our volunteers responded, serving there for seven to ten days. I volunteered in the second wave, which worked to make sure people had places to eat and sleep and also helped to provide medical support. Our second wave supplied all kinds of medical needs, along with food and temporary housing and other requirements.

Arriving in the camp, or *PosKo*, I was taken aback by the harsh living conditions. There, walking from one workplace or storage site to the next meant dodging the human excrement that was everywhere all over the ground. Our volunteer group was housed in a home rented with help from our Baptist mission. I bunked in the very back, with a room all to myself.

MY OWN BOUT WITH DENGUE FEVER

About halfway through the ten days I had committed to volunteer in the *PosKo*, I woke up with a rash all over my hands, arms, and chest, quickly followed by a high fever and chills. I remember trying to sleep but the chills making it impossible. There was no doubt I had dengue fever, which some call bone crusher disease. It produces such body aches that you imagine your bones are being crushed! Here is what Wikipedia says about it:

> Dengue fever is a mosquito-borne tropical disease caused by the dengue virus. Symptoms typically begin three to fourteen days after infection. These may include a high fever, headache, vomiting, muscle and joint pains, and a characteristic skin rash. Recovery generally takes two to seven days. In a small proportion of cases, the disease develops into severe dengue, also known as dengue hemorrhagic fever, resulting in bleeding, low levels of blood platelets and blood plasma leakage, or into dengue shock syndrome, where dangerously low blood pressure occurs. [9]

Doesn't sound like much fun, does it? It isn't, a fact I can give full witness to, especially since I had also had it four years earlier, when we lived in Solo. Honestly it took about a month for me to get over the dengue virus each time I contracted it. Still, it's worse for children than adults. Many children die from it (due to hemorrhaging), if they contract one of the fatal strains.

After it became apparent that I had dengue fever, a team of medical doctors with *Rebanna* (a Baptist group involved in social care and ministry) advised me to return to Kediri as soon as possible and seek medical attention at Kediri Baptist Hospital. That plane trip from Kupang to Surabaya and the subsequent drive to Kediri was the most difficult trip I had ever taken. It lasted ten hours but seemed like ten days. Shelly recalls that when I arrived at our house, I was soaking wet from sweating. I went to bed and was checked out the next day at the hospital. I was glad to hear that I could be an outpatient, but I would need complete bed rest for as many as ten days as I battled with the fever and body aches. I knew from experience it would take longer to really be well, probably over a month. When I had contracted dengue in Solo, during the second, third, and fourth weeks of being ill, I might wake up feeling better. But when I tried resuming some of my normal activities, thinking my condition was improved, I wouldn't even make it to noon before having to get back in bed.

Repeatedly perceiving myself to be—finally!—well enough to get busy, and then feeling all the symptoms return before afternoon, started to play with my emotions. Depression starts to set in as you wonder if maybe you'll *never* get well. Depression just goes with the dengue territory. But if you happen to be reading this while fighting dengue fever, let me reassure you. Your battle will be successful. You will get better, but you'll need to allow at least a month to get your strength back to usual.

9-11-2001

When America experiences some sudden, major crisis, a lot of Americans can remember just where they were when they learned about it. My dad had remembered being at a movie theater watching an Audie Murphy western when he got word that the Japanese had attacked Pearl Harbor, December 7, 1941. I remember very well how I learned that President John F. Kennedy had been assassinated. I was in the fourth grade and had been kept after school for being naughty that day. The horrible news that President Kennedy had passed away came over the school intercom, the principal announcing the news to teachers still in their classrooms.

And what about September 11, 2001, do you remember where you were when you heard about the Twin Towers and the rest? I remember it was a Tuesday night in Indonesia. I had spent the afternoon with a couple hospital workers from Kediri who were helping me with a church plant in Kertosono, about an hour northwest of Kediri. At the very moment I was arriving home from Kertosono, our neighbor Martha Clement was telephoning us. Martha and Shelly had been studying a Beth Moore book at our house earlier, finishing that day's study not long before I got there. "You need to turn on CNN and watch the news," Martha urged. "The World Trade Center in New York was just hit by a passenger jet." We turned on the TV, and minutes later, at 9:02 a.m. Eastern time, the second plane hit, even as we watched. While our instinct, like many others', was to consider the first crash a tragic accident, with the second plane, the whole USA could see the country was under attack. As millions watched the horrific event unfold in New York, another commercial jet circled over downtown Washington and at 9:45 a.m. slammed into the west side of the Pentagon. Within 15 minutes of that terrorist attack on the nerve center of our military, a catastrophic turn for the worse came in New York as the south tower of the World Trade Center collapsed in a massive cloud of smoke and dust. By 10:30 a.m., the north tower also gave way.

What on earth was happening? It took a little time—really very little—for officials to learn that radical Muslim terrorists had been at work for months planning their detailed and precise and above all diabolical plot. *But why?* The question was on the lips of millions of people in the United States, and Christians in Indonesia were asking the same thing: Why do Muslims hate us so much? Within a couple weeks, an awareness was growing that Muslims' hatred of the West, and especially of America and Christianity, existed because so many Muslims—in Indonesia and elsewhere—equated Christianity with Western Culture. (Doing that

CHAPTER SEVEN | CALL TO HUMBLE MYSELF

is a huge mistake.) Such awareness was brought home to me in early October, when I went to speak at a church in Bandung and encountered anti-American protests. The Bandung newspapers had printed editorials claiming the 9-11 attacks were carried out by Jewish Zionists, not Muslims at all. Clearly, the anti-American sentiment displayed so graphically before our eyes on September 11, 2001, was to be found in Indonesia as well.

And then a call came from Jennifer and Jonathan's school in Salatiga. Staff members had found a bomb in the grade school, not far from our kids' dorm. In the past, the school had dealt with a number of bomb threats, but always administrators had called the perpetrators' bluff, held off any dramatic response, and there had been no bomb. This time was different. Finding the unexploded bomb had administrators thinking seriously about closing the school. It was rumored that the bomb was only unexploded because its timing mechanism used "ABC" batteries, a cheap brand made in Indonesia.

Some Mountain View Christian School teachers with the New Tribes Mission were still pretty shaky following the killing earlier in the year of some fellow New Tribes Mission teachers in South America. They wanted the school closed. Most other teachers agreed with them, so administrators decided to close school for the rest of the semester. That presented us with a problem, since it was barely October and we couldn't let the kids fall behind by a whole semester. This was especially true for Jennifer, our firstborn, who was going to be graduating in the coming spring. In the end, the school was able to offer an online program to Jennifer and Jonathan that let them complete the semester. With the school closed, we thought of returning to the U.S. for a while as the worst of the anti-American protests played themselves out. We contacted some churches, including one pastored by a friend of mine, Westport Road

Baptist Church in Louisville, Kentucky. A member owned a house we could rent for as long as we needed. We were so grateful for the way this church took care of us! We ended up spending three months in Louisville after the 9-11 crisis. During our brief stay, we fielded many questions from Christians who were finding them hard to answer. Why would God allow such a tragedy to happen to Americans? Was 9-11 a judgement of God on our nation? And again, why do Muslims hate us?

These questions are still being grappled with today, as we confront perhaps the biggest catastrophe the United States and even the world has ever faced. The last sermon I was to preach inside a full church before Covid-19 quarantined us was preached on March 15, 2020, in Cisarua, West Java. I preached it in Taman Safari's church, and it was from Luke 13: 1–8, in which Jesus is asked about the tragedy that befell the Galileans who were murdered by Pilate, and also about the people crushed by the tower of Siloam when it fell. Did the people involved die because their sin was so much greater than that of others in Jerusalem? Jesus' answer is clear. A death is not necessarily an accurate measure of righteousness; neither is surviving some tragedy that others do not survive. This story and these verses are, in short, a call to repentance for everyone:

> **¹ Now there were some present at that time who told Jesus about the Galileans whose blood Pilate had mixed with their sacrifices.**
>
> **² Jesus answered, "Do you think that these Galileans were worse sinners than all the other Galileans because they suffered this way?**
>
> **³ I tell you, no! But unless you repent, you too will all perish.**
>
> **⁴ Or those eighteen who died when the tower in Siloam fell on them—do you think they were more guilty than all**

the others living in Jerusalem?

⁵ I tell you, no! But unless you repent, you too will all perish."

– Luke 13: 1-5

The news broke in the United States late in December 2019, that a new viral disease, Covid-19, which had originated in China in the city of Wuhan, was quickly becoming a crisis. How quickly people started to play the blame game. As I write, we are half a year into the crisis, and the rash of back-and-forth finger pointing goes on. We are doing what Adam and Eve did in the Garden, playing the blame game. Read Luke and see how Jesus turned that silly game on its head. Stop pointing fingers, He said. Focus only on getting in right relationship with God. The sole way to do that is to repent and come to Jesus. Right now, I and others are praying for a miraculous outpouring of the Spirit that leads to revival, which is God drawing near to us. Revival creates spiritual awakening, under which the Word of God gains power and spreads rapidly, throughout America, throughout Indonesia. We could see literally millions repent and come to faith in Jesus Christ.

CHAPTER 8

CALL TO TRAIN

Give a man a fish and you feed him for a day, teach a man to fish and you feed him for a lifetime.

– Lao Tzu

AN UNEXPECTED INVITATION

Before Jennifer and Jonathan's school went on hiatus until January 2002, Shelly and I received an invitation to make another move. It came from an unexpected source. The leadership of the Baptist seminary in Semarang (Indonesia's largest Baptist seminary) was asking us not only to move to Semarang to teach, but to move right onto the campus. We sure hadn't seen that coming! I want to say, first of all, we loved our ministry in Kediri. Working with the Association of Baptists there was a pleasure, and we just loved working with the Kediri Baptist Hospital Department of Evangelism. We loved each member of the IMB staff who worked and served at the hospital; we actually hated the thought of leaving them. Of anyplace we had lived or worked in Indonesia, Kediri was our favorite. So on the surface, there didn't seem much to mull over. Why would we make a move when we felt such a good fit with our ministry in Kediri? We'd been there for just four years, we were really only settling in and just beginning to see great things happen. My first inclination was *Definitely not moving*. I was also puzzled at being invited to teach at the seminary and live on campus. What was up with that? Sure, for eight years I had been teaching for the seminary extension program in Solo; I had even worked in developing a seminary extension program in Kediri. Still, to live on campus would mean adopting a brand-new focus for doing missionary work. It would be unlike anything I had done up to that point.

Everyone knew I was a field person, a church planter with a heart for sharing the Gospel. I just happened also to do some theological education, mostly so I could keep renewing my visa and working in Indonesia. But I was a field person. I was not fond of keeping office hours or being tied down in the classroom teaching two-plus courses all semester long, every semester. I was pretty sure they had picked the wrong guy. But incoming leadership at the seminary saw great value in a more practical approach to ministry and theological education. Pastor Sentot Sadono had recently been asked to take over as head of the Semarang seminary. Previously, he had served two five-year terms as the president of the Indonesian National Baptist Convention. Pastor Sadono, along with the man who was stepping down as seminary president, Pastor Eddy Wiriadinata, had decided the seminary needed some changes.

They hoped to address, first of all, the fact that the seminary lagged behind other evangelical seminaries in producing graduates with a heart for evangelism and church planting. The matter had been neglected to such a point that some students, asked to submit descriptions of their evangelistic experiences during the semester, complained such an assignment was legalistic, and refused to complete it. There may also have been some who fabricated stories of witnessing to people and submitted the fabrications to their teachers. The seminary had been on a quest to become the most respected seminary in Java, perhaps in all Indonesia, academically speaking. That had blinded the administration to the high numbers of their graduating students who not only did not witness regularly as a lifestyle, but who showed notable apathy or callousness about any effort to change that. Many of these students were forced to compare themselves and their seminary classmates in Semarang to students at nearby STII, the evangelical seminary in Yogyakarta. In order to graduate from STII, a student not only had to plant a new church during the four-year enrollment, they also had to baptize at least 15 people in that time.

Pastor Eddy and the new seminary president, Sentot Sedono, wondered what could be done and discussed some ideas. Mr. Sentot really liked the model down at "STII Yogya." It produced skilled graduates, men and women who knew how to share the Gospel, how to lead and disciple new believers, and how to congregate people in New Testament churches. Those graduates were the legacy of the founder of STII, Chris Marantika, a Baptist who came out of the Indonesian National Baptist Convention. Still, Mr. Sentot did have some reservations about adopting STTI Yogya's model. He argued that, in light of the role of the Holy Spirit, students shouldn't have annual or semester quotas for conversions and baptisms. He was aware of the widespread reports of STII Yogya's students paying pedicab drivers to be baptized so the students could graduate on time. While this probably has happened, I like to think of it as an exception, not the rule. Mr. Sentot, the new president, proposed an idea that Pastor Eddy liked. During the fall of 2001, the seminary in Semarang had hosted Mike Spradlin, the president of Mid-America Seminary in Memphis, Tennessee, and John Floyd, one of the school's teachers. The two had come to confer with the Semarang institution's leaders about, among other things, a future partnership between the two seminaries. Spradlin had talked with the Indonesians about the success of Mid-America Seminary's mandatory witnessing program. Each student had to witness sixteen times each semester, turning in written reports about their experiences to Mid-America's leadership. Students not submitting these reports were not allowed to progress to the next semester. Every Mid-America teacher had to participate in the witnessing program as well, witnessing sixteen times and documenting those encounters.

Mr. Sentot and Pastor Eddy agreed such a mandatory witnessing program was the way to go. As Mr. Sentot has pointed out on numerous occasions, it is our job to proclaim the Gospel: every student's job and every faculty member's job. Actually doing the job would bring new direction and greater evangelistic fervor to campus and from there, eventually, to the churches. Unfortunately, at that time a program mandating witnessing would also bring opposition and disunity among the faculty and student body. If the new vision for the seminary could take hold, however, the cultural landscape of the place would begin to change. Mr. Sentot could see that, and he had the mental and spiritual fortitude to implement the vision and see it through. It wasn't long before Mr. Sentot, with his faculty's support, approached Mike Shipman, a member of the IMB staff, to come to the seminary in Semarang to work on bringing the new vision to life. And I, apparently, was the second draft pick. I felt honored just to be mentioned in the same discussion as my longtime friend Mike Shipman! The seminary leaders asked us both to pray about it. I wanted to have an answer for them before making the unanticipated stateside visit in the wake of 9-11. Of course, as I said, continuing the work I loved at Kediri and not pursuing the seminary's invitation had at first seemed the obvious response. But then Mr. Sentot and Pak Eddy spoke with us about what they had seen in both Mike Shipman and me. As people who had been field persons for a long time, we could make a difference by training and mentoring the seminary's students. The proposed work began to feel more "right" for me.

SPIRITUAL MARKERS

Chapter 6 of Henry Blackaby's *Experiencing God* explains that in general there are four sources that, by the Holy Spirit, enable us to hear God's voice: the Bible, our prayers, the church, and our everyday circumstances. I was eventually able through my everyday circumstances (the fourth source) to discern God's voice on my possible move to the seminary. Blackaby's Chapter 6 talks about "spiritual markers." What are those? "A spiritual marker," we read, "shows pivotal moments in one's life, key decisions, or a new direction where you are sure you know that God has led you."[1] Blackaby gives a clear scriptural example, referencing the story of Joshua leading the children of Israel in crossing the Jordan River:

> [1] When the whole nation had finished crossing the Jordan, the LORD said to Joshua,
>
> [2] "Choose twelve men from among the people, one from each tribe,
>
> [3] and tell them to take up twelve stones from the middle of the Jordan from right where the priests stood and to carry them over with you and put them down at the place where you stay tonight."
>
> [4] So Joshua called together the twelve men he had appointed from the Israelites, one from each tribe,
>
> [5] and said to them, "Go over before the ark of the LORD your God into the middle of the Jordan. Each of you is to take up a stone on his shoulder, according to the number of the tribes of the Israelites,
>
> [6] to serve as a sign among you. In the future, when your children ask you, 'What do these stones mean?'
>
> [7] tell them that the flow of the Jordan was cut off before the ark of the covenant of the LORD. When it crossed the Jordan, the waters of the Jordan were cut off. These stones are to be a memorial to the people of Israel forever."
>
> [8] So the Israelites did as Joshua commanded them. They took twelve stones from the middle of the Jordan,

STRUGGLING WITH GOD IN THE DISTANT ISLANDS

according to the number of the tribes of the Israelites, as the LORD had told Joshua; and they carried them over with them to their camp, where they put them down.

⁹ Joshua set up the twelve stones that had been in the middle of the Jordan at the spot where the priests who carried the ark of the covenant had stood. And they are there to this day.

– Joshua 4: 1-9

The stones were *literal* spiritual markers. They would serve to remind the Israelites of the direction, the leadership, God delivered in that significant time of transition. Three things are key to remember. First, God works in sequence to accomplish His Divine purposes. Second, when He is ready for you to take some new step, that change will fit right into the sequence of things He has already done in your life. Third, there are times of decision making or life transition when you understand clearly that God is guiding you, and those times are spiritual markers.

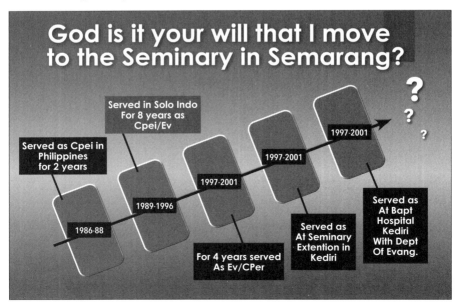

The graphic above describes my ministry, and it suggests how my decisions sometimes contradicted the second key thing above, namely, *When He is ready for you to take some new step, that change will fit right into the sequence of things He has already done in your life.* How could I best apply this principle to determine if God was leading me to make a change? To take up work as a member of a theological faculty appeared incongruent with earlier spiritual markers gained from the four sources of God's voice—at least, it seemed incongruent on the surface of things. But God was, in fact, calling me to Semarang. A theme did, in fact, tie the Word I had received in the past to the Word I was beginning to hear for the future. Those fifteen years of evangelism and church planting had taught me things that impressionable young seminary students needed to know. Thus looking *below* the surface, all the spiritual markers—including the most recent—appeared as a congruent sequence that made it clear God was calling me and my family to accept the seminary's offer.

LINING UP WITH GOD'S WORD

It was somewhat ironic that Sentot Sadono should be the person who started us on this move to Semarang. In his position in 1996, Mr. Sentot had been the leader bent on dissuading us from moving to Kediri. Now, six short years later, God had used him to bring us where He wanted us. Human instrumentality is a large part of God's plan. The important part is checking things against the Word of God. Any apparent use of God's body the church, or of everyday circumstances, must line up with God's Word. Such a check helped us decide to move to Semarang, just as six years before, a similar check had helped us decide Kediri was the place God called us to.

My family and I returned to Indonesia in January 2002 and moved into the house on "Holy Hill," as a new colleague called it. One of the fringe benefits of my new assignment in Semarang was that our children could come home from school in Salatiga each Friday afternoon, not just every six weeks! The now two-hour drive (also made each Monday morning) meant we would enjoy seeing much more of Jonathan and Jennifer, and later, Jamie Marie. It was an incredible blessing for our family. As for my work role, I was no longer a hands-on church planter, but rather a trainer. This chapter recounts a little of what was involved in the four groups for whom we would be providing training in Semarang during the next eighteen years. They were (*a*) seminary students; (*b*) United States churches seeking to partner with the seminary; (*c*) National Partners associated with Impact Center Boja; and (*d*) the Semarang Baptist Association's evangelism team. (Impact Center Boja is a sort of model farm just outside Semarang. It embodies a holistic approach to ministry modeled on operations in the Philippines and in Sumatra, where the whole person is the focus. The center serves people's physical needs by teaching skills of farming, fisheries, goat milk production, and micro-industries. It serves their spiritual needs, as well, by helping them understand the implications of the Gospel of Jesus Christ.)

TRAINING THE STUDENTS IN "THE NET"

By November of 2002, we were fairly well settled on campus. It was a kind of a fishbowl life. Our house was positioned in a way that had students passing in front of our dining room window all day. We would greet them as they came up or down those steep stairs leading from the road to the seminary buildings. Further, we found that some of the faculty were used to thinking of the house as their house too. Many times, someone came in through the front door without knocking or asking to come in. We worked to get used to it, but that wasn't easy. Still, living on campus was a joy, all in all. We especially loved all the impromptu interaction with the students.

CHAPTER EIGHT | **CALL TO TRAIN**

For the second semester, we started an evangelism group we called "the Net," based on the teaching of Jesus in Matthew: "'Come, follow me,' Jesus said, 'and I will make you fishers of men.' At once they left their nets and followed him" (Matthew 4: 19–20). We trained about ten students who had joined about how to share their faith. Then, we went out *dropping P.I.*, the equivalent of the evangelistic "push" still used enthusiastically by many International Mission Board personnel. In the 1950s (starting in October 1954, to be specific), former missionaries teaching at the Semarang seminary had introduced students to dropping P.I. and it had become pretty popular. So in actuality we weren't getting into anything new, just restarting what the students and faculty of STBI had started long before our day.

To add just a bit to the caption, the photograph above shows some of those we trained and mentored at the campus in Semarang. We have managed to stay in close contact with about half the folks in this picture, nearly twenty years after teaching and getting to know them at STBI, and have even visited them at the churches they now pastor. In addition to restarting the weekly evangelistic push, or dropping P.I., that semester, we would lead the members of the Net in studying Rick Warren's book *The Purpose Driven Life*. (It had recently been published in the Indonesian language.)

TRAINING WITH A PARTNER CHURCH IN ALABAMA

While we established partnerships with five congregations in the U.S. while serving the seminary, particularly close links were forged with Forest Lake Baptist Church in Tuscaloosa, Alabama. FLBC had sponsored two mission trips to Kediri during our four-year ministry there. Pastor Donnie Payne of FLBC had also been involved in the very first mission partnership we participated in, in Solo back in 1996.

Some of the first members of "the Net" evangelism team at STBI in Semarang, Central Java, 2002.

Now, the church was preparing for a mission trip in November 2002, when among other things members would join some of us on Sumatra to try to reach the *Anak Dalam,* or *Children of the Interior.* Pastor Sartono had been making arrangements for this trip meant to carry out evangelistic work with the very remote and backward people of this Unreached People Group. I had gotten FLBC's pastor and one of its deacons directly involved, even though their commitment would take up more than half the time they had in Indonesia, most of that time being needed for travel.

Pastor Sartono and I had gone to the Sumatran interior earlier that year, in May 2002. We went primarily to speak and lead seminars at Lubuklinggau Baptist Church. And we fellowshipped with people over local foods. I was in the middle of presenting evangelism training to a group from the church when, I remember, I became so sick so fast that I had to make a mad dash for the W/C, the bathroom, at the back of the church. In the end, I persevered and was able to finish our training. It was pretty clear what had made me sick. The day before, some folks had come to church from the remote area where the Anak Dalam tribal group was being reached. Wild boar is a staple of their diet, and they had brought some to share with us after morning worship. Who knows how long that wild pig meat had been sitting. I am sure it's what made me so sick.

CHAPTER EIGHT | CALL TO TRAIN

REACHING THE ANAK DALAM IN SUMATRA'S INTERIOR

Sumatra's Children of the Interior, or Anak Dalam, were unusual among Indonesians for being "nothing"—that is, for embracing no major religion, which is the category that polls as "none" in the USA. The Anak Dalam did tend to possess some animistic beliefs, however. One thing's for sure about them, they were not willing to give up their main food source, wild boar, in order to join the Islamic religion! And yet the Anak Dalam were very open to Christianity. A young pastor from Lubuklinggau Baptist Church, Pastor Budi, had helped open the work with this people, leading several to faith during previous visits he had paid them. He had made me aware that, not far from where he had led those people to faith, a different Anak Dalam village awaited evangelizing. He was planning out his visit there, and we were able to make it coincide with the Forest Lake Baptist team's upcoming visit to Indonesia. Unfortunately, back in Java, Pastor Sartono had gotten ill. He would not be able to go with our team to the interior of Sumatra.

When the team flew out of Semarang to Sumatra to engage the Anak Dalam Unreached People Group with the Good News of Jesus Christ, it was made up of Pastor Donnie Payne and Deacon Butch Kincaid of the church in Alabama, and me. We landed at the city of Bengkulu, where our Baptist mission had opened a rural development model in the early 1980s, one patterned after the hugely successful Rural Life Center in Davao City, Philippines. (The model at Bengkulu was the template for Impact Center Boja, on Semarang's outskirts.) We were most grateful for the rural development model, a comfortable place to spend the night. A long trip lay ahead the next morning, four hours or more of hard driving through the jungles of Sumatra to reach Lubuklinggau. When we obtained a vehicle with four-wheel drive, I realized the trip would not be as bad as I thought. With those miles behind us, we spent one night at Lubuklinggau Baptist Church. In the morning, the church's Pastor Budi and one member helped us navigate to the Anak Dalam village that was our destination. We crossed a river on a makeshift barge made of logs. According to Pastor Budi, we actually were drawing near the village. *"Tidak jauh lagi,"* he said, "It's not far away now." Then something strange happened. We had been traveling a dirt road, obviously, and one with lots and lots of potholes. (The Toyota van I used in Semarang would never get anywhere in such rough terrain.) But suddenly, very suddenly, even that simple road just disappeared. And Pastor Budi simultaneously said, *"Desa mereka di situ,"* "The village is just there." All I could see were weeds taller than me, so I asked, "It's *where?*" "There," he again indicated, pointing to a grove of trees in the background. I couldn't believe my eyes! There appeared to be tree houses in that grove. The tree houses were the village!

Forest Lake Baptist Church mission trip travelers meet with leaders from the Anak Dalam mission point, in one of the tree houses making up the tribal village. Pictured are (left to right), FLBC's Deacon Butch Kincaid and Rev. Donnie Payne, Pastor Ponco (who pastored the mission point), and Pastor Budi, leader of the mother church in Lubuklinggau.

We met with some of the leaders of the village, who took us on a tour. One man carried a rifle, which I took for an air rifle at first, given that in Indonesia, guns are outlawed for everyone except the armed forces. But that air rifle turned out to be a real rifle that used real old-fashioned bullets. The local government, I learned, allows the village's hunters to use a few rifles to hunt the primary Anak Dalam food source, the plentiful wild boar.

CHAPTER EIGHT | CALL TO TRAIN

WORSHIP SERVICE

Soon it was time for a real treat. We three Americans were asked to join the villagers, and even lead them in worship. Rev. Payne gave a simple Gospel message, which I translated for the Indonesians. Some who were present made decisions that day. The decision that most thrilled my heart was made by Ponco, the Indonesian man shown sitting in the middle in the picture above. There was a village not far from where we were worshipping, he said, that so far had not been given a chance to hear the Good News. He had decided to make a determined effort to reach them. Perhaps the thing that blessed us the most that day, though, was the people of the village joining in the singing of a hymn they were being led in. I was just struck by the expressions on the faces of the children as they sang. You could see they were truly worshipping! Most folks in that village could not read, but let me tell you, they knew how to worship!

The children knew how to worship, even though Christianity was new to them and they were as yet illiterate. The mother church was working on that, completing plans to bring literacy missions to this village.

Thanks to the local government and the rifles and the hunters and the villagers' hospitality, we were served boar during our visit (I somehow managed to avoid consuming it). The next day, making our way back to Bengkulu to fly on to Semarang, Butch Kincaid, the deacon from

As Jesus said, "God is spirit, and his worshipers must worship in spirit and in truth" (John 4: 24). Children from the Anak Dalam village we visited illustrate for us here how it looks to be worshipping in spirit and in truth!

Forest Lake Baptist, began to feel sick. Poor Butch started throwing up uncontrollably, and it became a very long ride in our four-wheel-drive vehicle. I told Butch what had happened to me six months before, on my visit with Pastor Sartono to Lubuklinggau Baptist Church. I jokingly offered him ice cream while he was still heaving, something he laughs about to this day!

Back in Semarang, we concluded our trip had been a royal success. While Butch still ailed and had to sit out the remaining four days of ministry, the three of us agreed that it had been an eye-opening, life-changing experience—and that we had genuinely helped provide some new direction for the ministry to the Children of the Interior. Pastor Sartono encouraged Kebayoran Baptist Church, a large church in Jakarta, to help with this ministry, in light of the fact that his own health was failing. The church responded and made follow-up visits to the village and helped an eventual church plant there to call Ponco as its first pastor. Ponco still pastors that church in the trees. Unfortunately, our good friend Pastor Sartono, with whom we worked so closely for the six years he coordinated evangelism for the Baptist convention, died the month after our trip, in December 2002. It was a sad day for us and a sad day for Baptists. Pastor Sartono exemplified the true servant of Christ, and serving with him was quite a joy. We miss him.

TRAINING LAY LEADERS AT IMPACT CENTER BOJA: MEET AJI SUSENO

On campus in Semarang, I was seeing more and more clearly that, as God had known, I could be an effective trainer and equipper of others to do church planting. I was sure doing my share of equipping and training through the seminary. Something that began to compel me more and more in those first years of my seminary ministry was the holistic approach to ministry exhibited in the work of Impact Center

Boja. As you know, the center was an hour from the seminary by car and patterned its ministry after the Rural Life Model established in Bengkulu, in Sumatra. That operation had in turn been modeled on Harold Watson's Rural Life Center in Mindanao, Philippines, which Jeff Palmer would later give strong direction to. Among our own center's practical, holistic tools that opened windows for sharing the Gospel were a FAITH garden (for "food always in the home") and a program importing Nubian goats to establish a supply of and a market for goat's milk (which doctors report to be three times as nutritious as cow's milk).

Thousands of people had come to Christ through Watson's Filipino center, and numerous house churches had been started, as well as several more-traditional churches. Blessed by God, Watson's project in Mindanao made a huge success. Its vision had been fully shared by the founders of the Bengkulu Rural Life Model in the 1980s and by the team that had pioneered Impact Center Boja, which opened in 2000. The linchpin of that team was Marvin Leech, who had been a missionary with IMB since early in the 1970s.

Impact Center Boja may not yet have seen quite the responsiveness to

Marvin Leech, right, and Pastor Sartono

the Gospel that was generated by its exemplar in the Philippines. Still, our center's holistic approach has helped with our Pantura Team's work to reach the residents of the seventeen North Coast regencies (roughly, counties). *Pantura* refers to the Unreached People Group residing on Java's North Coast. The Pantura number about twenty-two million souls; less than one percent of these people are Christians. The Pantura Team is an evangelistic and church-planting group of Indonesian National Partners dedicated to reaching the North Coast with the Gospel of Jesus and starting up house churches that multiply. Pantura Team members receive training at Impact Center Boja; I became the members' team leader in 2005. Impact Center Boja has hosted lay people from all over Java—farmers, fishermen, factory workers—whose studies last for up to six weeks. These folks returned afterwards to their places of livelihood, where they implemented the simple, reproducible tools and methods Impact Center Boja staff had taught them. Far more importantly, as they'd been teaching, the staff had built relationships creating opportunities to share the Good News. That was the center's strategy, and although it required constant reevaluation, I viewed it as a good strategy.

When I was teaching evangelism to those who staffed Impact Center Boja, a main component of training was how to share the Gospel in a way that balanced the requirement to be biblical with the need to be culturally acceptable. A further training focus at the center was personal evangelism and discipleship leading to small gatherings of new believers in house churches, for worship and "Cell Group," meaning small-group, Bible study. This strategy was known as the *Three Thirds Method and Big One Strategy*. (Incidentally, the strategy remains in use today on the mission field globally.) What everyone wanted to see was the formation of reproducible house churches.

CHAPTER EIGHT | **CALL TO TRAIN**

Aji Suseno, right, doing what he does best: sharing the Good News of Jesus with someone who hadn't yet heard it.

Aji Suseno and I met when I became team leader of the Pantura Team in 2005, and he was the team's secretary. He had gifts in administration, but I saw so much more potential in him that I asked him to become a key leader in a new evangelizing team the center was putting together to reach Java's North Coast. Aji developed into what would be considered the National Team Leader. He is a real servant-leader; he does so much that it's hard to know where to begin describing his role in the Pantura Team's growing capacity to reach so many areas. In 2006, we asked Aji to become the head of Impact Center Boja. He immediately started introducing better ways to reach people. One improvement he came up with was to rethink just how long our training sessions should be. In the past, the center had asked folks to train there for six-week stretches. It was a long time to be away from families and jobs. Aji thought it better to hold monthly three-day trainings and also offer month-long trainings twice a year. The new schedule seemed to increase how many folks came to train at the center, at the same time accommodating sessions for more-extensive training. All this was done in order to build up the number of *mitra kerja,* volunteer partners in ministry who do not work for pay. It was a good move and proved to be strategic in light of how many people were training and how many were being evangelized on the field.

TRAINING OUR BAPTIST ASSOCIATION'S EVANGELISM TEAM: MEET HAMID

I suppose a six-feet-two-inch tall Javanese student would stand out—literally—on a campus where most of those enrolled were at least six inches shorter than that, and sometimes an entire foot shorter. But for me, Hamid's contagious smile was what made him stand out. I met him at the seminary in 2005. He was a first-year student who came from Kediri. We felt he had important gifts, and it wasn't long after I had met him that Hamid was invited to pray about joining the Pantura Team of church planters. By the beginning of 2006, Hamid had officially joined us, taking on the task of reaching the regency called Purwodadi. This meant that every weekend, Hamid would travel almost four hours over rough terrain to get to his place of ministry.

Hamid excelled in presenting the Gospel of Jesus thoroughly, clearly, and boldly. But at his unusual height, equally important was the meek and gentle spirit he showed while engaging people with the Gospel. He was uniquely nonthreatening, even as he was firm. As a result, those he was speaking with typically remained very open to the Gospel. (And he had a knack for staying on track, knowing exactly how to return focus to the Gospel when a person he was sharing with made a move to "chase rabbits.") For similar reasons, perhaps, Hamid was just as skilled a trainer/discipler/mentor as he was a Gospel presenter. He viewed discipleship as being much bigger than imparting knowledge at weekly meetings with trainees or students. Discipleship was "life on life," meaning he emphasized on-the-job training at his side as he ministered to people. Training in the field was what Hamid was best at. He seemed to really enjoy it, based on the way he shone when he was at it—and on how often he would teach some way to share the Gospel and directly take his group out to put the lesson to use. Hamid was so good that I advised many a new IMB staff member in Indonesia to be mentored by him. How much he taught them about engaging people with the Gospel in a culturally acceptable manner!

CHAPTER EIGHT | **CALL TO TRAIN**

The inimitable Hamid, sharing his testimony at Impact Center Boja, outside Semarang.

In 2019, Hamid reached a milestone when the Semarang Baptist Association asked him to become its coordinator of evangelism. One of the first things he did in that position was to make plans to divide the association into districts, each one of which he could provide trainings for. Trainings would at various times cover evangelism, discipleship, prayer, and spiritual awakening. Hamid from time to time asked local IMB personnel, including me, for help putting on these associational trainers. We were glad to assist. We were also at times disappointed by the way churches didn't seem to see a need for them or show interest in attending. Comparing how a typical church responded to such opportunities in, say, 1989, when I first arrived in Solo, to how a typical church today responds, the difference is noticeable. In 1989 most within the Association of Baptist Churches were basically on board with its official program of evangelism. Trainings were well attended; nearly every church could be counted on to participate. And in Kediri, this response was actually outdone by the laymen's response! Over the past fifteen years or so, however, I have started noticing a general apathy and lukewarm attitude toward evangelism and missions. Churches in our association in Semarang participate at a rate below fifty percent. That is a big difference compared to the late 1980s, when I was in Solo, and the late 1990s, when I served in Kediri.

165

In addition, it used to be taken for granted that, once you were trained in evangelism, you went out and practiced it. As I've mentioned, we called it dropping P.I. or doing an evangelistic push. But nowadays Baptist churches just don't seem interested. On many occasions I have offered the pastors of my association opportunities for evangelism training at their churches. Unfortunately, getting little or no response to such offers has become common. I'm really not being critical; I just think this is a change that can be noticed across the course of two decades. The change brings to mind the church at Ephesus as described in Revelation 2: 1–7:

> ¹ **To the angel of the church in Ephesus write: These are the words of him who holds the seven stars in his right hand and walks among the seven golden lampstands:**
>
> ² **I know your deeds, your hard work and your perseverance. I know that you cannot tolerate wicked men, that you have tested those who claim to be apostles but are not, and have found them false.**
>
> ³ **You have persevered and have endured hardships for my name, and have not grown weary.**
>
> ⁴ **Yet I hold this against you: You have forsaken your first love.**
>
> ⁵ **Remember the height from which you have fallen! Repent and do the things you did at first. If you do not repent, I will come to you and remove your lampstand from its place.**
>
> ⁶ **But you have this in your favor: You hate the practices of the Nicolaitans, which I also hate.**
>
> ⁷ **He who has an ear, let him hear what the Spirit says to the churches. To him who overcomes, I will give the right to eat from the tree of life, which is in the paradise of God.**

The reason Jesus confronted the church at Ephesus was that *the church had lost its first love.* Pastor Michael Catt writes, in his book *The Power of Surrender,* that Ephesus lacked love. They were busy and energetic with a full church calendar and sound doctrine. They could debate the meaning of Scripture, but they didn't have any love—the one thing Jesus said would characterize His disciples. You can be as straight as a gun barrel doctrinally yet still be empty. When our love for Christ dies, so does our love for others, the Word, and the lost.[2]

There you have it. Losing love for Christ (vertical love) affects love for others (horizontal love). A lack of love for others influences how often we share the Gospel. How on earth can we say we love the lost, if we aren't actively sharing with them? Am I mistaken in perceiving many of our Baptist churches to have become like the church at Ephesus? They appear to have lost their zeal for sharing the Gospel. Even in Indonesia, Baptists have for decades joked about Baptists' three distinguishing characteristics. We are people of the Book, biblical in our methods and practices. We are evangelistic, known to be bold when it comes to sharing the Gospel. And we love to eat, not pray and fast! Numbers 1 and 3 haven't changed much, even today. But Number 2 has changed dramatically. I have used a famous Christian hymn about witnessing to describe how Baptists have lost their first love, which had been the sharing of the Gospel. My example employs a little wry humor, relying on a play on words in the Indonesian language. I say, "The following song used to be the Baptists' theme song." And the hymn is *"Aku Suka Mengabarkan,"* or "I Love to Tell the Story." Then I say, "But it has a new title now." That title is *"Aku Sukar Mengabarkan,"* or "I find it difficult to tell the story." Notice that adding an *"r"* to the middle word of the second title introduces brand-new meaning that is well—and somewhat humorously—suited to my point.

I sure would like to understand the reason for this change. I used to think it was primarily fear: fear of persecution, fear of not knowing what to say or how to answer someone's question. I think that must be a factor. But I'm not convinced it's the main reason for the erosion of churches' commitment to share the Gospel. I once heard a layman, Mr. Sarwo, who belonged to a Protestant church in Indonesia, explain his understanding of the phenomenon. This was during the lead-up to Indonesia's 2019 elections. He had a very interesting take. Mr. Sarwo said, "You know, people are scared what may happen if President Jokowi doesn't get reelected. But you know, I think the church would do more witnessing if we were persecuted. The church in Indonesia has had it too easy. Remember, this is a majority Muslim country. If things started getting harder and Christians started getting persecuted for their faith, it would refine our faith and we would be witnessing much more." His idea dumbfounded me. I think he hit the nail on the head. Because where is Jesus' church growing fastest at this moment? In Communist China and in Iran. What is the common denominator? Persecution. Thanks, Mr. Sarwo. And by the way, Mr. Sarwo is the guy who cleans our air conditioners. Although maybe he should teach at one of our Baptist seminaries!

Hamid "dunks" a new convert in front of the meeting place of Terang Dunia Baptist Church.

CHAPTER 9

CALL TO SUFFER

It is often through the deepest suffering that God teaches us the deepest lessons.

— Elisabeth Elliot

My family was on stateside assignment in 2008, a year that for us would prove to be a year of tragedy. One of three tragic events that happened within those twelve months was called the Great Recession. This economic tragedy was precipitated in the United States by the financial crisis of 2007–2008, and it quickly spread to other countries. The Great Recession started late in 2007 and would not be broken until the middle of 2009. For many nations, including the U.S., it was the longest and deepest economic downturn since the Great Depression of the 1930s.

I can remember a worship service we went to at the Brooklyn Tabernacle in New York City in October 2008. We attended with some Indonesian friends who lived in Queens. This was just three months or so after we lost our son, Jonathan, in an automobile accident. (I write about that tragic event below.) The tabernacle's pastor, Jim Cymbala, was recapping for his congregation what had happened over the previous week. Desperate residents of Manhattan and elsewhere were committing suicide following the economic collapse that had destroyed their investments and savings. The stock market had been crushed by the fallout from subprime mortgages and other loans granted to too many people with poor credit histories. But my pain at losing my only son left room for very little of the anxiety surrounding the Great Recession. I was still reeling from that blow in July. I could only think about how much I was missing him.

Rev. Cymbala's sermon that morning concerned the faith of the official's son, as told in John 4: 43–54. I remember that just before he preached, the famed Brooklyn Tabernacle Choir presented special music, "The Revelation Song," led by the pastor's wife, Carol Cymbala. Their singing was beautiful. Hearing it, and simultaneously taking in the sight of the multiple ethnic groups represented in the choir, I was nearly falling apart! I still wish I had gone forward and had Rev. Cymbala pray for me.

ANNA BORGER, AGE NINE

In May of 2008, about five months before this Brooklyn Tabernacle service, I was In Alabama, in the city of Tuscaloosa, to speak at my friend Donnie Payne's church. You remember that Donnie was the preacher whose 2002 mission trip to Solo had him going with us to reach the Anak Dalam in their remote tribal villages. I had been presenting a series of messages about missions to Donnie and the people of Forest Lake Baptist Church. One morning while I visited, I woke up and in short order went to read email, which I normally do in the morning. A message waited from Pastor Ardi Wiriadinata, a good Indonesian friend of mine who also taught at the seminary. I didn't like the way it started: "I am afraid I have some horrible news for you." Indeed, in was horrible news. Anna Borger, the daughter of colleagues who had served with us in Semarang, had died in an accident while riding on a bike path with her mother, in Salatiga, Indonesia. Anna was only nine. She had gotten separated from her mom, Timberley Borger, while the two of them were

CHAPTER NINE | CALL TO SUFFER

pedaling along the path. Anna rode over an embankment and in the fall, her neck was broken, instantly killing her.

Anna had been just a sweet and uniquely spiritual little girl. She loved to read the Word of God, even the Book of Revelation, since it had so much to say about heaven. The Apostle John's descriptions of the splendor and glory of heaven enthralled her. Shelly and I felt our hearts break each time we thought of her dying in such a tragic way. Timberley and Anna's father, Todd, had only recently moved to Salatiga from Semarang. Todd, who formerly had been teaching at the Semarang seminary and assisting the Pantura Team, had been appointed team leader for IMB personnel working to reach the Cirebon area. Among our whole group of Baptist missionaries, Anna's untimely death just tore us up. Over and again we asked *Why?* The question particularly haunted Todd and Timberley. And a day was coming when it would begin to haunt me and Shelly in the same way.

Here is a picture including Jonathan, our son, shown at left. The photo of our family was taken at Campbellsville University about two months before Jonathan's automobile accident (at roughly the time when Anna Borger passed away).

The Borger family brought the cremated remains of their daughter back to the United States in June 2008, wanting the closure that would bring. They held a memorial service one afternoon at Hurstbourne Baptist

Church in Louisville, where they had been members while Todd and Timberley were at Southern Baptist Theological Seminary. At Anna's memorial service, I remember, I thought more than once how I myself would simply be unable to face ever losing a child. I was certain of it as I looked on the pain so evident in Todd and Timberley's faces as they shared precious memories of their daughter during the memorial service.

JULY 18, 2008

The date July 18, 2008, marked a significant change in our family. We are forever unable to forget it. Jennifer, our firstborn, had driven all night long with her husband, Greg, to get to Louisville from Colorado Springs, Colorado. They had just ended a training experience at OC International (sometimes known as One Challenge), the Colorado Springs–based Christian faith mission sending agency. The air conditioning in Jennifer and Greg's car wasn't working, so they decided to drive at night, trying to beat the July heat. They left the evening of Thursday, July 17, planning to arrive by morning. I remember being a bit nervous about their long journey in the middle of the night. I remember being grateful to see them drive up early Friday to the "Road House," the mission house we were staying in through the graciousness of its owner, Westport Road Baptist Church. We had a family reunion planned for that night. I was going to cook hamburgers on the grill and have all my family there, including my mom. Jennifer and Greg decided to get a few hours' sleep before the reunion, in the late morning and early afternoon.

Jamie, our younger daughter, had just finished her second year at Campbellsville University in Campbellsville, Kentucky. She was with us at the Road House for much of her break, though. (Shelly and I had stayed at the house since returning to the U.S. toward the end of 2007, about eight months earlier. We had come home for my brother Tommy's funeral.) During the school year, Jamie and four of her close friends had shared a house very near the university. She loved spending time with them, and they had invited her to come visit for a couple days that week, when her brother, Jonathan, was heading to Campbellsville and could have provided a ride. But Jamie had elected not to go down to Campbellsville. She decided to stay in Louisville to greet Jennifer and Greg when they returned from Colorado. And, she thought that by staying in Louisville, maybe she could have her dad give her some more driving lessons.

Jonathan had been scheduled to graduate from Campbellsville University with a business administration degree that May but hadn't been able to pass a statistics class he needed credit for. (The photograph above was taken when our family attended the graduation exercises Jonathan really wished he had been part of.) I remember that he and I had talked over whether this particular degree was a wise choice, given the learning disability in math we knew Jonathan had. It had always been clear he would find it really hard to get a passing grade in statistics.

I tried talking Jonathan into majoring in drama or other arts, or in languages, which he excelled at. He had such a gift for learning languages. He was fluent in Indonesian, naturally, but also in Javanese, a local dialect. He had such a gift for meeting people and communicating with others, too. He had taken an aptitude test that suggested he showed unusual ability in social skills. So I encouraged him to play to his strengths, which revolved obviously around the arts. That was his true wheelhouse. But a couple of his friends were pursuing business administration in order to put those skills to use on the mission field. This was an influence on Jonathan. He had recently entered his own *bergumul* and was struggling with a possible call to return to Indonesia as a missionary. Much of Jonathan's *bergumul* struggle focused on whether "being led" to Indonesia had anything to do with the likelihood that missionary work would be "easier" for him there than somewhere else, since he had grown up in Indonesia. Further, it was important to Jonathan not to be thought of as an "MK" (missionary kid) for whom "reverse culture shock" in the U.S. was so difficult that the idea of going back to the more-familiar land offered comfort.

In 2007, Jonathan and another former Indonesia MK had spent their summer in Surabaya on a two-month mission trip. There, in East Java, two of the missionaries saw how particularly well our Jonathan navigated the Javanese culture. They had invited him to return as a journeyman using his growing interest in photography. While that sounded good, he would have to graduate first, and to do that he had to pass statistics. So in summer 2008, Jonathan was enrolled in a business admin course, putting time to good use while waiting for the fall semester, when (with university funding arranged by former Bangladesh missionary Jim McKinley) he would get another chance at the dreaded subject. He was also working as Campbellsville Baptist Church's custodian. And so Jonathan was up in Campbellsville that week. Thursday night, he played basketball with friends at the church gym. He loved playing ball and could really get heated up from three-point range.

LAST CONVERSATION WITH MY SON

I remember vividly my last conversation with my son. It was about 2:30 on Friday afternoon. I was busy at the Road House, catching up with email on my computer. Jonathan called, saying, "Dad, I just got off work and am going home to shower. I have a date tonight, so I'll be going out after I eat at the family reunion." Jonathan was smitten with a young lady who was from Louisville. We had met her a couple times and she was really cute. Anyway, once dressed and ready, he was going to pick up a watermelon and head to our house to eat. I said to Jonathan, "Well, we're going to eat at six, and I'm cooking hamburgers on the grill, so don't be late." That was it.

Grilling the burgers, six o'clock came and went. I can remember I tried to call Jonathan on his cell phone, but he didn't pick up. I got very concerned when it was well past six and he still had not arrived. Shelly also sensed something was wrong, which was confirmed when two people from Westport Road Baptist Church pulled up into the driveway. It fell to Jim McKinley along with Larry Pursival, one of the church staff, to deliver the horrible news of Jonathan's wreck along the road from Campbellsville to Louisville. He had been under way for just five miles. His car had been hit head-on by a lady using her cell phone. Jonathan had been killed instantly. The lady had two broken legs and had been taken by helicopter to a hospital in Louisville. Shelly and I were in shock, or worse. We heard the tragic news, and then I don't remember a lot: Jamie screaming, Jennifer crying out, "My brother, my brother!" In the hours after, I knew we had to be in a nightmare, unable to wake up. There was numbness and a failed attempt at sleep. In the morning, we had the grim task of going to the funeral home to identify Jonathan's body. As we entered the room where his lifeless body lay, more screams and wailing. We stayed there perhaps thirty minutes, then left to go home and start the grieving process. The pain we were feeling only intensified over time. It didn't go away, it still won't go away; there is a permanency to it.

CALL TO SUFFER

I was reluctant to name one of this book's chapters "Call to Suffer." To be honest, excepting the loss of Jonathan, I haven't experienced much suffering in life. Although we had lived and served in a Muslim country, we had not personally experienced the kind of suffering the Bible speaks of: "In fact, everyone who wants to live a godly life in Christ Jesus will be persecuted" (2 Timothy 3: 12). I had always understood how grateful I should be for that. Clearly, the suffering the verse mentions is suffering that one experiences as a result of living a Christian life. Sure, in Indonesia we had sometimes felt a certain amount of rejection for being believers, occasionally bordering on a feeling of being ostracized. Often, too, we wondered if we were being rejected more because we are American than because we are Christian. Either way, we felt some feelings of rejection, but at the same time we knew our experiences did not amount to persecution like this biblical text speaks of. In some areas in Indonesia, the actual life of someone who becomes a believer is from then on in danger. Once in a while, a believer's life is actually cut short as a result of belief. That is true suffering.

Philippians holds an interesting passage: "For it has been granted to you on behalf of Christ not only to believe on him, but also to suffer for him" (Philippians 1: 29). Here too, scripture seems to be advising believers to expect suffering, to understand it is part of a Christian life. It's perhaps especially part of life for those who share the Gospel actively. Although Paul considered it a privilege to suffer for Christ, in truth I don't think of suffering as a privilege. Nevertheless, I know that when Christians do suffer, that is a new opportunity to witness for Christ. Shelly always has good insights on subjects like this. She has explained that when she lost Jonathan, that one catastrophe weaned her away from anything the world had to offer her in the way of comfort. Food, entertainment, work, family—once upon a time, these were comforting and joy-inducing or at least distracting. They no longer helped after Jonathan died. Once she saw this, she knew she would be forced to rely on God. In that instant, she drew near to Him, her sole source of comfort. She drew near to God. And God drew near to us!

Paul knew that such comfort would come in times of suffering. He wrote about it in 2 Corinthians:

CHAPTER NINE | CALL TO SUFFER

> ³ Praise be to the God and Father of our Lord Jesus Christ, the Father of compassion and the God of all comfort,
>
> ⁴ who comforts us in all our troubles, so that we can comfort those in any trouble with the comfort we ourselves have received from God.
>
> ⁵ For just as the sufferings of Christ flow over into our lives, so also through Christ our comfort overflows.
>
> ⁶ If we are distressed, it is for your comfort and salvation; if we are comforted, it is for your comfort, which produces in you patient endurance of the same sufferings we suffer.
>
> ⁷ And our hope for you is firm, because we know that just as you share in our sufferings, so also you share in our comfort.
>
> – 2 Corinthians 1: 3-7

C. S. Lewis, in his book *A Grief Observed*, talks about his own grief and concludes that working through grief in a healthy way brings you to a point at which you can love the Lord Jesus more than the person you have lost, and likewise you can love the person you lost more than you love yourself. This is a paraphrase of what Lewis writes, but the idea was very helpful for Shelly and me as we grieved for Jonathan. Lewis sees suffering to be God's "megaphone." What he means is that when we suffer—and losing one's only son definitely falls under that category—that very pain creates a chance to amplify to the world what's in your heart. That can be a good thing. At the same time, it can be a bad thing. What if we respond negatively to the suffering and question God's goodness and love? Well, in that case that's the message that will be amped up and heard by others.

There is that story of two men sharing a hospital room, each diagnosed with cancer. One is angry and bitter, basically cursing God (and cursing the pastor who comes to the hospital to pray for patients there). The other man has an entirely different response, never wavering in his trust in God's goodness and love, even if unable to fully understand why he had had to develop cancer. This man was just as sick as the other, but he felt gratitude toward God instead of anger. He was thankful to have seen the Lord bless him so much already, with a family, a church, and his faith. A well-known proverb teaches that "The same sun that bakes clay and makes it hard, makes a candle soft and pliable." One sun, yet two different results.

Whenever you face confusing circumstances, stop and ask, "What is God saying to me by all of this?" Many are asking this question during the Covid-19 crisis. What is God trying to get us to hear with this pandemic? Like Job, we must not stop following God when suffering and pain enter our lives, we must go to Him in prayer! So ask Him to explain the truth about whatever it is you personally must face. Ask God to show you His perspective on the matter. Do you remember when Jesus showed Mary and Martha God's perspective on the tragic death of their brother Lazarus? They learned about an aspect of God's nature that they had not experienced before: "Jesus said to her, 'I am the resurrection and the life. He who believes in me will live, even though he dies; and whoever lives and believes in me will never die. Do you believe this?' 'Yes, Lord,' she told him, 'I believe that you are the Christ, the Son of God, who was to come into the world'" (John 11: 25–27). Before this interchange, Mary and Martha knew Jesus as the healer, the great Rabbi, the one who could do many miracles. But now He took them to a deeper level of understanding of who He was. He was the Resurrection and the Life. He was the one with power over not only Life but also Death!

When we lost Jonathan, God gave me a verse to hang on to. It comes from John's Gospel, reading "I have told you these things, so that in me you may have peace. In this world you will have trouble. But take heart! I have overcome the world" (John 16: 33). Jesus reminds us here that all, believers and nonbelievers alike, are sure to have any number of troubles in life. And not of the kind that merely disappoint us, like when our favorite team gets defeated in the playoffs, or the mall parking space gets taken before we can double back. No, Jesus promises all of us a life with at least some significant troubles. The question is not *Is trouble coming?* Rather, the question is *How will I respond when trouble comes?* When I'm troubled, what will I amplify to others? Or, what is truly in this heart of mine that others will encounter and take to heart?

In the passage that includes this verse (John 16: 33), Jesus talks about people living on two levels. The first level is where we find people who live without God and experience life's troubles without Him. The second level, the higher one, is where we find people who are in Christ and experience life's troubles in Him. These people's troubles are just as troubling as any other. But they are in Christ, and they have His peace. His peace is given even in the midst of life's difficulties. The fact that some live without God and some live in Christ gives rise to two views on life. One of them stresses self-preservation. Viewing self-preservation as our task drives us to try to be sure that we and those we love most will do okay in life. This aim isn't an absolutely bad thing, although it sure shouldn't be the highest priority in life. The other view on life stresses making much of Jesus Christ and glorifying God. As a Christian, hardship, suffering, death cannot stop my life mission to shine my light on Him! These "bad" things, in fact, let me speak louder than ever to the world. Bottom line, Lewis had it right. Suffering is God's megaphone.

PREPARATION FOR SUFFERING

Suffering is difficult, but it can be prepared for. What do we do to get ready for suffering? First, embrace God's higher purpose:

> ¹⁶ Therefore we do not lose heart. Though outwardly we are wasting away, yet inwardly we are being renewed day by day.
>
> ¹⁷ For our light and momentary troubles are achieving for us an eternal glory that far outweighs them all.
>
> ¹⁸ So we fix our eyes not on what is seen, but on what is unseen. For what is seen is temporary, but what is unseen is eternal.
>
> — 2 Corinthians 4: 16-18

Second, expect suffering to come. Third, remember that our hope in Christ and the Cross is our anchor. An anchor's purpose is to keep a ship from being tossed around by tumultuous waves on the sea:

> ¹⁹ We have this hope as an anchor for the soul, firm and secure. It enters the inner sanctuary behind the curtain,
>
> ²⁰ where Jesus, who went before us, has entered on our behalf. He has become a high priest forever, in the order of Melchizedek.
>
> — Hebrews 6: 19-20

Fourth, use your suffering for His Glory. Suffering should and can be our servant; we are not its servant. When the bottom falls out, when you find yourself in a situation so awful it would've been impossible to imagine until then, when life hurts almost unbearably, what do you do? I would say, you just listen for God. For me, God spoke in the midst of my suffering and gave me John 16: 33 to cling to. With the words of the passage, God spoke out of horrible circumstances to urge me to focus on the Cross of Jesus and literally cling to it! Each time we sing our great hymn "At the Cross," it helps us remember what He did for us on Calvary. Out of Jonathan's accident and tragic death, God led me to that Cross for, I believe, five strong reasons, listed below.

- The Cross offers us the anchor of hope we need (Hebrews 6: 19).

- The Cross settled the matter of whether or not God loves us (John 4: 9).

- The Cross is evidence of God in control of a free mankind (Acts 2: 22–24). For God there is instrumentality in flawed, sinful human beings; they are useful in accomplishing His purposes. It was no accident that Jesus went to Calvary. God the Father orchestrated the Cross to bring about His redemption and carry out His purposes in a lost and dying world.

- The Cross shows how, out of the absolutely worst things, God fashions eternal good. The obvious illustrative scripture is Romans 8: 28.

When Jonathan died, my mind and Shelly's mind were swirling with unanswered questions. Particularly, I wondered why God would call Jonathan to Indonesia yet not allow him to return as a journeyman with our IMB. John and Glenn Ingouf, who lost their daughter to cancer while they were serving in Indonesia, gave me a book about the American scion Bill Borden. Bill was an honor student at Yale University and, when he had graduated, would become an instant millionaire as sole heir to the Borden Dairy fortune. Bill felt led to go to China to reach the western part of that country's Uighur Muslims for his Lord. He wrote in the flyleaf of his Bible, "No Reserve, No Retreat and No Regrets." And on his deathbed in Cairo, Egypt, where he had contracted spinal meningitis while traveling, he pointed to those words. He said aloud, "No regrets," and then he passed away.

Why did God call Bill Borden to the Uighurs yet not allow him to fulfill that calling? I think God looked at Bill Borden's heart and was pleased to see it was prepared to serve in China. Bill's life just happened to be cut short. Jonathan's passing was also so untimely! But as I say about Bill Borden, I think God looked at Jonathan Bruckert's heart and was pleased to see it was prepared to serve in Indonesia.

We read in I Kings 8 that, "My father David had it in his heart to build a temple for the Name of the LORD, the God of Israel. But the LORD said to my father David, 'Because it was in your heart to build a temple for my Name, you did well to have this in your heart.'" Apparently, God was pleased to know that David wanted to build a temple, even though the Lord's own plan was for David's son Solomon to build it. The Lord's own plan for Jonathan and Bill Borden was different, in the end, than anyone had expected. But these two men's hearts desired to share the Gospel with the lost, and I believe this pleased the Father. I'll just have to wait until we get to Glory to ask Him why their calls could not be fulfilled in China and Indonesia.

- Fifth and finally, God is at work on a much larger canvas than we can perceive, and the Cross is His most brilliant brushstroke of all. The presence of the Cross brings to life the whole picture of God's activities in this world. Without the Cross, the things that make up a human life can seem needlessly harsh, pointless, disjointed, nonsensical, chaotic. When viewed separate from God's crowning brushstroke, the things that so often make up life lead to inaccurate conclusions about what life means and what God's nature is. Humans' painful experiences, looked at in isolation, lead to misinterpretation. Once shaped by the brushstroke of the Cross, however, our life events come into true focus. We see then that God is a suffering God. God has not exempted Himself from suffering. When He suffers and when we suffer, it is so that God can render the bad and the good together into something beautiful.

CHAPTER NINE | CALL TO SUFFER

The writer C. S. Lewis thought of suffering as "the megaphone of God."

TWO QUESTIONS

There were two questions we heard frequently after losing Jonathan. Many people asked us whether we were going to bring charges against the lady driving the car that killed Jonathan. She was clearly at fault. The numbers of Americans killed due to drivers' use of cell phones is off the charts, so wouldn't it be right to press charges? For vehicular manslaughter at that time, sentences could reach up to five years in jail. My whole family prayed about this. We felt led not to press charges against the lady. All of us agreed about it, although many outside our immediate family did not agree. They felt she needed to pay for what she had done and be made an example of. However, Shelly, Jennifer, Jamie, and I felt the Lord did not want us to press charges.

Many people also asked about our family's future, saying that they supposed since we had lost our son, we would not be returning to the mission field. We knew of missionaries who lost a child and returned to the States never to go back to the field. We also knew of missionaries who lost a child and did go back to the field. As we prayed together as a family, we all felt that it was right for us to return to the field when we reached the appropriate time in the grieving process. I remember both of my girls saying, "Dad, I think Jonathan would want you guys to return to the field and fulfill your calling there." Once again, that need to pray about every key decision you make regarding ministry. It is the theme of this book: praying to God, knowing that He hears, and struggling until we hear His direction for our lives. A passage of Holy Scripture ties in well:

> [17] When the Philistines heard that David had been anointed king over Israel, they went up in full force to search for him, but David heard about it and went down to the stronghold.
>
> [18] Now the Philistines had come and spread out in the Valley of Rephaim;
>
> [19] so David inquired of the LORD, "Shall I go and attack the Philistines? Will you hand them over to me?" The LORD answered him, "Go, for I will surely hand the Philistines over to you."
>
> [20] So David went to Baal Perazim, and there he defeated them. He said, "As waters break out, the LORD has broken out against my enemies before me." So that place was called Baal Perazim.
>
> [21] The Philistines abandoned their idols there, and David and his men carried them off.
>
> [22] Once more the Philistines came up and spread out in the Valley of Rephaim;
>
> [23] so David inquired of the LORD, and he answered, "Do not go straight up, but circle around behind them and attack them in front of the balsam trees.
>
> [24] As soon as you hear the sound of marching in the tops of the balsam trees, move quickly, because that will mean the LORD has gone out in front of you to strike the Philistine army."

> [25] **So David did as the LORD commanded him, and he struck down the Philistines all the way from Gibeon to Gezer.**
>
> –2 Samuel 17-25

Notice that each time David faced a decision, he prayed about it: in Verse 19, in Verse 23. Even more important, each time David heard from God, he obeyed God's direction: in Verse 20, in Verse 25. It's a pretty simple formula. You ask the Lord. You wait and listen for his voice. You obey. For us, the formula produced our return to Indonesia to continue our ministry.

WE RETURN TO INDONESIA

We were away from Indonesia for almost thirteen months, the longest StAs we ever took. I remember that the Member Care staff was so helpful to us throughout the process. They took care to let us grieve at our own pace. When we arrived back in Indonesia in January 2009, I was amazed at how many things triggered memories of Jonathan. Entering our house on the campus and seeing Jonathan's empty room made it feel again like we had just lost him. Our Indonesian friends kindly expressed their condolences and comforted and helped Shelly and me immensely. You have probably heard, like I had heard, that losing a child is something you never recover from. If you can manage to successfully work through your grief, you settle into a new normal, but you do not "recover." One person told me, "Losing a child is like losing a limb, losing a leg. You can still walk, but you will now walk differently." That describes it well. You live in the new normal, and at the same time there is no getting rid of the noticeable limp that results from your insurmountable loss.

I have introduced you to my son Jonathan in this chapter. Let me close it on a happy note by introducing you to my wife, Shelly. The story I'll tell about her has this book's theme at its center, which is *how necessary it is to struggle with the Lord until we know His Word for us personally.* In this case, Shelly also struggled to maintain her composure and sweet disposition!

DOG GONE

In Indonesia the Bruckert family hobby was raising boxer dogs. I guess we had about eight boxers in succession. One thing we found out was that the life expectancy of a boxer isn't very long. A missionary in Bengkulu who was a vet told us that boxer dogs were known as *tumor hounds.* The way they were bred has left them susceptible to cancerous tumors. Our boxers all died kind of tragically: Amanda died from tick fever, Thelma Lou died from cancer, Elmo was poisoned, Bailey died early because she had heart worms. Then there is Daphne. I will tell her story shortly.

I can remember being at a meeting in Surabaya, riding in an elevator and talking about having boxers that just didn't seem to last long. One of guys in the elevator asked, "Why don't they last long?" "Well, there's really more than one reason," I told him, "but I've had eight here in Indonesia, and they just haven't lasted." He looked totally taken aback. He repeated, "You've had eight pairs of boxer shorts in the whole time you've served in Indonesia? Are you kidding me?!" Well, folks, here is what you call a classic misunderstanding.

Although I can remember one occasion on which *that* kind of boxer was involved. I had gone to a meeting of church planters in Lampung back in 1996. All of us guys decided to play basketball one afternoon. I had the dubious job of guarding Don Dent. Don hit everything he shot that day, probably due to two problems I was having. I don't want to make excuses for being torched by Don, but the truth was I had just finally recuperated from dengue fever, which had caused me to lose quite a bit of weight. Without those pounds, the boxer shorts I wore while playing kept falling down. And it was no help at all that the elastic waistband in the shorts had given out. I ended up tying the loosened cotton knit in a knot, in order to finish the game. Indeed, boxers literally don't last long in Indonesia!

DISAPPEARANCE OF DAPHNE

In all seriousness, we had a boxer by the name of Daphne that we brought to the seminary with us in 2002. We thought Daphne was a great dog, but the students were terrified by her, and we had to keep her penned up behind our house, in our yard. Being confined that way took a toll on Daphne. We wanted to make it up to her at the first opportunity. So right before Christmas break, when students had for the most part gone back to their places of ministry, we let her out to roam the campus and get some much-needed exercise. It did seem to help. But one Sunday morning we returned from church to find her missing. We figured someone had stolen her.

Fast forward three years. While I attended a Big One training in Lembang with our Pantura Team, Shelly stayed back in Semarang, translating for a medical team from South Korea that had come to the seminary campus. The training in Lembang turned out to be a turning point in our team's direction. Our whole team was captured by the way Mike Shipman's "Be-New Team" presented the materials on Big One strategy. After hearing numerous testimonies from people who had come from Islam and turned to *Isa Almasih,* Jesus the Messiah, we were convinced the Pantura Team needed to adopt the program. It was a historic moment for our team. And yet it was the simultaneous events back in Semarang that we would be talking about for years afterward. Enter Mrs. Shelly Bruckert.

The leadership at the seminary asked Shelly particularly to work with a dermatologist on the Korean team, talking for the doctor to the patients and vice versa. A makeshift examination room had been set up in an auditorium where, usually, chapel was held. At the back, a temporary pharmacy was created where the drugs prescribed could be given to patients on the way out. Shelly had a bit of a break translating and noticed a young man waiting outside the examination room. She started to jot down the needed information about his condition, which was eczema all over both arms. They went over how long he had had the problem and where he might have come into contact with potential allergens.

Then their conversation took a strange turn. He asked, "You and your husband live here on campus, don't you?" Shelly answered, "Yes, we have since 2002." The man continued, "Your husband used to walk your dog, a big brown boxer, down on the soccer field. And when he went to shoot baskets, he would tie that dog up to a tree near where we live in the *kampung* [neighborhood] just south of the seminary. We always saw the dog when we looked through the fence, day after day." What does that, Shelly was thinking, have to do with this, a visit to the clinic? About then, the man said, "You know, we Javanese believe that if you have a skin condition, it can be cured by eating dog meat. We waited for an opportunity to get your dog."

WHO LET THE DOG OUT?

Shelly stood there and listened to this unbelievable story. She heard out the description of how poor Daphne was lured close to the fence the Javanese neighbors looked through, using a piece of meat to trap her and proceeding to throw a fishing net over our beloved boxer and take her off to the execution. The whole time, Shelly maintained her composure, keeping her anger under control. Maybe she distracted herself with that silly song famous at the time, "Who Let the Dogs

Out?" by the Baha Men. Really, the question wasn't who let the dog out, but rather who let those bozos in to steal our dog? Security guards kept an eye on the seminary campus, but they apparently fell asleep that Sunday before Christmas 2006 when Daphne was taken. We couldn't have imagined, when we let her out in the interests of her good health, that dog-eating neighbors would actually be able to enter the campus and snatch our Daphne.

Shelly was acutely aware that the gap between our world view and that of the Javanese was huge. To us, a dog is not a source of food (or medicine), but a pet we feel great affection for and consider almost a family member. When it came to our boxers, we were American through and through. But we were not in Kansas anymore (or even Kentucky, for that matter). We were in Java, and to the Javanese—even those Javanese who are "folk Islam"—dog meat is a rare delicacy and treat. When they butchered sweet (my term, not the eczema patient's) little Daphne, they gained meat to feed their families, enough even to serve at their kampung version of a block party, Shelly was told. The meat was so plentiful that some was actually sold to *kaki lima,* street vendors, for a bit of cash.

Shelly simply didn't know how to react. It always takes a lot for Shelly to get angry and show it. That's why people ask, *"Apakah ibu Shelly pernah menjadi marah?"* or "Has Mrs. Shelly ever gotten angry?" For three years, Daphne's fate had been unknown, but thanks to the South Koreans' clinic, the secret was out now. Still, Shelly didn't express anger to the Javanese man. Until. Until it seems he offered to buy Shelly some replacement meat, like a fish or some *kerbau* (water buffalo). He clearly wanted to be a good neighbor, and never mind that he stole our dog and worse.

SHELLY'S STORY

And then Shelly was angry. But she had her own way of dealing with anger, which was by being passive aggressive. When the man's consultation with the dermatologist was over, he wanted to introduce his grandfather to Shelly. His grandfather was waiting for his grandson outside the makeshift examination room. The grandfather also seems to have been examined; the tumor on the back of his neck was diagnosed as inoperable. This is where—whether or not you think it's possible!—the story gets even stranger. Shelly looked at Grandpa and she knew he was one of the main culprits in Daphne's sad end. So she decided to retell the story she had been told, only she told it in a way only Shelly would:

"Oh, *bapak* [grandpa], you didn't know, but our dog had been diagnosed with cancerous tumors just a few months before your grandson and the others took her. Our veterinarian friend in Bengkulu discovered her illness. But you do know that if you eat an animal that has tumors, then you will get them as well." In case you missed it, this is the classic passive aggressor handling her pent-up anger. If you're tempted to criticize Shelly for frightening that old man, first, know that a Bengkulu vet truly had diagnosed cancer in Daphne. Still, Shelly could not diagnose Gramps. But really, were her words much different from the pat answer most doctors in Indonesia give patients concerning their symptoms, which is *"Masuk angin,"* or "Wind (air) has entered your body"? Shelly merely changed *"Masuk angin"* to *"Masuk anjing,"* or "Dog has entered your body"!

Deep down, Shelly has a compassion for people. She is always asking questions like, "God, what are You saying to us in all this?" or in the case of this story, "What good can You bring from the tragic tale of Daphne becoming sate?" Shelly recalls that I had recently been preaching on how we can recognize the activities of God around us. I had preached specifically on the subject of looking for things happening around you that seemed strange, since it would be there that God was at work. The classic example, finding a man up a tree, comes from Luke:

> ¹ **Jesus entered Jericho and was passing through.**
>
> ² **A man was there by the name of Zacchaeus; he was a chief tax collector and was wealthy.**
>
> ³ **He wanted to see who Jesus was, but being a short man he could not, because of the crowd.**
>
> ⁴ **So he ran ahead and climbed a sycamore-fig tree to see him, since Jesus was coming that way.**
>
> ⁵ **When Jesus reached the spot, he looked up and said to him, "Zacchaeus, come down immediately. I must stay at your house today."**
>
> ⁶ **So he came down at once and welcomed him gladly.**
>
> ⁷ **All the people saw this and began to mutter, "He has gone to be the guest of a 'sinner.'"**
>
> ⁸ **But Zacchaeus stood up and said to the Lord, "Look, Lord! Here and now I give half of my possessions to the poor, and if I have cheated anybody out of anything, I will pay back four times the amount."**
>
> ⁹ **Jesus said to him, "Today salvation has come to this house, because this man, too, is a son of Abraham.**
>
> ¹⁰ **For the Son of Man came to seek and to save what was lost."**
>
> – Luke 19: 1-10

This story's main point isn't that Jesus was drawn to the little tax collector and interacted with him. It's that He ever noticed Zacchaeus in the first place! He was met by throngs of people when he entered Jerusalem, and he focused on this one sawed-off scoundrel whose name was Zacchaeus. Have you ever considered why Jesus focused on him? Clearly, He was taking notice of where the Father was at work. It was strange for a guy to be up a sycamore tree; it was also God's clear signal that He was working in this Jewish tax collector's life! That day, Jesus won not just Zacchaeus, but many of his friends in his *oikos*.

In the solution of our "dog gone" mystery, was God showing Shelly and me where He was at work in our world? We decided to pay a visit to the young man, the grandson, from the clinic. We took him some medicated cream the Korean medical team had provided for any follow-ups. We shared the Gospel with him before we left. We also called at the young man's father's house, having gotten his address from his son. The house was right next to the fence to which Daphne had been lured. Not that we were holding a grudge, mind you. We shared the Gospel with the father, too, and he seemed very open. Perhaps he found very strange this attention from a husband and wife from America whose dog he had devoured long ago but who were only now dropping by to visit. As I shared the Gospel, though he was very agreeable I sensed that his *"Nge, nge"* (or "Yes, yes") was intended to pacify us by telling us what we wanted to hear. We had no luck in our subsequent efforts to disciple him, so becoming a follower of Jesus perhaps wasn't ever really of interest to him. But at least we put forth the effort to try to reach the family that stole our pooch.

The day Shelly called me at my meeting to tell her story, she had me laughing so hard I could hardly finish my lunch, which was *sate ayam* and definitely not sate dog. That night I went into town with Mike Shipman, and we witnessed to someone at a Starbucks. When it was time to be leaving, we went to the car, parked on the top floor of the parking garage, and climbed in. We'd borrowed our friend Keith McKinley's car to get our assigned evangelism done. Mike reached into his top pocket, but he couldn't find the key. I said the key had to be here, because Mike had just opened the car door. Mike searched everywhere, though it was dark and hard to see well. I asked if it could have fallen out of his pocket. He pulled off his shirt to be sure it wasn't there somewhere. After a frantic hour of searching, still no key. So we called Keith to ask about an extra key for his car. I'm not sure I would have been willing to hand over another key to two buffoons who lost theirs in a mall parking garage. In answer to our question, I think Keith said he would need to go look, but he never got back with us. Can't say as I blame him.

At last I did have a brilliant idea. "Hey, Mike," I said, "let's turn on the lights in the car *and* use the flashlights on our cell phones and search this car again." It didn't happen right away, but finally we located the keys lodged and hiding between the front seats, where they had surely fallen from Mike's pocket as he got into the car. Mike beamed, still shirtless. Well, that was fun. It had not been a secret that when you go out with Mike Shipman, you should be prepared to focus on the lost. Until that night, though, never did I imagine that included lost keys!

CHAPTER 10

CALL TO PREACH

> To love to preach is one thing, to love those to whom we preach is quite another.
>
> – Martyn Lloyd Jones

I love to preach. To read the words of Martyn Lloyd Jones, perhaps the greatest pulpiteer of the twentieth century, is very sobering. Loving those to whom we preach can be challenging. It reminds me of the story of a missionary in Southeast Asia who was experiencing extreme culture shock. She said, "I hate the food and the climate; why, I even hate the people." A seasoned colleague responded, "Then let me give you some advice. If you can't *love* the people you're here for, do the next best thing." "What's that?" the discouraged missionary asked. "Just go home," her colleague said.

Preaching is something I have always enjoyed. Ever since God called me to preach, I recognized it as the highest honor entrusted to individuals. For me, to preach is to be entrusted with the sacred task of breaking the Bread of Life so that it feeds the many with the Word of God. Preaching in English was great, but I took special delight in preaching in *Bahasa Indonesia* and knowing that the glorious Truths of the Gospel were being communicated cross-culturally. Maybe not everyone shared my opinion. I can remember being questioned about why I preached so much in *Bahasa*. The churches have Indonesian preachers available for that, don't they? That question and similar ones were swirling in my head one night as I lay on my bed at the old guest house on *Gondangdia Lama* Street. I was really struggling about whether to continue to preach the Word in the way I'd gotten so accustomed to doing since arriving in Indonesia. I was going through some real doubts about my call to preach and my role in working with the traditional churches in Indonesia.

This was at a time when there were two basic missionary "camps" in that nation, *Indonesia S* (for Singapore) and *Indonesia J* (for Jakarta). The Indonesia J folks worked with the traditional churches, churches our missionaries had worked with since the churches had been birthed in the 1960s and 1970s. They felt most comfortable with our office in Jakarta and were forthright about why we were in Indonesia. Most under the Indonesia J umbrella were getting their visas through Indonesia's Department of Religion and were theological teachers plugged into one of our seminaries or satellite seminaries. For example, I was a teacher for the satellite seminary in Kediri at that time. In turn, the Indonesia S folks were more secretive than the Indonesia J folks. Their platforms differed from those of the Indonesian National Baptist Convention, and they were very reluctant to be identified in any way with the convention. This dichotomy set up a real gap between Indonesia S and Indonesia J personnel. It's safe to say it created mistrust and even dislike that set back by light years Baptists' work to advance God's Kingdom among Muslims. Gracious alive, how could we bring the power of the Gospel and of reconciliation with God to Muslims in Indonesia when even we Baptists couldn't get along? Thinking about it now, I suppose the turmoil of my doubts about the preaching I'd been doing was mostly due to the two camps' lack of unity. Then, awake in my bed and in prayer in the wee hours at that Jakarta guest house, I heard the Lord speak very clearly to me. I didn't hear an audible voice. Nevertheless, it was one of the rare times I have felt permeated with Truth embracing my whole heart. God clearly said to me, *"Keep preaching my word."* That was all. And it was the exact Rhema Word I needed.

I often review in my mind that night that God spoke to me on *Gondangdia Lama* Street. At the risk of sounding charismatic, I want to emphasize this pivotal time in my life and ministry. This book's main concern is when and how God speaks to us, and for me that night, He spoke through prayer. Why did He speak *then*, at that point in my life? His purpose was twofold, I think. It was an affirmation of the call to preach I'd heard way back in July 1975. And it was also an instruction to continue using the gift I had received from Him as I strived faithfully to advance His Gospel in Indonesia. That night, the Voice of God gave me direction for the future of my ministry in Indonesia: *Stick to what I called you to in the first place, keep preaching the Gospel.* That Word became a spiritual marker for me, providing God's guidance and assurance. Thanks, Father!

PREACHING GOD'S WORD—
JAVA, SULAWESI, SUMATRA

My preaching ministry would take me to three of Indonesia's most populous islands, as earlier chapters have indicated. Each place—Java, Sulawesi, Sumatra—would be the site of pivotal moments. It will be helpful here to discuss a revival I participated in on the island of Java, in the Indonesian capital, Jakarta, in 2012. I was invited by Pastor Edwin of the Jakarta Baptist Community to come lead a three-day revival service. Two things stick out about those days, one of which is kind of negative. On the first night, a young member of the community had apparently been asked to sit on the front row to watch the time and tell me when to stop preaching. She was about sixteen, if I remember right. And she followed her orders, since I remember she eventually began pointing to her wristwatch by way of signaling me. Let me just say that in the U.S., I expect pastors or worship leaders to hand me an order of service showing just how long I'll have to preach: "Pastor Greg, you will enter the pulpit at 11:26 a.m., and you'll need to finish preaching at 12:02 p.m. Then invite the people to come forward and make decisions, and take four more minutes for that, bringing us to 12:06 p.m." In America I expect something very like that. Everything done to schedule, neatly packaged up in an hour-long service precisely, I understand that. But Indonesia had been different. I had never been tightly scheduled during a revival service there. In Indonesia you preach until you're done, simple as that. Because no one minds if the service "goes over." This girl on the front row had somehow wound up on American time, though, and kept indicating her watch! When I finished my preaching, I found her and said next time I would need longer to preach than she'd given me before, and would appreciate it if she didn't interrupt my sermons again. If this sounds like I got a little angry that first night of the revival, I did. And my timekeeper didn't interrupt me in the middle of my sermon again on either of the next two nights.

A VISIBLE FAITH

The second very clear memory I have of that revival was a significant occurrence that absolutely amazed me, on the second night of our services there on Java. I preached on a verse in Mark and focused on the faith so visible in the lives of the men who brought their paralyzed

The Sumampau family, Taman Safari, Java, Indonesia, in 2012.

friend to the Lord Jesus. I emphasized how all four had a faith that could be seen: "When Jesus saw [emphasis added] their faith, he said to the paralytic, 'Son, your sins are forgiven'" (Mark 2: 1–12). When I finished preaching and began inviting people to come forward, a woman made her way up front whom I recognized as Mrs. Yanny Sumampau. We had been introduced by my mentor John Smith some twenty-five years earlier, when I was still in language school! Now, weeping at the front of the church, Yanny began to *curhat*, or pour her heart out, for her family. She had a burden alike for her husband and her three sons, none of whom were diligently serving the Lord. She came forward with this burden just like the four men in Mark had brought their burden for their friend to Jesus. I prayed. Yanny believed. And in the years since, God has miraculously answered her prayer. Her husband, Tony, has rededicated his life to Christ and is actively serving Him at the church that meets at Taman Safari in Cisarua, Java. (Taman Safari, again, is one of three theme parks the Sumampau family operates in Indonesia.) Among other things, he heads the Full Gospel Men's Fellowship based in Jakarta. Yanny and Tony's sons, John, Michael, and Aswin, have seen God do mighty works in all three of their lives since that second night of the revival, when Yanny and I prayed for them. Michael and John are active in Abba Love Church in Jakarta, and Aswin belongs to a Baptist church that has been meeting for two years at the Aviary Hotel in Bintaro, Tangerang, Jakarta. Shelly and I have actually been mentoring Aswin and his family in their Christian life. We have grown close to Aswin, his wife, Jacqueline, and their children, James and Lisa. I've taken Aswin through a couple of courses and book studies that have been consequential for his spiritual foundation in Christ. He has become an active leader at The Light Communities Church in Jakarta. Truly, God answered Yanny's prayer for her family.

PREACHING IN SULAWESI

The western coast of the Indonesian island of Sulawesi is home to the city of Palu. Sulawesi is the island with a peculiar shape. Four long peninsulas branch off of a single central body, making the island resemble an octopus. In March 2012, I preached a revival in Central Sulawesi province, at a location three hours' drive from Palu. When the revival concluded and I left, I little knew the circumstances under which I'd eventually return. It would not be until 2018. On September 28 of that year, a 7.5 earthquake rocked Palu and was followed by a tsunami, causing a tsunami alert to be issued for the nearby Makassar Strait. Palu was hit by a localized wave that swept shore-lying houses and other buildings off their foundations. Between them the earthquake and tsunami killed some 4,340 people, making it Indonesia's deadliest earthquake since the 2006 Yogyakarta earthquake (and the deadliest worldwide in 2018, far surpassing an earthquake in Lombok, Indonesia, a few months before that had killed more than 500 people).

When I heard about the devastation in and around Palu City, I became increasingly burdened to try to help the city. I didn't fully understand it at the time, but the Lord was giving me an incredible burden for Palu and Central Sulawesi. I didn't have any contacts in the Palu area, so at first I encountered roadblock after roadblock hindering my wish to help. It was different from 2004, when all help from NGOs and church groups outside Indonesia was welcomed by the Indonesian government in the days and months after Aceh was devastated by the infamous December tsunamis. Southern Baptists kept one hundred volunteers on the ground in Aceh every day of 2005. It was an incredible number of volunteers, especially considering Aceh's status as Indonesia's strongest bastion of Islamic religion. They call Aceh the "front porch of Mecca." In Palu, thirty percent of the population is reportedly Christian, but relief efforts of churches and NGOs there after the 2018 tsunami and earthquake were being blocked at every turn. The Indonesian government wanted complete control of the response; they didn't want any other government or faith-based group taking credit. Maybe they didn't want to be embarrassed like they had been in Aceh in 2004. They wanted the world to see them handle the crisis well on their own. Still, I couldn't deny the burden I felt to try to help.

I learned that my pastor, Mr. Bambang, had contacts among the members of *Perkantas*, an international fellowship of evangelical students based out of England. Mr. Bambang had formed a network of students from Perkantas who planned to go to Palu to help the relief work there. Our church in Semarang had signed up additional volunteer workers to join these students in helping. As well, Mr. Dukri, an itinerant evangelist who, like me, was a member of Pastor Bambang's church, would be sent to Palu to help with relief work. This seemed like my chance to help, too. Perhaps if Mr. Dukri started a few projects like distributing food and providing tents to those who had lost homes, doors could be opened for evangelism and maybe even a church plant. That was what was on my heart, but I ran into another roadblock.

Pastor Bambang has a heart for missions and evangelism. He wanted to bring more than disaster relief to Palu, he wanted to bring a social ministry of evangelism and church planting. So, by October, the church had brought Mr. Dukri to the outskirts of Palu, where people had lost everything—sometimes even numbers of loved ones—to the quake or tsunami. I asked if I could join Mr. Dukri and the team our church in Semarang was sending. But the pastor felt it was still too early to send anyone who was not a *pribumi*, a native Indonesian. He also feared terrorists from the outlying jungles around Sulawesi, who had recently started trickling into Palu. I could become a target in that city, he feared. Prevented from traveling to it for the time being, I kept praying for

Palu. At least our church now had someone on the ground in the city. I felt that would be a foot in the door for a new work there. Mr. Dukri had been helpful in visiting Palu's Unreached People Group areas and completing surveys of various UPGs. As a church planter, though, he really didn't have much skill. To start a new mission point, we needed to plant a new church in Palu City. I believed that should be our focus. If we wanted to reach UPGs in Central Sulawesi, a more-traditional church plant in Palu should mark our start, followed by working our way out to each village and then moving farther out even than the villages, in order to reach UPGs using less-traditional approaches. Between October and mid-December of 2018, our church had not established a base camp, but that was going to change.

JESSICA

On December 18, my good friend Aji Suseno contacted me about a young lady from Palu who was being treated in the hospital just down the street from where we lived. The young lady, a student from Palu attending a university in Semarang, had been in a motorcycle accident a day earlier and was comatose and on a ventilator. Aji—who is, I should say, the brother of Pastor Bambang, my pastor in Semarang—asked me if I would go and have prayer for Jessica and members of her family who were waiting with her in the hospital. When I arrived at the hospital, I met her mom and dad and her sister and two brothers. I was allowed into the ICU to see Jessica and pray for her recovery. She was in critical condition, still in a coma, her head shaved from the surgery that had relieved the pressure on her brain caused by bleeding. Later, I remember being with her family reading John 15: 7, about abiding in Christ and having an authority in prayer because we are in Jesus. We all prayed together for Jessica. Afterwards, her father, Mr. Kaleb, and I moved across the waiting room from the others to talk. As it turned out, he was the head of the Protestant branch of Central Sulawesi's Department of Religion. He ended up inviting me to preach at a Christmas service on December 26.

What was the Lord God saying to me through this situation? It seemed to me He was pretty clearly ushering us into an opportunity to take up a new work in Palu. Jessica's father appeared to be the "person of peace" who was giving me an invitation not merely to preach but to come to the Palu area to start a new Baptist church. Eventually, not only did this man give us official permission to plant a church in the city of Palu, he gave us an official Department of Religion document allowing us to open up Baptist work anywhere in the province of Central Sulawesi! God had indeed thrown wide open a door of opportunity for the Gospel:

> **7 To the angel of the church in Philadelphia write: These are the words of him who is holy and true, who holds the key of David. What he opens no one can shut, and what he shuts no one can open.**
>
> **8 I know your deeds. See, I have placed before you an open door that no one can shut. I know that you have little strength, yet you have kept my word and have not denied my name" (Revelation 3: 7-8).**

For two months I continued to visit Jessica in the hospital. She showed steady signs of improvement. Bulu Baptist Church, the church my family belonged to, took an interest in praying for Jessica and sent her a steady stream of visitors from the congregation. After Jessica left the hospital, a journeyman couple from IMB repeatedly took time to visit her as she recuperated in accommodations on the campus of our Baptist seminary (her family with her), less than a mile from the hospital. The couple, Jeremy and Beka Simmons, had just moved to Semarang just a few months prior to Jessica's accident.

Jessica continued to recover at our seminary. We were confident the Lord had opened up an opportunity—that door that no one could shut—to open up a work in Palu. Mr. Kaleb was grateful for how Jessica had been cared for by our community. He gave us a place to congregate in Palu and promised that a facility he was currently building would be our new church's to use for as many as five years, including as its pastor's home. The Lord provides! That building went up and the church slowly began to gain members and meet formally. The search began for a pastor to lead the young church. A few names had been suggested; a young graduate of the Baptist seminary in Bandung came to interview for the role. He said all the right things, but it didn't really feel right. So we asked him to complete an orientation and training at Impact Center Boja. He agreed right away, but only a few days later he got sick and started having second thoughts about Palu. He was realizing how tough it would be for him to minister cross-culturally. Politely, he ended the interview process, returning to Bandung a few days later.

Jeremy and Beka Simmons visiting Jessica at the Baptist seminary in Semarang, during her recovery from a motorcycle accident in that city.

I was grateful to the Lord that the young man hadn't actually moved up to Palu before deciding the job wasn't for him. I think his was a classic case of inexperience or lack of maturity, and the job needed someone more stable in his relationship with the Lord, more seasoned and perhaps already proven in ministry. Guys like that tend to be in short supply, but we kept praying that God would lead us to the right person, and we kept searching.

Pastor Bambang, my pastor at Bulu Baptist Church (and, again, Aji Suseno's brother), sent many of those prayers to God. The search for a pastor always topped his prayer list at Wednesday night prayer meetings. I tried to remain patient, but I found myself battling anxious feelings whenever I thought about the situation we were in. Where on earth could we find a pastor willing to go live where major earthquakes, aftershocks, tsunamis, and terrorist encampments all belonged to the landscape? Finding one seemed unlikely at best. Who would God send who could actually help the church grow and develop? Well, think back to that celebration, described in Chapter 6, at which I had sampled my first bowl of "dog soup." Think back to the young man, Fernandez, who had landed on that particular special dish to feed the gathering that evening. We had led him to faith and he'd gone on to help us start a church in his village just outside of Solo. More than twenty years has passed since we'd seen each other in person, although from time to time I'd get news about where Fernandez was.

Among other places, he had served in Lampung, from 2002 to 2014. I learned this from some former seminary students it had been my privilege to teach, who happened to serve in the same Baptist association as Pastor Fernandez. Pastor Bambang had also told me about a long-ago occasion on which he had met a certain couple in Lampung. He had gone to Lampung to teach a *Kairos,* or *Perspectives,* class. When Pastor Bambang and I had been brainstorming about who could possibly plant the new church in Palu, he had remembered this church planter, a Javanese from near Solo, and his wife, who was from Central Sulawesi. It definitely sounded familiar, and I asked the pastor the man's name—which was, of course, Fernandez Paiman. "I *know* him!" I blurted out proudly. "Fernandez is my *anak rohani,* my spiritual son in Christ. He's like a Timothy to me! I led him to faith in 1992, and we ended up leading more members of his family to faith, too, and his family became the nucleus of a church start at a place called Selo Katon." When Pastor Bambang began telling his story of the couple in his class circa 2008, who would have guessed the tale would lead to my preaching on the island of Sumatra, at Fernandez's Sinar Kasih Baptist Church in Medan? And who would have guessed what came next after my reunion with Fernandez?

RETURN TO MEDAN'S SEMINARY, DECEMBER 2019

Early in November 2019, a mission team came to us from Arkansas led by Jon Mark and Amanda Page, former IMB missionaries in Semarang. They brought the whole family with them, along with their pastor and four members of their church in Arkadelphia. On the last day of their work in Semarang, we had planned a sending-off party for the team at a local restaurant owned by a friend from one of our Baptist churches. I remember sitting with Aji, the head of Impact Center Boja and the person who had called me on behalf of Jessica (Mr. Kaleb's daughter) after her motorcycle crash; we talked about Palu. The two of us had gone there the past September to present some training. Aji, Pastor Bambung, and I all shared a burden for a new work in Palu, and I remember Aji saying at the party that we needed to get someone up there quickly, or what we'd started was going to come to an end. And we had to get someone up there who had real pastoral skills. I asked Aji if he had any ideas about such a someone. He told me his brother, Bambang, knew a couple with experience in church planting who had, furthermore, family

CHAPTER TEN | CALL TO PREACH THE GOSPEL

connections in Central Sulawesi, where the wife was from. I asked him their names. "Pastor Fernandez Paiman and Asni Paiman," he answered. "I *know* them, I know them both well!" I blurted with some degree of enthusiasm. "Fernandez is actually my son in the Lord!"

An hour later I was on my cell phone with Pastor Bambang, asking his permission to represent our church at a meeting with Pastor Fernandez and Mrs. Asni in Medan on Sunday night, December 1. They were then pastoring Sinar Kasih Baptist Church in Medan. As it happened, I was scheduled to speak at Medan's Baptist seminary's graduation service that weekend, and also at a different Medan church's two-day revival event. The pastor agreed, and I became the official designee of Bulu Baptist Church charged with inviting Fernandez and Asni, face to face, to serve in Palu. (A few weeks before my visit to Medan, I had tossed out the possibility to Fernandez on the phone, but the in-person meeting would allow for a truly open discussion of whether a move to Palu was within the realm of possibility.) I took a taxi to meet the Paimans at a restaurant—which this time I made *certain* was one serving good Indonesian food. I had *nasi goreng,* fried rice, one of my favorites, and Fernandez and Asni enjoyed some *cap cay,* Chinese vegetables, along with prawn soup. The food was delicious, yet we quickly got down to business. I presented what I thought were the advantages Fernandez would gain by moving to Palu. Not only would his family be close to all of Mrs. Asni's family, Palu was a great place to start a new work. I explained what the head of the province's Department of Religion had promised out of gratitude for our efforts for his family. Mr. Kaleb had already given us a letter of permission to open Baptist churches all over the province. And in starting a brand-new church, Fernandez would have the ability to shape and develop it along whatever lines he had in mind concerning what a church should be. Pastors who join established churches often find themselves having to conform to the existing (or old) leadership's ideas of what their church was. Now, conforming may be no problem at all, if the church is biblically based and exhibits all nine of the characteristics of healthy churches listed in Mark Devers' *Nine Marks of a Healthy Church*. But having all nine is a tall order, and new pastors regularly discover that the church to be served is controlled by a few men and women whose vision for the church feels incompatible. A pastor in that precarious position must submit to the powers that be, and disillusionment and frustration set in, with burnout close behind. But with a new church start, a new pastor—the first pastor, in fact—is much more likely to be free to shape and craft his vision for the new church.

His work to date showed that Fernandez loved evangelism and church planting. Because he would be starting with only fifteen to twenty committed members in Palu, he could focus on reaching new people. He wouldn't be tied down by an overwhelming amount of pastoral care or administration. He could instead pursue a good deal of outreach and evangelism. Fernandez seemed to like that idea. Then he showed me straightforwardly the salary he would need to live on. To live in Palu would cost him much more than it cost him to live in Medan (or me to live in Semarang). It concerned me that what Fernandez and Asni needed in salary wasn't much different from what Pastor Bambang was receiving. That could be a problem when the figure was brought back to the church in Semarang to contemplate its financial responsibility in taking Fernandez on.

Two other problems came up. Fernandez explained one. He was worried that his children, Brian, about fourteen years old and in junior high, and elementary-age Lois might not be on board with the call. He was reluctant to move and then have to deal with kids and perhaps a wife who were not on board. I planned to address this concern of Fernandez's at length when he and I set out on our upcoming survey trip to Palu in February, just a few weeks off.

CHAPTER TEN | CALL TO PREACH THE GOSPEL

The second problem was Mrs. Asni's to explain. She shared at length how the Lord had spoken to her seven years earlier about moving from Lampung to Medan. She had had a struggle in prayer, a *bergumul*. I sensed, however, that Mrs. Asni did not look favorably on another move because she really liked living in Medan now, having adjusted to the new culture since 2014. "What about going back to your hometown?" I asked. "Going home was always nice," she said, "like going home for Christmas or something." She liked it when she could return home for short stays. "To serve full-time in the place where I was raised, well you know what Jesus said about that," Mrs. Asni said. Oh, no, I knew what was coming: "Jesus said to them, 'Only in his hometown, among his relatives and in his own house, is a prophet without honor'" (Mark 6: 4).

It was a good meeting with Fernandez and Asni. They wanted time to pray about our invitation and to take a survey trip to Palu to learn about options for their children's school. We agreed such a visit would help them weigh all that might be involved in moving to Palu, especially where Brian and Lois's education was concerned. They thought it might also be a good idea to meet with the folks at the sending church, Bulu Baptist Church in Semarang. Fernandez could preach at the mother church, and they could introduce themselves to the members and interview with the missions committee. We roughed out a timeline for the two trips before leaving the restaurant and saying good-bye. Sometime in February or March sounded good, and then by the beginning of April, the couple would have had time to pray through whether God was leading them to Central Sulawesi. A plan was made for Pastor Fernandez and Mrs. Asni to fly from Medan to Yogyakarta on February 14, then take a bus to his hometown of Solo. They would stay there Friday night, then hop another bus on Saturday to Semarang. There they would be guests in a church member's home, and Fernandez would preach at our church on Sunday.

Fernandez's preaching at our church in Semarang was marvelous. He also took questions about what the sending church expected of him, and he asked some questions of his own. The next day, Fernandez, Asni, and I flew to Palu. It was a bit tense, because strong winds forced our plane to circle the airport for close to an hour before we landed. The night had gotten late, as a result. When we finally landed, we were picked up by Mr. Kaleb, Jessica's father and head of the association of Protestant churches of Central Sulawesi. We stayed with him and his family, and they took care of our every need, even providing a car we could use to survey the city of Palu. For four full days, we looked at schools, met with the core group ready to start meeting as a Baptist church, and sharing the Gospel with various folks around Palu. It was a great opportunity for Fernandez and Asni to get an overall feel for Palu and Central Sulawesi today. As we left to return to Semarang, it was hard for me to read Fernandez about how he was leaning. Javanese are really difficult to read, I can give you lots of testimonies about that. I'm not the first to say that with Javanese, you never know if they love you or hate you. They keep all emotions to themselves as much as possible. Every now and then, you'll think you've had a brief glimpse of what they're feeling, but chances are you're misreading it. So I could only guess, and boarding the plane for Semarang, I felt there was about a fifty-fifty chance the family would come to Palu. But I could pray, between that day and the day their decision was due, in early April. From the moment I got home, Shelly and I prayed that the Lord would make it clear to Pastor Fernandez, Mrs. Asni, and the kids what His will was for their life.

In Palu I had talked quite a bit with Fernandez about hearing God's voice. I had told him how, in my own spiritual markers, God had spoken to me about His will for me concerning Semarang and the Baptist seminary. I explained to him that what I'd given most attention to in my ministry in Indonesia and what I'd most loved doing in the field—evangelism and church planting—seemed to point clearly to the move to Semarang and were in line with what Shelly and I felt was God's leading. I brought up my call to the seminary campus. It seemed clear that in light of the seminary's new direction focusing on personal evangelism and church planting, and stressing practical approaches to theological education, we were the right people for the task. I had been focused on personal evangelism, church planting, and practical methods of Gospel sharing for fifteen years.

Fernandez asked me then about his children and what it might mean if they were not on board with the call. I said that my own view of God's call in ministry was that He speaks to the husband and to the wife as well. From the first time I thought maybe God was directing me to serve Him in another country, I needed Shelly to receive that same call. It only made sense that if God called the husband, He would also make that call known to the wife. It had happened for Shelly and me, despite a slight difference in the call's timing for each one. Eventually, God brought us both to the same sense of being called. I added that my view of God's call in ministry included no need for our children to approve of it. Parents' job is to protect kids and provide a daily environment in which they feel safe. I asked Fernandez, "Say Brian was sick with a high fever. You were going to take him to the doctor, but he said he didn't want to go. Would you hesitate to take him then? No, of course not," I answered for him. "You'd make him go and you'd make him take medicine, too, if that was what the doctor ordered, even if Brian at first refused. It's the same thing when a call comes. We can't let children dictate whether we answer a call just because they don't like the idea of moving."

A text message came on April 2 from Pastor Fernandez. It read,

> Shalom Pastor Greg. Praise the Lord. Three days ago, our two children, Brian and Lois, gave us the answer that they

support our move to Palu, Central Sulawesi. Even though at the beginning they really had a hard time, to the point of throwing a fit about the whole idea of moving there. Thanks for praying for our family during this time and we will be letting our church where I pastor in Medan know about this along with your church at Bulu Baptist Church in Semarang on April 19, 2020.

The children's ultimate response didn't surprise me, really. It's hard for children to be uprooted and have to start from scratch in a totally new place. But if the call is real, the move may be unavoidable, and God will give the children of the called all the grace needed to adapt. I admire Pastor Fernandez and Mrs. Asni for seeking God's will, for being able to clearly hear His voice, and for accepting the direction they received from Him for their ministry in Palu.

CHAPTER 11

CALL TO STAY

> God has a huge heart for the nations. He's got a plan to reach them, and it involves us, His church. But not all are called to go—some are called to stay.
>
> — Frontiers USA

David Platt talked about how God calls all of us in the Church to be involved in missions. Some are called to go and serve as cross-cultural missionaries. But not every one of us is called to go; some are called to stay. David explains:

> For this reason, I would not say, "Every Christian is a missionary." Actually, to be completely frank, I have said that before! But I wouldn't now, and here's why. I appreciate the impulse behind this statement, wanting to emphasize how every Christian is on mission to make disciples. But that's also the problem. As much as I want to encourage every Christian to be on mission right where they live, if that's all we do, then thousands of people groups and billions of people will continue without even hearing the gospel. At some point, someone has to leave where they live to proclaim the gospel and plant the church where the gospel hasn't gone and the church doesn't exist.[1]

Chapter 3 told about the call Shelly and I received to go to the mission field. We had to struggle, or wrestle with the Lord in *bergumul*, to hear His Word about going overseas and serving in cross-cultural ministry. Whether or not we were called to go was a matter we had settled with God some thirty years ago. We had gone and we had served. And as it turned out, there would again be a call to grapple with in *bergumul*.

As Chapter 9 describes, losing our son, Jonathan, brought us home to the U.S. in 2008. Once time had gone by and we had grieved some and begun to live our new normal, we faced a decision on going back to the field or calling it quits. We were called to go. A handful of years later and under entirely different circumstances, it looked like another decision was necessary. Our International Mission Board acted in September 2015 to offer voluntary early retirement to its personnel age fifty years and up. The board was addressing some revenue shortfalls. I can remember David Platt, who was the IMB president then, asking us all to pray to discern whether the Lord was leading us to retire and return to the U.S. If God was once more extending to us His call to go—to go stateside, this time—then the IMB would provide as generously as possible for those called to this transition. By September 2015, I had been serving a little more than a year as the cluster leader on the island of Java. In that position supporting our personnel on Java, Shelly and I had found fulfillment and joy. That was in spite of all the stress it produced. We were usually tied to our cell phones, making decisions constantly (many of them seeming to have little to do with advancing the Kingdom of God in Java). Among the things that gave us a sense of buoyancy while we served as cluster leader for Java was new friendships with others serving on our Affinity Group leadership team. Team members came from all over Southeast Asia. Working with these folks for six years, we became very good friends with all of them. When the meeting was held at which we first heard about IMB's voluntary retirement incentive, in Bangkok, I remember several of us crying and then going to our knees together, seeking God's face and wanting to know His will for each one of us. Of our group from Indonesia, several faithful servants knew very quickly that they would seriously consider IMB's offer. Critical family needs had been requiring ever more of their attention, and the timing seemed right for their return to the U.S. The departure of several key families in the Java cluster would be a blow. After all, being over fifty, they were the folks with the most experience ministering to the Indonesians. In total, five of our units eventually accepted the early retirement offer from IMB, meaning the Java cluster took quite a hit.

Shelly and I needed time to pray and think. We returned to Semarang from that emotionally charged leadership team meeting in Bangkok still undecided about whether to stay in Indonesia. We were carefully weighing our options. But many of our best friends in our age bracket had decided to retire.

KUDOS, MARK BRUCKERT AND TERRY MANTELL!

Perhaps the main reason that friends in Indonesia and elsewhere (for example, the Philippines) opted to retire was their aging parents. My mother and Shelly's mother still lived in their own homes. My mother's place was a second-floor condominium in Louisville, Kentucky, where my two brothers lived as well. We paid the lady across the hall to fix Mom's evening meal and make sure she got into bed all right at night. In 2015, my mother was ninety and her health had really begun to go down. I called her from Indonesia every day and we talked via Skype, too. Our conversations were never long ones, but it did give me the chance to touch base with her, and she kept me updated on how she was doing.

I owe a whole lot to my brothers, Mark Bruckert and Terry Mantell, for the way they carefully looked after our mom the whole time Shelly and I were in Southeast Asia serving Jesus Christ on the mission field.

Neither of my brothers complained about my being half a world away in Indonesia, fulfilling our call. Humbly, they were there for Mom, taking care of her without much thanks or praise. It must have been especially demanding in the final three years of her life, as her health gave out. Because of Mark and Terry, our decisions over the years to remain in Indonesia were that much easier to make, and I appreciate them for that.

My mother, Peggy Bruckert, and my two brothers, Mark and Terry, at Parkland Baptist Church in Louisville, Kentucky, in 2017.

Once Shelly and I had prayed IMB's offer through, we had a peace about God leading us to stay in Indonesia. As I mentioned, already several of our most experienced missionaries were accepting the offer and leaving Indonesia. Seasoned personnel would be in short supply. We felt led of the Lord to stay, knowing that our scaled-down missionary forces would need more than ever the mentoring and leadership of veterans like us. When all the early-retirement activity wound down (eventually, IMB missionaries *under* age fifty received their own offer), the number of departures surprised even the IMB, which reported to the *Baptist Press* that 1,132 missionaries and other staff had accepted its early-retirement or early-return offers.[2] Included in that number were our daughter Jamie and her husband, Jeremy Phillips. They had served faithfully for a term in the city of Balikpapan in East Kalimantan province and would now return stateside with our two grandchildren.

CHANGE ON THE HORIZON

Toward the middle of 2018, we got wind from our leadership of a shake-up to come within our mission structure on the field. We heard what it all might look like during a retreat for Affinity Group leadership teams (AGLT) at Phuket, the beautiful resort town in Thailand. Over three days at a luxurious hotel with beautiful ocean views, we feasted on delicious Thai food and enjoyed getting acquainted with Greg Mann, newly arrived Affinity Group strategy leader, and his wife, Sarah. Greg and Sarah had been in the position for less than two months. They wanted the time in Phuket to be one of bonding for our AGLT. In various meetings—one-to-one, with Shelly, in groups—with Greg and with Mark Moore, the Affinity operations director, it had become clear that change was on the horizon that would affect a lot of us in the field. "Restructuring" was coming, an effort to streamline our Affinity Groups and clusters in order to gain adequate resources and focus on three goals:

1. Empower Indonesian National Partners to reach remaining unengaged Unreached People Groups.

2. Balance our teams to secure proper shepherding of and care for our personnel.

3. Mentor and equip new teammates for missionaries.

We would need to wait until September for the real details, but before we left Phuket we began to get a pretty good idea. In mid-2018, our work in Southeast Asia involved eight cluster leaders, one each in Vietnam; Cambodia; Thailand/Laos; Myanmar; Malaysia/Philippines/Brunei (the "Southern Crescent"); Sumatra (Indonesia); Java (Indonesia); and East Indonesia and Beyond. A consensus seemed to have been reached that these eight needed to be reduced to five. Such streamlining of the Affinity Groups would make the strategy leader's job less cumbersome, supervising five cluster leaders rather than eight. During the retreat in

Phuket, one cluster leader volunteered to step down, and it was agreed that our Cambodia and Vietnam efforts would merge under a single cluster leader. Over dinner, discussions seemed to be heading in the direction of restructuring all our Indonesia efforts in one cluster, not three. Jobs would be lost. That had the present cluster leaders from Indonesia praying a lot over the next few months. Our Indonesia effort's three cluster leaders were, truthfully, all for the status quo. But the writing was on the wall; things could not stay the same for our Affinity.

CALLED TO LET GO

Our Thai retreat finished, it was time to await September's announcements—and pray. Our routines in Semarang didn't need to change yet, and mine included swimming at a fitness center Shelly and I had joined. I tried to get there four times each week. Sometimes, the exercise turned out to be "prayer swimming." It may sound strange, but God spoke to my heart about the future of my ministry while I was swimming laps. In the pool, I heard His Word directing me to let go of my role as cluster leader. I did not need to hold onto it for dear life. Ever so gently, God was readying my heart to lay down my "CL" role willingly, instead of seeing it taken from me. To lay down my work of my own volition would demand humility, something that has not tended to come naturally or easily to me, to be honest. At the time, I remember this passage from Philippians 2 being helpful:

> [6] **Who, being in very nature God, did not consider equality with God something to be grasped,**
>
> [7] **but made himself nothing, taking the very nature of a servant, being made in human likeness.**
>
> [8] **And being found in appearance as a man, he humbled himself and became obedient to death—even death on a cross!**

CHAPTER ELEVEN | CALL TO STAY

> ⁹ Therefore God exalted him to the highest place and gave him the name that is above every name,
>
> ¹⁰ that at the name of Jesus every knee should bow, in heaven and on earth and under the earth,
>
> ¹¹ and every tongue confess that Jesus Christ is Lord, to the glory of God the Father.
> — Philippians 2: 6-11

God wanted my humility. But when it came time to cast individual votes for the best candidate for our new all-Indonesia cluster leader, I felt tempted to write my own name. We had been instructed to vote for ourselves if indeed we thought that was best. I took time to pray then— *bergumul!*—and seek God's face. He led me to let go, to turn from the old role and position in Java and turn to the comfort of knowing He was leading me. I prepared my ballot, writing down another's name. It did not surprise me, later, to learn that the name I wrote was our *unanimous* choice for the new cluster leader. God had been at work. I happened to read a verse in the Psalms through which, I recognized, the Lord was speaking to me: "The boundary lines have fallen for me in pleasant places; surely I have a delightful inheritance" (Psalms 16: 6).

I drew comfort from the verse, but at the time, I only partially understood what God was saying to me. His Word here had ramifications I didn't fully comprehend when I first voluntarily stepped out of the role of cluster leader for Java. We were to transition immediately to service as associate cluster leader for the Java sub-cluster. I felt at first that this job offer illustrated for Shelly and me God's goodness to us right through the worrisome restructuring of the Affinity Groups. I felt again, truly, "The boundary lines have fallen for me in pleasant places." The Lord had led us as a shepherd leads his flock. We shared that with the AGLT in our last meeting with them, in Jakarta in October 2018, and Shelly and I also expressed our appreciation for their encouragement during the past six years. It wouldn't be long before I could fully understand what God intended for us and how that intention tied into that verse from the Psalms.

CHAPTER 12

CALL TO FINISH WELL

Richard Owen Roberts is known for his writings on revival and spiritual awakenings. Still serving at the age of 89, he talks about the importance of "finishing well" in his series of sermons on the Book of Hebrews. The text of Hebrews falls into two parts, although the two have been interwoven, Roberts explains. One part avows the preeminence of Christ over all others. Christ is greater than the angels, greater than Moses, and greater than the Hebrew sacrificial system. Roberts identifies this avowal as one of the purposes of the writer of Hebrews. The purpose of the other part of the book is to encourage followers' unwavering faith. Many Jewish followers of Christ appeared to be shrinking back, no longer faithfully following the Lord. This problem among the Hebrew Christians happened because of their persecution by the Roman government, which demanded the worship of the emperor. Emperors like the evil Nero required people's ultimate allegiance, and when the Hebrew Christians instead followed Christ, the Romans made things tough for them. Threatened by the powers that be, many were choosing not to follow Christ anymore. Word had spread about Nero's "garden parties." Reports had been confirmed that Nero, in order to light up the gardens where his infamous nighttime orgies were hosted, impaled on poles Christians who refused to deny Christ, pouring flammable substances over them and setting them ablaze. The reports caused the Hebrew Christians to weaken in their faith and draw back from following the Lord Jesus. As well, some younger Hebrew believers were persecuted by their own family members, who chided them for abandoning their

Jewish heritage and religion for this new sect called Christianity. Faced with these things, even Jewish believers who had started out well decided to get out of "the race."

It is clear that the author of the Book of Hebrews wants to remind the Hebrew believers not only that Christ is preeminent—over every other power, principality, leader, system—but that if they truly believed, their faith would persevere until the end. I had a favorite teacher at seminary, Wayne Ward, who said the main message of the Book of Hebrews was that "He whose faith fizzles out in the finish was faulty at first." It really sums up what the ancient author says in this important book: Finish well, *believers.*

MISSIONS CATALYST/INDONESIA CHURCH MOBILIZER/REVIVALIST

Welcoming in the new year 2019, I little knew how the depth and scope of the truths that can be mined from Psalms 16: 6, the verse the Lord had given me in October after the retreat in Phuket, would soon be clarified for me. With the new year, three Indonesian clusters were officially restructured into one Indonesian Leadership Team. Not long after, I met for the first time with its new leader, Ken Jacks. Our one-to-one meeting happened early in the morning, before his scheduled meeting with all the associate cluster leaders working with the newly formed Indonesian Leadership Team. Right away after Ken and I had exchanged pleasantries, he said he had something to ask me. "Greg, I want you and Shelly to pray about something," he opened. "I want you to step out of the ACL position and be the missions catalyst/Indonesia church mobilizer/revivalist. I know that's a long title!"

He offered a quick job description that had me wondering if I was dreaming. It sounded like my dream job, too good to be true. The missions catalyst/Indonesia church mobilizer/revivalist would have five tasks. He would engage the Baptist conventions at organizational levels (church, association, and institution). He would be a voice for revival, spiritual awakening, and spiritual renewal. He would broadcast a missions challenge, reminding the church that the Gospel is entrusted to it and must be shared with all of Indonesia. He would walk alongside churches and other organizations willing to take the next step to engage new segments of lostness. Finally, he would help establish a network of visionary Indonesian churches committed to reaching the edge of lostness. I felt Ken's take on the spiritual condition of Indonesia's National Baptist Convention was correct. It was in a lethargic state after being in decline for a long time. Ken was one of the few leaders I had encountered who had a burden to continue working with the national convention and who thought the convention's potential was off the charts. As Todd Lafferty, IMB's executive vice president, once described Indonesia's Baptist convention, it was "the sleeping giant," in Ken's view. If it ever roused from its spiritual slumber, watch out!

In Ken Jacks' vision, the sleeping giant could wake. Ken grew up as an MK in Indonesia and has a deep love for its national convention. Others with IMB chose not to work with that convention, because of its lack of concern for reaching the Unreached People Groups of Indonesia. Around one hundred twenty Indonesian UPGs remained virtually been untouched by the Gospel. The convention, however, focused narrowly on its own organization, summoning little apparent interest for reaching these UPGs. Unfortunately, the churches of the Indonesian National Baptist Convention have generally become so self-focused that very few still resemble the churches I worked with during my first assignment, in 1989. Sadly, many churches resemble the church in Ephesus said to have lost its first love.

That loss, that self-focus, was why a missions catalyst/Indonesia church mobilizer/revivalist was needed, Ken told me in so many words. He reminded me that Steve Sanders and his wife, Joy, continued to work with our national Baptist convention. (Like Ken, Steve had been raised in Indonesia, in a missionary family.) Most of the missionaries serving with IMB in Indonesia do not look primarily to churches as the avenue for achieving their Gospel mission. While a significant number of us still receive our visas through the Baptist convention, as well as the Baptist Foundation, IMB missionaries working exclusively with the Baptist convention had dwindled down, basically, to just Steve and Joy. Ken told me Steve and Joy needed some help with the workload, and Ken had thought of Shelly and me.

DECISIONS, DECISIONS

As I hope this book has clearly shown, whenever Shelly and I faced a major decision in our life or ministry, we sought the Lord's Word and His guidance. We tried never to take for granted His leadership in our lives, although we knew we could trust in it. We knew we needed to humbly and faithfully seek His will in times of potential change. We missed the mark sometimes, like with our one-time transfer to the Philippines, but we learned from our mistakes and we are sincere in wanting God's input concerning every step we take. So, the morning of my conversation with Ken Jacks, I promptly called Shelly over WhatsApp to let her know of his offer. She asked me a good question during that call, namely, what about my role as assistant cluster leader? Ken had said I would remain an ACL through April 15, 2019, then become the full-time missions catalyst/Indonesia church mobilizer/revivalist for the convention. Seeing Shelly's response via our video call, I thought she appeared very open to the change of roles.

As I prayed about it again and again, I gradually recognized that I could think of no better way, really, to finish up our career in Indonesia. Serving the national convention by presenting to churches seminars on spiritual awakening and revival not only on Java, but across Indonesia! What a joy! In my heart the Lord was reigniting the fire to preach and teach and excite the Baptist churches and pastors of our convention. Shelly and I both wanted to finish well in the years we had left in Indonesia. The proposed change in our role, as we interpreted it, was nothing less than God allowing that to happen, out of the blue, so to speak. In retrospect, we see how God sovereignly used important people in our lives to open this opportunity to us. We were very ready to move forward into the new assignment.

When Ken had brought up to me the idea of a new assignment, he had also asked if there was anyone I would recommend for my old job, associate cluster leader for Java. Indeed, I had already considered who would be best at taking over when I retired from IMB, something I had placed about four years down the road. God's sovereign plan had changed the timeline, but my choice for the new associate cluster leader, Java sub-cluster, was John Trout, and he agreed to take on the associated responsibilities beginning in April 2019.

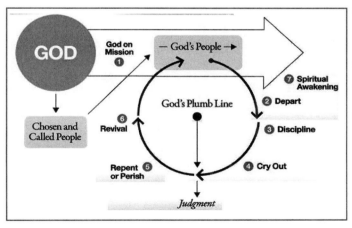

The cycle that Henry Blackaby conceived of for his *Fresh Encounter* curriculum.

A TEST RUN IN BOJA, MARCH 2019

In March, a month or so before I was to move into my new role, I decided to test the waters by teaching Henry Blackaby's *Fresh Encounter* materials to a group of pastors and laymen at our Impact Center Boja. The center was about an hour's drive from our house, and every Tuesday for the next three months I made the trip. The pastors went through Fresh Encounter in its entirety and also studied in Richard Owen Roberts' classic *Revival*. Their response impressed me. Each week we met at six for supper, which was followed right away by prayer time. Hamid, who was the association's evangelist, led our prayers for each part of Indonesia in turn that remained untouched (or nearly so) by the Gospel. Following prayer time, teaching of the materials lasted two hours. Then, to conclude, we had a time for sharing about what God was saying to us individually and how God was working in our lives. I perceived real hunger in the hearts of the pastors and, especially, the laymen attending those twelve Tuesday sessions. They wanted to do better, so they gave testimonies about their failings. One confessed that telling lies about his handling of the family finances had become habitual, even in talking with his wife. More than one confessed to a variety of other problems in their marriages. One man testified he had joined our study group at his wife's urging. She wanted him to hear from God and commit himself deeply to Christ, because he feared that a curse had been placed on his home and his store, something that many Indonesians believe is possible. The work on the Blackaby and Roberts materials had reassured him, he said. He had experienced a real peace and felt he was no longer oppressed by evil spirits. One pastor, Mr. Matris, confessed to being greatly distracted by the approaching Indonesian political elections. He had lost his focus on shepherding his people and hearing from God in prayer and bible study. The seminar, he said, got him back on track. I shared my own backsliding, which had taken the form of too much interest in the NCAA basketball tournament as opposed to my need to seek God's face. (Roberts' *Revival* includes a

CHAPTER TWELVE | CALL TO FINISH WELL

Pastors and laymen who completed the *Fresh Encounter* seminar at Impact Center Boja.

chapter containing twenty-five signs that a believer may be backsliding.)[1]

In June, we traveled to Thailand for the annual Great Meeting. We were in for a treat, as the keynote speaker for the week was Bill Elliff, pastor of the Summit Church in Little Rock, Arkansas, and pastor/church director of OneCry. Bill has years of pastoral experience to draw on for his talks, but what touched all of our hearts during our time with him was his passion for spiritual awakening and revival in our churches. Throughout the meeting it was obvious that a groundswell of prayer revival appeared to be starting up among our missionaries serving in Southeast Asia. When it was time to go back to our places of ministry, I sensed that most of us would carry along a new or renewed passion to pray for revival and spiritual awakening in Indonesia, especially for the region we were connected to through our service.

PASTORS' RETREAT AND REVIVAL

In late May, a steering committee meeting was called to begin ironing out with the leadership the details of a three-day pastors' retreat. It would take place in Salatiga, Central Java, during the second week of September.

Indonesian Baptist pastors attending the Fresh Encounter retreat and revival held September 10-12, 2019, in Salatiga.

All pastors within the Indonesian National Baptist Convention would be invited. I was well acquainted with the people on the steering committee, including Steve Sanders, my closest colleague in my new assignment, with whom I would work to prepare for the September retreat. Steve and I decided early on to fast and pray on the twenty-ninth day of each month until the retreat, beginning with May. From May until August, our days of fasting would focus on prayer for revival and spiritual awakening. As well, I compiled the prayer requests I had asked for from our steering committee members, sending a copy to them all so that our prayers ahead of the retreat would be well focused.

As the plan for the retreat was developing, I let the committee know in a clear statement that my purpose for the seminar portion of this retreat was to review the principles and practices of revival, according to the "cycle of revival" explained no fewer than seven times in the Book of Judges. This cycle of revival is also illustrated in the Book of Revelation, through the churches that Jesus beckoned to repent. Richard Owen Roberts was first to identify the cycle in the Book of Judges and Book of Revelation, then Henry Blackaby reshaped Roberts' argument into perhaps its best-known form, the *Fresh Encounter* materials designed for study groups. Interestingly, Blackaby had help in writing *Fresh Encounter* from a former IMB missionary to Indonesia, Avery Willis. The cycle of revival comprises seven stages, and their workings are at the heart of the

Fresh Encounter materials. The cycle would be the focus of the September retreat.

POWERING UP VS. STUDYING UP

At the outset it seemed like Indonesians on our steering committee weren't fully on board with a cycle of revival "theme" for the pastors' retreat in September. They hadn't ever experienced a seminar whose purpose was seeking God and praying for His presence to be manifested in a powerful way. For them, a seminar was basically an academic pursuit. I asked them to think of this revival-themed seminar as a revival service for pastors, who needed to hear directly from the Lord to recharge their spiritual batteries.

Pastor Ngatimin, who is the head of the Pastors Fellowship, wondered why ours wasn't taking the shape of typical seminars, at which lecturers impart information and knowledge. I explained that we hoped for something far better than information: We wanted to see God show up and bring revival and renewal to the hearts of our pastors. Pastor Ngatimin wasn't easily convinced. He is a good friend of mine, having been the pastor we called to shepherd the first church I ever planted in Indonesia, in Palur, Solo. Eventually, he yielded to Steve and me and our idea, demonstrating respect for us and perhaps acknowledging the significant proportion of the funds for the retreat that would be provided by our organization. Pastor Yosia Wartono likewise didn't at first seem to see what we were trying to accomplish. He kept suggesting the typical seminar format, with a panel of experts up front answering questions from the participating pastors. In Indonesia, he said, a seminar normally features three or four very knowledgeable people who address the audience and then sit together to take questions from audience members. I explained for him that we were interested in preaching strong sermons on seven topics, each one a "stage" in the revival cycle, and then inviting the pastors to give testimonies about what God was speaking to their hearts, what God seemed to be teaching them as they listened to the sermons. We really wanted these pastors to hear from God.

Finally, I think, every steering committee member from the Baptist Convention comprehended and was on board with what we sought to accomplish in September. As September approached, I felt pretty sure all of us were prayed up and anticipating that the Lord would do great things during our three days in Salatiga. When the three days of the *Fresh Encounter* retreat came to an end, I wrote an account to send the members of our Indonesia Leadership Team. It read:

> We just returned from the Fresh Encounter revival meeting that was held for our GGBI [Indonesian National Baptist Convention] pastors at a retreat center about an hour from where Shelly and I live. There were about 300 pastors in attendance in addition to 8 of our IMB personnel. We had been praying (and in some cases fasting) for this gathering for the past 4 months, and we were expecting God to show up in a mighty way. We were not disappointed! God's manifested presence was evident in our midst. Many of our pastors made public commitments and came forward asking for prayer that God would pour out His Spirit on them to enable them to more effectively shepherd their people.
>
> In the first session, which opened on Tuesday afternoon, John Trout preached a powerful sermon on "God's vision and mission for His church," the first stage in God's pattern of renewal and spiritual awakening. Afterwards, the head of our Indonesian Baptist Convention, Pastor Yosia Wartono, preached on the 7 churches in the Book of Revelation, giving special attention to the church at Ephesus, which illustrated

the second stage in God's cycle of revival and spiritual awakening, that God's people have a tendency to turn away from Him and choose to go their own way. Then the final sermon on the first night was preached powerfully by Steve Sanders, on the life and reign of King Asa in 2 Chronicles 14–16, illustrating how God disciplines His people when we turn away from Him.

I was the first one to preach on Wednesday morning and preached on the role of prayer in revival and spiritual awakening, using the revival during the time of Ezra and Nehemiah to illustrate the importance of crying out to God as we repent and turn to Him. The second session on Wednesday was led by Ken Jacks, who preached a powerful sermon on the Laodicean church (from Revelation 3) to illustrate the need for repentance. We counted 32 people that came forward during the invitation as Ken encouraged them to come forward to ask prayer for the churches that they lead. Interesting enough, during each session we had 8 counselors at the front of the church to receive and pray for those that came forward. It was a wonderful blend of some of our National Leadership and some of our IMB personnel. What a sight to behold, to see us working together to cry and embrace our pastors and pray for their ministries!

After lunch on Wednesday our next session was led by Pastor Ardi Wiriadinata, who is the pastor of First Baptist Church in Bandung. He preached a riveting sermon on the reign and revival under King Josiah in 2 Chronicles. It was entitled, Could I be the cause of Revival in my Church? In a very creative way, he showed how we, like King Josiah, can be the cause of positive change in the spiritual climate of our church by taking the initiative to bring spiritual renewal to our churches. He illustrated the sixth stage in God's cycle, and that is renewal that is brought about by the Spirit of God. Finally, the head of the Department of Evangelism, Pastor Eko Kurniadi, preached a sermon on the call of Isaiah (chapter 6), emphasizing the need to have a renewed view of God's Holiness that would in turn become the foundation for spiritual renewal and revival for our churches.

During the evening on Wednesday we heard three very different, but at the same time very interesting, testimonies about how God was working in the lives of all three men. On the final day, much time was spent sporting our new tee shirts with the Fresh Encounter theme printed on the back of them, along with the text from 2 Chronicles 7: 14 the theme was based on and also posing for numerous group photos. The final session was led by Pastor Wartono, who spoke on the signs of spiritual growth/decline in our churches. He then passed out an evaluation form that contained criteria that that they could use to honestly evaluate the spiritual health of their churches. Afterwards, a final invitation was given, where numerous people made public commitments to follow through with some of the steps spelled out in Pastor Wartono's sermon, in order to help lead their own churches in spiritual renewal and also lead their churches to pray for spiritual awakening.

[1] **Finally, brothers, pray for us that the message of the Lord may spread rapidly and be honored, just as it was with you.**

— 2 Thessalonians 3: 1

Not only did every person receive a free tee shirt, but we also gave out the classic book on revival by Richard Owen Roberts, Bangkitlah dari Kesuaman Rohani (simply "Revival," in English). There was definitely a consensus that God had moved in a mighty way among us, and there was much chatter about the need for follow-up at the local level as we seek to see the spirit of renewal spread among the churches that these pastors lead. Please pray that this will not stop with the meeting coming to an end yesterday, but that the Holy Spirit would continue to work in our National Baptist Pastors and their churches and that a spiritual awakening would come like a mighty river flowing through the world's largest Muslim nation to bring thousands, if not millions, into the Kingdom.

Counselors praying for pastors who had come forward to ask for prayer during the pastors' retreat and revival in Salatiga, Central Java.

One way to follow up on what took place in Salatiga was to go to individual churches and lead revival services; another was to present seminars at our Baptist seminaries. Immediately after the *Fresh Encounter* revival in Central Java, I went on a preaching circuit that took me twice to Jakarta, for revival services, as well as to Kupang in the eastern part of Indonesia and Medan in North Sumatra. The people were very open, and I was able to meet with key leaders from all of these areas, including the leaders of the Baptist seminary in Medan. Here is my report to our Indonesian leadership team about my ministry at that seminary:

> On Thursday of this past week I returned from Medan after five days of ministry in Indonesia's third largest city. I preached at the Indra Kasih Baptist Church on Sunday October 12, and then began the Fresh Encounter seminar at Medan's Baptist seminary. I was given three hours each night, Monday through Wednesday, to teach the main portion of the materials. In addition, I was also given a chance to preach in their chapel service on Tuesday morning. I preached on Isaiah 57: 15, the importance of humbling oneself to experience God's presence and blessing for ministry.
>
> The final night of the revival service, I felt led to give an invitation for both the seminary students and faculty to respond. Normally when I give an invitation, it is two-pronged, toward the lost and then toward Christians who have backslid and need to rededicate themselves to Christ afresh and anew. The last night of the seminar, I included an emphasis on being burdened for family members, friends, and neighbors who are lost and need to be prayed for specifically. Wednesday night, I really emphasized quite a bit about what salvation is and how to submit oneself to Christ.
>
> I felt the invitation and response went exceptionally well the last night of the seminar at the seminar, because of the following evidence:
>
> 1) The Holy Spirit was moving among us, both in the students and also among faculty members who were there.

We sure can't minimize the role of the Spirit as we call folks to make decisions (see Acts 2: 37).

2) The music was soft and worshipful. I can't emphasize this enough. We need to hear what is being said, to not only be able to pray intelligently for those that are coming forward, but so that they can hear us, as well.

3) I made preparations early on to make sure there were at least 5 of us praying for the students. I was anticipating a response, but honestly, the response that night went beyond my expectations (Ephesians 3: 20–21).

One thing to note is that Mr. and Ms. Baskita invited me to speak at the graduation service in late November at the Baptist seminary. Only one shot to speak to them, but I think this might be worth a trip there to fortify our relationship with one of our four Baptist seminaries. Any input from you guys about this would be welcome.

Indeed, I did return to Medan in late November and spoke at the seminary graduation service. In addition, I was able to speak at the Helvetia Church in Medan two times, once for a youth revival where

Speaking at the graduation ceremony at Baptist Theological Seminary in Medan, North Sumatra, in November 2019.

a significant number came forward making decisions. The highlight for me, though, was being able again to meet with my son in the Lord, Fernandez Paiman, pastor of the Indrakasih Baptist Church in Medan. I shared in a previous chapter about my meeting with Fernandez and his wife, Asni.

On December 2, 2019, Shelly and I were also able to attend the inauguration ceremony for the seminary's new president, Pastor Rimun Robinson. Many pastors belonging to the convention attended, to show their support for the new leader of our oldest and most established Baptist seminary.

At the inauguration ceremony for the new president of our Baptist seminary in Semarang, Central Java, in December 2019.

FRESH ENCOUNTER AT THE SEMINARY IN JAKARTA

In February of 2020, Shelly and I had the opportunity to teach at the Baptist seminary in Jakarta. We conducted the same seminar I had taught in Medan the past October. Our purpose was the spiritual formation of the students, for which Henry Blackaby's *Fresh Encounter* materials were well suited. The seminar went well, with about forty students attending. When the seminar was over, one of our IMB personnel followed up with four students who expressed interest in being trained in *Any 3*, the evangelism training that focuses on Muslims. The four also went out sharing with our IMB colleague and his Indonesian National Partner.

COVID-19

In January and early February, we had begun hearing about a new coronavirus infection that had originated in Wuhan, China, and spread to a number of countries, including Italy and South Korea. This infectious disease, Covid-19, was getting more of our attention by early March, when a pandemic was officially announced and infections were gaining traction in Indonesia. The World Health Organization made the announcement on March 11. On March 14, Shelly and I were scheduled to fly to Jakarta to preach at the church at Taman Safari and lead a two-day seminar on spiritual leadership for church members. I taught on Saturday night and on Sunday morning preached about the church at Thyatira, in Revelation 2. We flew back to Semarang on Monday, March 16. At home I started second guessing our wisdom in being so often away at so many church meetings. There was increasing buzz about sheltering in place and social distancing. Not long after we returned from Jakarta, the Indonesian government called for churches and mosques and all Indonesian citizens to begin taking these precautions, or face legal consequences.

Sheltering in place and social distancing were strange ideas that I really didn't understand. I understood the words just fine, but I could not imagine how a nationwide crackdown to separate people and keep them from gathering together was going to look. I heard Dr. Ralph Neighbour discuss what was happening. He founded TOUCH Outreach Ministries and has written more than forty-five books on Cell Group life and leadership. He is also the founding pastor of Encourager Church in Houston, Texas (formerly West Memorial Baptist), and at age eighty-nine has a lifetime of experience equipping the church to reach the world, starting with our neighbors. Dr. Neighbour said something very perceptive about the Covid-19 pandemic: "The Father has sent us all to our rooms to think about what we have done."[2] I remember that, as just a little fellow, whenever I was naughty—and actually, that was quite frequently!—my father would send me to my room and instruct me to stay in it until I'd had "enough time to think about what you've done." I might make it fifteen minutes, and then I'd open the door a crack and ask, "Dad, can I come out now?" "Not until you've thought about all you just did," came the stern reply. Thinking about social distancing and about how all our churches, everyone's churches, have had to give up meeting together to worship, I think of Dr. Neighbour's analogy. And I take it a step further. Not only has the Father sent us to our rooms, He has taken all our toys away from us! Most everything that gives us stability and pleasure is gone as a result of Covid-19. All we focused on, our entertainment (for instance, sports events), our stock portfolios and bank accounts, our ability to pursue fame and fortune—all gone, or at best indefinitely on hold. Why, the Father has even taken away our church buildings! *And what an opportunity this presents for a great revival and spiritual awakening among the people of God in Indonesia and the United States of America.*

In terms of historical cycles, Americans are due a major spiritual movement; fifty years have elapsed since the last. I hope all of us will use this virus-dictated time of relative confinement for some serious reflection. I advise us all not to try to leave our rooms too soon after being disciplined by the Father. We need to think about all that we have done. Through this new coronavirus, God is giving us time for introspection, reflection, and, as needed, repentance and restoration of our walk with the Lord. It would be tragic for American pastors and believers not to take this opportunity to pursue deep soul searching and contrite repentance. I fear too many are ignoring it—as are some Indonesian pastors and believers, though the problem seems a lesser one here. I thought what Lane Johnson said as he led a prayer session on OneCry on April 4, 2020, was interesting. He said,

> There are lots of interpretations about how we might interpret this Covid-19 pandemic. The passages that seem to explain clearly what God is up to like 2 Chronicles 7: 14 and Jeremiah 18, seemingly are not being paid attention to. The churches are having a difficult time seeing this as anything other than asking for God's help to get us out of this.[3]

This message is clear in 2 Chronicles 7: 14: Whenever there is some kind of natural disaster, if God's people would humble themselves, repent, seek His face, and turn from their wicked ways, then God will respond with His forgiveness and restoration. That humbling, repenting, and seeking are what is required of us, now that our Father has sent us to our rooms. Are we genuinely taking time to search our souls and reflect seriously on any sin in our hearts that might be grieving the Father? The prayer of David seems appropriate here: "Search me, O God, and know my heart; test me and know my anxious thoughts. See if there is any offensive way in me, and lead me in the way everlasting" (Psalm 139: 23–24).

> **When God intends great mercy for His people, he sets his people a-praying." "**
>
> — Matthew Henry

Hunkered down in our house and social distancing, Shelly and I (like so many others) needed some support and fellowship with Indonesian believers who had a kindred passion and heart for revival and spiritual awakening in Indonesia. Some pastors up in Jakarta had been leading The Light Communities Church in daily Zoom-based prayer meetings.

The people were praying for revival. The pastors invited us to join them for the meetings. As we prayed for revival, we felt burdened to involve all of our Baptist pastors and lay people in prayer meetings like the one we had joined. So we started *Baptist Berdoa* online, gathering to pray at six o'clock on Thursday evenings. (means "Baptists praying together.") We borrowed the talents of Ronny Serworwora, a media expert who was working with The Light Communities Church Zoom gatherings. With a team from his church, Ronny has put together quite an impressive program for us. He works on both sides of things, not just helping handle the technology but also interviewing people from our churches and calling on participants in turn to lead everyone in prayer. Ronny's role in our media project has been key, helping us link Baptists together in prayer during the pandemic that has so impacted our churches.

In the photo accompanying this passage, Ronny leads me in an interview online during our Baptist Berdoa prayer time. We met Ronny when he was just a teenager, when he helped move our things from Jakarta to Solo for our first assignment. He has now graduated with a Ph.D. from Southwestern Theological Seminary. The session during which this photo was taken saw more than three thousand people log on to pray, hearts in unison praying for revival and spiritual awakening to take place

Ronny Serworwora asks me to pray for Rene Sahir, the pastor of the Indonesian Church in Queens, New York.

CHAPTER TWELVE | CALL TO FINISH WELL

in Indonesia. During the years 1966 to 1971, God did send revival and spiritual awakening to the nation, happening simultaneously with the Jesus movement revival in the United States. In those years, more than two million Muslims came to faith in Jesus Christ. Our prayers online through Baptist Berdoa are for another spiritual awakening in the world's largest archipelago nation. God has done it before, and we Baptists in Indonesia believe He will again send spiritual awakening, a movement of epic proportions, even in the midst of trying times.

After the first few prayer meetings, I realized two things could improve our *Baptist Berdoa* program. It needed to spend less time on interviews and information sharing and discussion, and it needed to spend more time on our praying. I encouraged Ronny to tune in three times a week to the OneCry prayer website. Anyone may log on to it and join the prayer meeting. During each of the one-hour meetings on the website, the structure of which was devised by Byron Paulus and Bill Elliff, about six people take turns leading prayer. Prayer covers several different topics, all having to do with Covid-19 and the need for revival and spiritual awakening. I encouraged Ronny to listen and learn from what Byron and Bill were doing and to pattern the *Baptist Berdo*a gatherings after their example. The more time in prayer, the better, so we needed ways to minimize discussions with people as they logged on. Such minimizing began to happen naturally after we suspended our six o'clock Thursday gatherings in favor of ten o'clock Tuesday prayers involving only pastors. (The pastors now gather online at eight o'clock Tuesday evenings.)

After a couple of online meetings of pastors, we decided to change our approach, and it was a grand success. In our "prayer room" were myself and three more of our IMB folks. Pastor Muksin served as emcee, and he kept the prayer time moving, asking each of us to share one prayer request and also to pray for another's request. I felt like it went really well, though there are still kinks to work out. For instance, I wondered if there hadn't been too many Westerners from the IMB praying in our prayer room on Zoom, and too few Indonesians. I voiced my concern to Ronny as well as Aswin, who is a lay leader at The Light Communities Church. Ronny responded that the Westerners' praying would, he thought, motivate the nationals to do more. We should certainly prioritize encouraging the nationals to pray, Ronny explained, because if we do, in time they will pray more and be a more central presence in the prayer meetings. Well, we will see how things develop. I am optimistic that lots of Baptist people in Indonesia are today praying for revival and spiritual awakening. It encourages me to remember Matthew Henry's words: "When God intends great mercy for His people, he sets his people a-praying."

Late in April of this year 2020, a one-day prayer event called "Praying on the Mountain" was held, an event that ninety-five-year-old Pastor Fred Lunsford was burdened with. Pastor Lunsford has been praying for years that God would send revival and spiritual awakening. Baptist Press reported on the event and how Pastor Lunsford's burden had started:

At age 93, after pastoring 70 years, fighting in World War II and preaching at revivals all over the U.S., Fred Lunsford was ready for the Lord to take him home.

But, Lunsford recounted, God had different plans for his life and was just getting started laying a new path that would expand well beyond the mountain town of Marble, N.C., where he'd lived all his life.

Pastor Fred Lunsford, whom, at age 95, God used to start the "Praying on the Mountain" meeting. More than 299,000 people participate in "Praying on the Mountain."

CHAPTER TWELVE | CALL TO FINISH WELL

Lunsford said he spent many hours every day frequenting his personal prayer garden and a mountain on his property he called "Light House Mountain" asking God to reveal His purpose.

It was in that prayer garden, two miles from his house, that God told him to begin praying for spiritual revival, Lunsford said. Eventually, those hours in prayer led to an event, scheduled for May 5, in which more than 100,000 people are expected to pray with Lunsford.

"He [God] extended my years for a reason, and He wanted me to pray for spiritual awakening and to get as many people praying as I could," Lunsford said. "God spoke into my heart, and I yielded to it. It's not me; it's the Lord."

For the next two years, Lunsford told everyone he could about his mission to pray for revival and believed that it would come. During this time, Lunsford shared his testimony at a conference where David Horton, president of Fruitland Baptist Bible College in Hendersonville, N.C., was speaking.

Horton, inspired and impacted by Lunsford's testimony, shared the mission with Greg Mathis, pastor of Mud Creek Baptist Church, also in Hendersonville.

Horton, Mathis along with Fruitland Baptist Bible College professors Michael Horton and JD Grant, went to spend a day with Lunsford, praying with him and listening to the ways God had impressed the call to revival on him.

While the men sat inside their vehicle January 20, 2020, Lunsford prayed for the spiritual awakening to begin, and said that with the pastors' visit, it had begun.

"I don't know how to explain to you what happened that day," Mathis said. "I have never felt a manifestation of the Spirit of God like I did in that vehicle that day."

In the following days, Mathis said, he could not get the idea of the spiritual awakening out of his mind. He and Lunsford began planning for a gathering of 100 pastors at the top of Lunsford's "Light House Mountain" to pray for revival and awakening.

But 100 pastors quickly turned into 200 who planned to dedicate one day to gather on the mountain and, led by Lunsford, pray for God to move.

But as their plans took shape, the COVID-19 pandemic began to unfold. Social distancing requirements made it clear to Mathis, Lunsford and others involved that gathering in person was no longer an option. But, Lunsford said, those 200 pastors who initially committed to the idea were only sparks for a global movement.

"By phone we began to pray with Fred as to what else God would want," Mathis said.

Lunsford said he believed it was never about gathering 200 preachers atop the mountain, but that God was getting their attention.

"He said, 'I now believe God wants 10,000 people from wherever they are to join me on that day praying for spiritual awakening in this country,'" Mathis said, recounting Lunsford's words.

Setting aside May 5 for Lunsford to go alone to the mountain to pray, with others joining him in spirit, Mathis began to reach out to other North Carolina pastors, asking them to encourage their congregations to commit to prayer.

But word of the event spread, and soon Mathis and his team saw over 100,000 individuals pledged to pray on that day.

CHAPTER TWELVE | CALL TO FINISH WELL

Working through the Mud Creek Baptist Church website, Mathis" team created the webpage "Praying on the Mountain," drawing global attention. The number of those committing to pray has grown each day.

Mathis said the entire experience confirmed his belief that God is working and prayer is powerful.

"It's made me feel that God truly wants to do something," Mathis said. "I think God is giving a spiritual awakening through this and many other things, many other prayers."

Mathis said God is using COVID-19 to call people to Himself and get their attention. "God's doing something and God's prompting the hearts of Christians to come together."

Lunsford said the response has been more than he ever expected.

"It's been amazing how it's all happened, what's taken place," he said. "It's beyond my comprehension. I just can't understand it. It's all because of His grace. I know this is of God, and on May the 5th something big is going to happen.

"I believe honestly that God is going to do something extraordinary, that will get the attention of people all over the world. I don't know what it is, but I believe it with all my heart."

Lunsford said he believes the day of prayer will be a launching pad for something bigger down the road.

"I believe God is moving, and we need to listen," Lunsford said.[4]

As it turned out, more than 299,000 people joined that website and prayed with Pastor Lunsford. Shelly and I joined in at 3 a.m. Indonesian time!

PRAYING AND FASTING OVER COVID-19 CRISIS

In April 2020, regional leaders of our International Mission Board asked that every member of the IMB staff in Indonesia devote considerable time to prayer on April 19, 2020, while also fasting, to seek the Lord's will about accepting an assignment to the U.S. for two months or declining it and continuing to serve in the world's largest archipelago nation at what seems to be the front end of its Covid-19 crisis. We had been sheltering in place for more than a month, working to develop creative engagement strategies. For a month, Shelly and I had been praying daily via Zoom with the people of one of our Baptist churches in Jakarta, and we had also become involved in work on *Baptist Berdoa's* once-a-week prayer meeting and its offshoot. But on April 19, our leadership wanted us to fast and pray over the health situation and related offer of furloughs, weighing all of the available information.

Information we had received included an emotional plea from the Embassy of the United States to the Republic of Indonesia, located in Jakarta. Embassy leaders wanted American citizens in Indonesia to return to the U.S. Their message stressed, in part, that "The window of opportunity for leaving Indonesia narrows every week as international flights decrease. For those US citizens who want to leave, now is the time. For those who decide to stay in Indonesia, count the cost and do so of your own volition."[5] Such a warning was pretty much to be expected from the American government. We found the email from our leadership more sobering, with its message encouraging all with an impending stateside assignment to carefully consider leaving even earlier than planned. Shelly and I had been scheduled to begin our next stateside assignment on August 1, 2020. The email from our leadership stated the real possibility that by that date, leaving Indonesia might have become very difficult, perhaps even impossible. That April 19 day of fasting and praying would be an absolute necessity for us. Our leadership team in Indonesia had reiterated for each one of us serving IMB in Indonesia how pivotal this moment was. *We must seek the Lord!*

It will serve us well here to consider the four things that characterize authentic revival and spiritual awakening. First, God acts to revive His Church. Second, the Lord awakens the lost. Third, He brings about cultural transformation. And finally, there are significant advancements in missions.

1) First, God acts to revive His Church.

It is Thursday night, April 23, 2020, and I am writing the final chapter of my book. For Indonesia's Muslims, tonight starts a significant time of year, the fasting month of Ramadan. Ramadan's culminating holiday, *Idul Fitri*, will fall on May 23, but President Joko "Jokowi" Widodo has recently announced a ban this year on the usual *Mudik* "exodus" marking the *Idul Fitri* holiday and the end of a month's fasting. For millions of Indonesians, *Mudik* means traveling to home villages to join family members and make the traditional requests for forgiveness of any wrongs done to each other in the year just ended. Thus the holiday involves large groups, and the ban is intended to curb the spread of Covid-19 by those groups. (Many Christian Indonesians take advantage of Idul FItri to visit their homeplaces for a week's vacation or more. Trains and buses become *packed*.) Tonight, many IMB personnel are concerned about whether President Widodo's decision could spark unrest and even rioting in major cities including Jakarta, Medan, and Surabaya. The president's ban on *mudik* is more fuel for the powder keg on which Indonesia is sitting. This powder keg has already been stoked with pandemic-related unemployment and economic struggle, the specter of food shortages, xenophobia, and hints that rival religious and political factions plan to leverage opportunities in provocative ways. The situation has left us feeling unsettled and at times fearful of what may happen.

SEEKING THE LORD IN *BERGUMUL*

Readers of this book by now understand that when you face a big decision, it's time to seek the Lord, listen for the Lord, and, perhaps, struggle with the Lord in prayer. After hearing from our leadership, Shelly and I sought His will in *bergumul*. We remembered how He had led us, sustained us, and blessed us during our thirty-five years in Indonesia, so of course we wanted to do what had gotten us exactly to the place we were in. We prayed, struggling to hear His voice. Shelly and I wanted once again to receive God's leadership and guidance about staying in Indonesia or leaving. When we had prayed it through, Shelly and I both knew God was leading us to stay. It feels to us that Indonesia is on the cusp of something great that God is doing here. It feels to us there is a groundswell of prayer, a revival of sorts, beginning among Baptists in this land we have come to love. Believing that God is in the process of doing something significant in Indonesia's Baptist and other evangelical churches, I fear that leaving early could mean missing out on it.

When I had begun praying about leaving or staying as the pandemic descends on Indonesia, the Lord had begun waking me up every night at one or two, the wee hours. I'd been using the time not only to pray about our decision but to pray for revival and spiritual awakening in Indonesia as well. I asked God to rend the heavens, as Isaiah describes in Chapter 64:

> [1] **Oh, that you would rend the heavens and come down, that the mountains would tremble before you!**
>
> [2] **As when fire sets twigs ablaze and causes water to boil,**

come down to make your name known to your enemies and cause the nations to quake before you!

³ For when you did awesome things that we did not expect, you came down, and the mountains trembled before you.

⁴ Since ancient times no one has heard, no ear has perceived, no eye has seen any God besides you, who acts on behalf of those who wait for him.

⁵ You come to the help of those who gladly do right, who remember your ways. But when we continued to sin against them, you were angry. How then can we be saved?

⁶ All of us have become like one who is unclean, and all our righteous acts are like filthy rags; we all shrivel up like a leaf, and like the wind our sins sweep us away.

⁷ No one calls on your name or strives to lay hold of you; for you have hidden your face from us and made us waste away because of our sins.

⁸ Yet, O LORD, you are our Father. We are the clay, you are the potter; we are all the work of your hand.

⁹ Do not be angry beyond measure, O LORD; do not remember our sins forever. Oh, look upon us, we pray, for we are all your people.

¹⁰ Your sacred cities have become a desert; even Zion is a desert, Jerusalem a desolation.

¹¹ Our holy and glorious temple, where our fathers praised you, has been burned with fire, and all that we treasured lies in ruins.

**¹² After all this, O LORD, will you hold yourself back?
Will you keep silent and punish us beyond measure?**

I thought of how Bill McLeod's testimony once touched my life. McLeod had testified about waking up in the middle of the night to pray for revival. For a year, each night, when God woke him from his sleep, McLeod prayed for about thirty minutes for revival in Saskatoon, Canada. In 1971, revival came. McLeod has continued to pray nightly for revival. I regret that, while I've often gotten up in the middle of the night for a University of Kentucky basketball game on television, until this pandemic, I've rarely gotten up in the middle of the night to pray for revival. But doing so became my pattern. I've been praying for revival for Indonesia and the USA during these days, fully trusting God to come down in His manifested presence in a way that causes the mountains to quake and tremble before Him.

In Verse 8, Isaiah uses the image of the Potter with His clay. Richard Owen Roberts has explained that when this image is used in the Word of God, it usually points to revival, when God comes near to His people. Isaiah 64: 1–12 clearly describes an epiphany of some sort that occurred as God drew near His people and revived them. It took an epic catastrophe to bring that epiphany about, however, as the prophet describes in Verses 10–11. Undoubtedly, the verses refer to the ransacking and total destruction of Jerusalem that happened in 586 BC. From Verse 11, "all that we treasured lies in ruins" reminds me of our sudden loss of the things from which we Americans derived security and pleasure—our economy, our sports and entertainment. All that we treasured was destined for ruin within a month of the new coronavirus's introduction in our own land.

But Isaiah goes on to tell that Jerusalem's ruination won't last. Instead, God magnanimously poured out His grace on His people. The cry for mercy (Verse 12) from God's people as they took in what had happened while they have been exiled, is a prayer God loves to hear from His own. As H. Kent Hughes has commented:

> The greatest prayer we can pray is for God to do his will, for his glory, in his way, by his gospel, in our generation, without restraint. That's a prayer God loves to hear and is ready to answer. He's the one who gave us this prayer in the first place. He creates newness out of ruins when we bow low before him and say, "Lord, as far as I'm concerned, don't restrain yourself at all. Have your way with me and with us all, freely and entirely. Just let us be a part of your movement today."[6]

2) Second, the Lord awakens the lost.

In Chapter 65: 1–3 of Isaiah, we find the answer to the prayer the people prayed in Chapter 64: 12:

> **[1] I revealed myself to those who did not ask for me; I was found by those who did not seek me. To a nation that did not call on my name, I said, "Here am I, here am I."**
>
> **[2] All day long I have held out my hands to an obstinate people, who walk in ways not good, pursuing their own imaginations—**
>
> **[3] A people who continually provoke me to my very face, offering sacrifices in gardens and burning incense on altars of brick . . . .**

In the latter days, God would answer their prayer, which would open the door for the nations, meaning the Gentiles, to come into the Kingdom to be part of God's people. The notion of the Gentiles coming to faith made the Jews angry in the time of Jesus and Stephen, the church's first martyr, and the notion of Gentiles coming to faith will stir up the Jews in the last days, provoking jealousy but ultimately bringing them to faith before Jesus' Second Coming.

The heart desire of those who cry for revival is that, once God has made His manifest presence known to His people, He will draw near to us who are seeking Him with all our hearts. God's drawing near is the first thing we see in revival and spiritual awakening. The second thing we see is, as the Book of Acts describes beginning in Chapter 2, the Holy Spirit received by the church, reviving it, and leading the Gospel to begin flowing like a mighty river, gaining power and bringing many into the Kingdom of God. We see three thousand come to faith during the Pentecost event. Then, the Book of Acts is careful, throughout the remainder of the text, to note the progression of the Gospel surge (see Acts 4: 4, 5: 15, 6:7, 11:21). God continues adding to his church, in incredible numbers. This is spiritual awakening!

Paul, too, talks about the spiritual awakening to which he was an eyewitness. In 2 Thessalonians, he writes, "Finally, brothers, pray for us that the message of the Lord may spread rapidly and be honored, just as it was with you" (2 Thessalonians 3: 1). Paul wanted to direct the churches to the source of spiritual refreshment, to the incredibly great power that energized a small band of ragtag disciples into a spiritual entity that would turn the world upside down. The Thessalonians alluded to this great power in their response to the preaching of Paul and Silas: "And when they found them not, they drew Jason and certain brethren unto the rulers of the city, crying, These that have turned the world upside down are come hither also . . . ." (Acts 17: 6). What a difference the Holy Spirit makes in our lives! He not only changes our character, conforming us to the image of the Son of God, He also gives supernatural power, as the people in Thessalonica gave witness to.

The prophet Isaiah was able to look seven centuries into the future.

CHAPTER TWELVE | CALL TO FINISH WELL

There he saw the result of the revival described in Isaiah 64: an incredible spiritual harvest of people the prophet said *did not seek God*. The result was, in other words, God "reaching out to an obstinate people" (Isaiah 65: 1–2). These verses spring one of the surprises that fill Holy Scripture. It is that the revival is going to bring about a harvest of souls, but the harvest is going to take place primarily among the nations, among the Gentiles—not among the Jewish people. The missionaries who are serving in Indonesia have hope that the people described by the prophet in Isaiah 65: 1–2 include the people of the many islands of Indonesia, for example those in the one hundred-plus Unreached People Groups that remain virtually untouched by the Gospel. As it says in Isaiah 11: 11:

> **And it shall come to pass in *that* day, that the Lord shall set his hand again the second time to recover the remnant of his people, which shall be left, from Assyria, and from Egypt, and from Pathros, and from Cush, and from Elam, and from Shinar, and from Hamath, and from the islands of the sea.**

Indonesia comprises over 18,000 islands with 6,000 inhabited. It seems to me, then, that the "islands of the sea" in that amazing prophecy of Isaiah's will include many that today belong to Indonesia. And so we are believing that God is creating something in the midst of our Covid-19 crisis. He is in the process of reviving His church, and He is also bringing in perhaps a final harvest of souls, through a spiritual awakening arising from a revived church! In a recent *Baptist Berdoa* meeting, the pastors talked about John Piper's e-book *Christ and*

the Coronavirus. All of our Indonesian pastors had been sent a copy to prayerfully read, and I had asked them all to write to me with their opinions on Piper's argument. His book's final chapter calls us to good works based on faith. More important, Piper shares his realization that God is using Covid-19 to get us to look afresh at the Great Commission. At many times in history, He has used catastrophe to cause the Gospel to spread more rapidly. Think for instance of Acts 8: 1. Just as He used persecution to shake the early Jewish believers from their comfort zone, He can use the current pandemic to shake us out among Indonesia's Unreached People Groups to bring them the Gospel.

Late in this spring of 2020, evangelist Nick Hall, the leader of the movement known as Pulse, reported on the "Great Quarantine Revival." During virtual and broadcast services marking Easter week, nearly 120,000 chose Christ. Pulse's Easter worship reached over 1.7 million people in more than one hundred sixty-five nations, using the Facebook and YouTube platforms. Why shouldn't this be the beginning of a great spiritual awakening that will sweep across the USA and the other nations of the world as well? Our hearts rejoiced to learn that a significant proportion of those responding to Pulse's invitation were in Indonesia! Personally speaking, I am grateful that Shelly and I are alive for such a time as this, experiencing this fresh awakening that we have seen only the first fruits of.

3) Third, the Lord brings about cultural transformation.

Many people, when they hear the word revival, may think of protracted evangelistic meetings led by some guest speaker from out of town. Or perhaps they have more-negative thoughts, writing off revival as mere emotionalism, or even bizarre behavior. They would be correct in this, to some small degree, if revival brought to mind the "Toronto Blessing" and the strange uncontrollable laughter its participants displayed. That seemed to be (at least in part) a case of emotions and induced antics bordering on the ridiculous. One neutral observer who was there noted that people were rolling around cackling hysterically, showing no regard for the Word of God as a man tried to preach from Isaiah. You'd have to be completely naïve to call *that* revival. A lot has been written by Christians and the secular press alike about another revival, in Pensacola, Florida. Was it a true revival, though? It's been claimed that several people were saved in the Pensacola revival. In fact, the daughter of a friend and high school classmate of mine was saved during that meeting. She had been addicted to drugs, and her parents were at a loss as to how to help her. When they heard of the revival, they decided to invite their daughter on a vacation in Pensacola Beach. A vacation, they knew, would sound good. Their underlying plan, though, was to somehow get her to the revival meeting. If their invitation was a half-truth, or even a lie, it has to be remembered that they were desperate parents needing their child to be delivered from addiction. Of course at first the daughter refused to attend the revival. On the second night, however, she did attend, fuming inside about her parents' scheme. She got radically saved and is today, with her husband, serving as a missionary in Ireland. That's certainly a fact.

And yet, concerning the Pensacola revival in 1995, people whose opinions I respect when it comes to the genuineness of revivals say that emotionalism made up the better part of this one, too. Richard Owen Roberts has told the story of a lady he knew well and thought a lot of who called one day inviting him to this revival meeting in Pensacola. He declined to attend, and in fact he directly encouraged her not to attend. He told her that before she chose to go to the revival again, she should perform a test gauging whether the revival truly was from God: Ask Pensacola's police chief whether crime in the city had dropped drastically since the revival started. If so, Pastor Roberts said, ". . . I will concede that there has been a major revival and spiritual awakening that has come to Pensacola. However, if there is not a sharp reduction of crime," he added, "Then, just as I have thought, this is mere emotionalism."[7] Asked if the Pensacola revival had shown an effect on society at large, the police said no radical reduction of crime followed the revival. It was just as Pastor Roberts had perceived would be the case. So, what is the verdict? I do know a young lady who was radically saved at the Pensacola revival, but Richard Owen Roberts is the most-read scholar of revival and spiritual awakening in our time, and I tend to trust his take on what went on there.

Was God moving in the Pensacola revival like the reports said? Most likely He was—at the beginning. Once men led of the flesh rather than the Spirit tried to produce what their minds presented as manifestations of the Spirit, authentic revival closed down. This should be a warning to us that, despite the best intentions, trying to force God to send revival can end up quenching the Holy Spirit. When unwise men, acting more like paganistic shamans than Christians, try to manipulate God into action, what results is sensationalistic manmade manifestations that make the church look foolish. As Pastor Roberts says in his classic book *Revival*, man cannot force God to send revival. God sends revival solely according to His schedule and His sovereign plan:

> Upon hearing of the refreshing rain from heaven upon others, rush to your prayer closet and there beseech the Almighty that you may also know this divine blessing. Urge your family and friends to effectual, fervent prayer. Appoint special seasons of prayer throughout your community. Let a mighty concert of prayer demonstrate to the Father above your eager yearnings for His favor in your community. But steadfastly resist all urges to get up a revival by human effort

or means. Do not suppose that by duplicating methods used elsewhere you can also duplicate results. Remember Satan is eager to produce a counterwork, which will run parallel with God's great work. Do not allow your zeal for having what others are enjoying provoke you to acceptance of a cheap substitute.[8]

One of the main dangers of "revival" that Pastor Roberts warns against is a focus on the peculiar or sensational. He adds that the real work of any true revival is

to quicken the Body of Jesus Christ, turning it into a vibrant, moving spiritual force, arresting the attention of a lost world and turning the minds and hearts of countless millions to the much neglected Savior. All eyes should be focused on this Savior. If the focus is drawn from the Savior to some sensational feature of the awakening, there is sure evidence that Satan has triumphed in this instance. Let every eye be fixed on Jesus. He is the reviver.[9]

WELSH REVIVAL-CULTURAL TRANSFORMATION

The revival that exemplifies what cultural and moral transformation really looks like is the Welsh Revival of 1904–1905. Donald Elly has written about the early twentieth-century revival in Wales. At his site on WordPress.com, he explains this:

Effects of the WELSH REVIVAL 1904–05: Whole communities were radically changed FROM DEPRAVITY TO GLORIOUS GOODNESS. The CRIME RATE dropped, often to nothing. THE POLICE had little more to do than supervise the coming and going of the people to the chapel prayer meetings. The UNDERGROUND MINES echoed with the sounds of PRAYER and HYMNS, instead of nasty jokes and gossip. People who had fallen out became FRIENDS AGAIN.[10]

It was obvious that Welsh culture was transformed! Yes, a hundred thousand people were saved, eighty percent of whom were still faithfully attending churches two years later. But the key indicator that spiritual awakening took place was that the whole culture was transformed by the power of Christ.

REVIVAL IN RENO

Not long ago Shelly and I again joined the online OneCry prayer team, which is based in Reno, Nevada, to pray for revival and spiritual awakening in the U.S. and the rest of the world. This is something we have been doing since March 21, as the Lord has shuttered us in our home. Though we are separated from other Christians in physical space, we are connected via the Internet to hundreds of other believers, through OneCry's prayer call. When we first listened to the pastors in Reno, we were quickly drawn to the unity and love displayed in the lives of these men of diverse racial backgrounds, cultures, and languages. Those taking part in the prayer sessions are variously black, white, Hispanic, evangelical, and charismatic. Despite such differences, they are bound together by their love for the Lord Jesus Christ and the love that they have for one another.

I marveled at the things the pastors told us God was doing in Reno. Reno is "Little Las Vegas," a small "Sin City," known for gambling, divorces, and vice. I visited it in 1980, preaching at my father-in-law's church on its outskirts. So I've seen Reno with my own eyes—the casinos on every corner, the legalized prostitution, the general dedication to the god of hedonism. It compels you to ask how revival could possibly take place in

CHAPTER TWELVE | CALL TO FINISH WELL

Reno, where you could look fruitlessly all day long for a trace of Christian discipleship or even simple selflessness? Who laid the foundation for this amazing event? Looking closely, we find the answer is the same one as in most other situations where God is at work: Good things happen when Christians hear the voice of God and courageously step out of their comfort zones and move when He calls them to move. OneCry journalist Randy Hekman offered an explanation of what is going on in Reno:

> Many years ago, God gave former banker and current stockbroker Dave Quinn what he considered to be a prophetic vision in which he saw a flood of water coming out of the mountains surrounding Reno and descending into the Reno area. The water was rushing to the door of every church in town. Those doors that were opened even a crack, allowed this water of life to come in. Those doors that were totally closed, however, received no life-giving water. Dave took this as a sign that God was going to move in many of the churches of Reno.[11]

These are admirable goals. It's hard to doubt that the fires of revival have started in Reno. Randy Hekman asks an interesting question pertinent to the requirement for cultural change this chapter is focused on. "There is," he notes, "incredible optimism in Reno that what was begun there will grow until the entire Reno culture is changed. Could this unlikely city, far from the 'Bible Belt,' be the spark for the Great Awakening our nation desperately needs?"[12] He uses the words "Spiritual Awakening" instead of the word "revival." I have tried to differentiate between these two terms, but they have sometimes been used interchangeably. For example, in England in the 1730s, the "Evangelical *Revival*" took place under the leadership of men like George Whitfield and John and Charles Wesley. In the same decade, what would come to be called the First Great

Awakening was happening in Colonial America, under the leadership of Jonathan Edwards. The two phenomena were not different in substance, although different terms were used in naming them.

On the other hand, there are cases in which revival means one thing and spiritual awakening another. Take what God does periodically in His church, the body of Christ. He revives it. He makes it come to life spiritually after it has been asleep spiritually. Thus the term *revival* denotes God's doing something in Christians or in His bride, the church. The term *spiritual awakening*, in contrast, denotes the spread of the Word of God when it has become a tsunami sweeping over a region or a nation, bringing thousands and millions to faith and rousing many to be born again, in a drastic movement of His Spirit. Such spiritual awakening is described in the chapters of Acts (Chapters 2–28) and also by Randy Hekman in commenting on the praying in Reno.

The beginning of a Great Awakening our country desperately needs? Maybe so. Note Hekman's statement that precedes his question: "There is incredible optimism in Reno that what was begun there will grow until the entire Reno culture is changed."[13] Focus on that awhile. Shelly and I considered it, asking each other, "Can you imagine how the cultural landscape in Reno would change if a revival, then spiritual awakening of gigantic proportions, would take place? What would happen if the legalized prostitution shut down, the casinos boarded up, and the city that leads in divorce filings closed all doors to that process? You'd have a lot of unemployed people, wouldn't you?" In the Reno *Gazette*, Ed Komenda has reported an estimated 206,000 Nevada casino employees were out of work after the state's unprecedented "shutdown" meant to fight Covid-19.[14] The history of revivals and spiritual awakenings in the United States and places like Wales suggests that a true spiritual awakening would similarly impact industries like gaming and prostitution. If the pandemic resulted in more than 200,000 layoffs, I think it's reasonable to expect that, in a Great Awakening, a similarly massive number would decide to find employment elsewhere, after they had been reborn of the Spirit of God. It's something to consider.

4) Fourth, there are significant advancements in missions.

We can't think about the results, including supernatural impacts, of revival and spiritual awakenings without considering the influence true revival and spiritual awakenings have had on church missions all around the world. In the introduction of this book, I note the impact of the Pyongyang Revival not only Christianity's spread throughout South Korea, but on its spread across the globe. The Pyongyang Revival made South Korea a center of worldwide missions. According to Jae Kyong Lee, a Southern Baptist missionary,

> Less than one hundred years [after the revival], twenty-four missionaries were officially sent out by the Korean churches in 1974. Their number grew exponentially, and forty years after Korea [had] sent out its first missionaries, 27,436 Korean missionaries from various denominations were serving in 170 countries.
>
> This growth has caused Christians worldwide to marvel at how Korea so quickly went from a country void of the gospel to one of the biggest exporters of it."[15]

Another example of the impact of revival and spiritual awakenings occurred during the time of Nikolaus Ludwig von Zinzendorf. This Moravian nobleman was of great interest to John and Charles Wesley and to George Whitfield, the men who would heavily influence the Evangelical Revival in England in the early 1730s. They carefully observed what was going on among the Moravians in von Zinzendorf's circles.

The Wesleys and Whitfield wanted what was happening in Herrnhut, where the fires of revival were racing across the land, to happen in their own country of England.

It is simply remarkable to see the influence this revival in the tiny enclave in Bavaria ultimately had on world missions. One of the remarkable things that laid the groundwork for the spread of the Gospel of Jesus Christ was the prayer chain that started in 1727 and went on non-stop for one hundred years! Consider the results of that unceasing, desperate praying. In 1792 the Moravians sent out three hundred missionaries to various parts of the world. By 1930, however, the number of Moravian missionaries was three thousand. Not only had the number grown ten times in size, it represented one out of every twelve members of the Moravian Church. *One in twelve serving as a foreign missionary!* That is a jaw-dropping statistic. The Southern Baptist denomination—the largest missions sending organization of all—currently supervises about thirty-five hundred foreign missionaries, despite having over fourteen million in its pool of church members.

HAYSTACK REVIVAL

One of the most remarkable revivals and spiritual awakenings, in terms of its footprint on world missions, was the Haystack Revival at Williams College in Massachusetts in 1806. America still felt, then, the powerful influence of the Second Great Awakening, which had taken place in 1800 and 1801. But this much more localized revival among college students would generate new influence. It began in the middle of a thunderstorm, in of all places a pile of hay in a field. Five students from Williams College had met in a meadow near campus to hold a prayer meeting. A summer storm came up suddenly, and the students sheltered under a haystack. Clearing the hay away from their faces, they could speak with each other in their unusual shelter. They continued their meeting. They cried out to the Lord to allow them to be part of reaching the world with His Gospel.

Ultimately, out of this spur-of-the-moment gathering in a haystack, the American Board of Commissioners for Foreign Missions formed. It was the very first U.S. missions organization to send missionaries overseas, starting with Adoniram Judson and Luther Rice, famous Baptist missionaries to Burma and India, respectively. A monument has been erected at Williams College to mark the revival in the meadow that day. It proclaims, "The field is the World!"

DECIDING TO STAY

As the pandemic had unfolded throughout the spring, Shelly and I had spent much time in prayer with our Indonesian brothers in Christ, asking for the nation to be delivered and for revival and spiritual awakening to come to its many islands. And once again we entered *bergumul* in prayer. When that wrestling was concluded (for now, at any rate), we knew that to leave Indonesia at this time would be out of step with what the Lord seems to be doing. We have prayed for years for revival to come to the churches of Indonesia. We have prayed more intensely than ever since February 2019, when my potential new role with the Indonesian National Baptist Convention was described. God guided us into that role for a reason, which may turn out to be that we can help with what some are calling the "Great Quarantine Revival" that has begun to touch the far corners of the world, even Indonesia.

We truly don't want to miss what God is about to do here in this, the most populous Muslim nation. We have served here for thirty-five years, and it would be nothing less than thrilling to witness a great movement of God where we have found community. We fully understand and honor some of our colleagues' decisions to complete the two-month IMB assignments stateside. A decision made in prayer is a valid one and entails no guilt; all of us probably anticipated the Lord would lead some in one direction, others in another. As we told one young couple, when you're seeking God's will and want to hear His voice, don't look to the right and left to see what others are doing. You can wind up confused that way. Instead, look to the Lord with myopic vision, and *He will lead you.* King Jehoshaphat said, "O our God, wilt thou not judge them? for we have no might against this great company that cometh against us; neither know we what to do: but our eyes are upon thee" (King James version of 2 Chronicles 20: 12).

May the Lord give us all grace to keep our eyes on Him and our ears attentive to His still small voice. Amen.

ENDNOTES

Struggling with God in the Distant Islands

INTRODUCTION

1. Platt, David, Sermon at Foundations meeting, 2018. Exodus, "The Spirit of God, the Missionary Task, and the Glory of God."
2. https://www.history.com/topics/1960s/1968-events
3. https://www.youtube.com/watch?v=AzCfHhpMi6c- The manifested Presence of God- Richard Owen Roberts

CHAPTER 2 – CALL TO SERVE

1. https://www.azquotes.com/quote/1403544

CHAPTER 3 – CALL TO GO

1. Brown, Sherrie Willis, *"I Aim to Be That Man": How God Used the Ordinary Life of Avery Willis Jr.* Copyright 2018, Christian Faith Publishing, Inc. 832 Park Ave, Meadville, Pa. P. 2478

CHAPTER 4 – CALL TO WAIT

1. https://www.desiringgod.org/messages/battling-the-unbelief-of-impatience, John Piper

CHAPTER 5 – CALL TO PERSEVERE

1. https://blogs.transparent.com/language-news/2015/04/15/why-learning-a-language-is-like-running-a-marathon/ Brian Nelson

CHAPTER 6 – CALL TO LEARN

1. http://theaquilareport.com/how-to-prepare-for-your-short-term-mission-trip/ Annette Adams
2. Rankin, Dr. Jerry. *Spiritual Warfare* (Nashville, Tenn.: B & H Publishing Group). PP. 201–203. Kindle

3. Catt, Michael. The Power of Surrender (Nashville, Tenn.: B & H Publishing Group, 2010). P. 170.
4. OneCry: Catt, Michael, Interview with Michael Catt, March 27, 2020.
5. Drummond, Lewis A. *The Awakening that Must Come* (Nashville, Tenn.: Broadman Press, 1978).
6. Elliff, Bill, *OneCry: A Nationwide Call for Spiritual Awakening* (Chicago: Moody Publishers). Kindle Edition. P. 609.
7. Ibid.

CHAPTER 7 – CALL TO HUMBLE MYSELF

1. *"Humility is not thinking less of yourself but thinking of yourself less,"* Ron Mader (CC BY 2.0) via Flickr "Humility is not thinking less of yourself but thinking of yourself less," C. S. Lewis.
2. Jim Halla, https://biblicalcounseling.com/the-difference-between-humility-and-humiliation/
3. Wikipedia http://en Wikipedia.org/wiki/ecclesiastical polity
4. Hughes, R. Kent, *Preaching the Word Book of Acts,* Chapter 28, "Rejuvenating God's Servants."
5. Identity Politics, Citizenship and the Soft State, Internet Google.
6. Wikipedia, Suharto's forced Step Down, 1998 Riots
7. *Ibid.*
8. Wikipedia, Dengue Fever Symptoms

CHAPTER 8 – CALL TO TRAIN

1. Blackaby, Dr. Henry T., and Claude V. King. *Experiencing God: Knowing and Doing the Will of God* (Nashville, Tenn., B & H Publishing Group, 2008). P. 204.
2. Catt, Michael. The Power of Surrender (Nashville, Tenn.: B & H Publishing Group, 2010). P. 47.

CHAPTER 11 – CALL TO STAY

1. Platt, David. https://www.missionfrontiers.org/issue/article/we-are-not-all-missionaries-but-we-are-all-on-mission
2. www.bpnnews.net/46374/imb-1132 -missionaries-staff-accept-vri-hro

CHAPTER 12 – CALL TO FINISH WELL

1. Roberts, Richard Owen. *Revival* (The Richard Owen Roberts Publishers, 123 N. Washington St., Wheaton, Ill. 60189). P. 39.
2. Neighbour, Ralph. OneCry Prayer Meeting, April 8, 2020.
3. Johnson, Lane. OneCry Prayer Meeting, April 5, 2020.
4. http://www.bpnews.net/54719/95yearold-preacher-prompts-thousands-to-pray-for-global-revival
5. Health Alert: (COVID-19 Update #51) U.S. Embassy Jakarta, Indonesia, April 19, 2020.
6. Hughes, R. Kent, *Preaching the Word Book of Isaiah*, "God Saves Sinners," p. 436. Copyright 2005, Raymond C. Ortlund, Jr., Database 2008 WordSearch.
7. "Marks of True Revival," Richard Owen Roberts—YouTube—Sermon Index.net
8. https://www.gatsonline.org/wp-content/uploads/level/3/322REVIVALPRINCIPLES.pdf
9. Ibid.
10. https://donaldelley.wordpress.com/2016/02/02/welsh-revival-1904-5-effects-and-influence-of-the-welsh-revival/
11. Randy Heckman, OneCry Ministries, *Winds of Revival in Reno*
12. *Ibid.*
13. *Ibid.*
14. https://www.bing.com/search?q=ed+komenda+reno+gazette&form=EDGEAR&qs=PF&cvid=def8a2f5026a4e068b61781fd5d2f8b4&cc=US&setlang=en-US&plvar=0&PC=HCT
15. https://www.baptistpress.com/multi_author/jae-kyeong-lee/

ENDORSEMENTS

The genuine warmth and passion of this missionary shines through. Greg shares openly and honestly a lifetime of following God through both glorious and gut-wrenching moments. Missionary biographies are always inspiring. Through his story, Greg shares how he and his wife Shelly have sought to find and follow God's will, practical advice for all of us. I am blessed to personally know them and deeply admire them. If you have ever wondered if God still works like He did in Acts, reading their story will confirm that He does. Greg will open a window for you about God's work on Distant Islands!

–E. Randolph Richards, Ph.D.
Provost and Chief Academic Officer
Professor of Biblical Studies
Palm Beach Atlantic University
Author of Misreading Scripture with Western Eyes
RandolphRichards.com

* * *

What a privilege it has been to know Greg and Shelly Bruckert. I was on my 5th venture in short term missions, responding to the Indian Ocean tsunami with a team from Lake Ridge Baptist, when I met Greg and his son Jonathan in Aceh on the Island of Sumatra in 2005. What started as them translating for members of our team has continued for almost two decades as a partnership with our church to help serve an unreached people group on the Island of Java. I laughed and cried through this book knowing many of the people and places in the stories that describe God working in these distant islands. Under Greg's leadership our team members became disciples of Jesus ready to replicate in the USA what we learned in the field. Thank you, Greg and Shelly, for sharing your lives, your passion for service, and now your "callings" with so many who are and will follow in your footsteps.

–Ruth M. Anderson
Lieutenant Colonel, United States Air Force Nurse Corps (Retired)
Former Occoquan District Supervisor, Prince William Board of County Supervisors
Co-Lead, Reach Out Pillar, Lake Ridge Baptist Church, Woodbridge, Virginia

I enthusiastically recommend this book to every Christ follower who is struggling to know and do the will of God. In this book you will find a powerful testimony of a true servant of the Lord. Greg"s story reminds me of a promise given to us by our Lord in John's gospel, "In this world you will have trouble. But take heart! I have overcome the world.If you are looking for something that will encourage you on your journey of faith, this is a book you need to read.

    – Ron Lentine
    President/ Director
    Lentine Outreach Ministries,inc.

In full disclosure for this recommendation of Greg Bruckert's book, *Struggling with God*, the reader should know that I am no impartial judge of Greg's work. Greg and Shelly Bruckert are my heroes. For over twenty years, I have had the joy of working alongside them and watched them closely and have seen in them what it means to follow the Lord faithfully at all times, all circumstances.

I have met few couples as godly, as passionate for Jesus's glory, as consistent and persistent in their walk of faith. Do yourself a favor and stop what you are doing, find a good chair, pray the Lord would open your heart and mind that you would hear what his Spirit has to say to you through his faithful servant, and read this book.

Greg Bruckert writes with an easy style and carries the reader through his missionary experience as the Lord leads he and Shelly from one challenge to the next. Greg uses the notion of calling to carry us along, building a deep and abiding theme of faithfulness peppered with the Scriptures that have been Greg's sail and rudder.

May you be as blessed in reading *Struggling with God* as I have been in being called a friend of Greg and Shelly Bruckert.

    In Christ,
    J. Keith McKinley
    Associate Professor of Christian Missions
    The Southern Baptist Theological Seminary
    Louisville, Kentucky

Everyone would be better off if they could meet Greg Bruckert. First of all, they would hear the gospel and have a chance to respond. Second, they would experience Greg's passion for spiritual awakening and discerning the will of God.

Greg's book, *Struggling with God in the Distant Lands*, gives readers an opportunity to meet Greg up close and personal, as he reflects on his extensive spiritual journey as an international missionary. By unfolding the critical decision points in his life, with humor and transparency, Greg shows how he discerned God's will and followed it.

Although applicable for all believers, those called to ministry, especially missionaries, will be able to immediately relate to the specific kinds of decisions Greg mentions. I highly recommend Greg's book.

—Mike Shipman
Evangelism and Church Planting Consultant
International Mission Board, SBC

For much of their adult life, Greg and Shelly Bruckert have devoted their hearts to the Kingdom of God and to His mission field. Together, they have had profound impacts in the lives of others in faraway places, just as they have had profound impacts in Northern Virginia in the lives of the Anderson family and in our home church of Lake Ridge Baptist, Woodbridge, Virginia. In "Struggling with God in the Distant Islands," Greg steps us through his mighty struggle "with God in prayer for revival and spiritual awakening," and he does so in the spirit of *bergumul*—the Indonesian word for the struggle to discern God's voice. Greg's work is one for the ages and for believers who strive to discern God's will and do His work on earth. It's a must-read for any believer ready to obediently sacrifice the time it takes to hear God's voice.

—*Richard L. (Rich) Anderson*
Colonel, United States Air Force (Retired)
Former Member, Virginia State Legislature